HOMETOWN KILLER

The big, old house on South Fountain had been empty for about five years when Robert and Molly Warner moved there in 1994. On Saturday, July 8, 1995, Molly decided to participate in a "neighborhood cleanup" by cleaning out the debris-filled, double-car garage. While working in the south bay of the dilapidated garage, she moved an old wooden door and saw part of a tennis shoe stuck in the dirt floor. She reached down to pick it up and realized, to her horror, there was something inside of it.

She quickly ran out of the garage to find her husband. Frantic, she told him about the discovery, "There's something inside that shoe, Robert! I think it's a body."

When the officers and detectives arrived they cordoned off the area with crime scene tape, and began the gruesome job of uncovering the body.

The tennis shoes had torn through the large trash bags that the body had been buried in.

BOOK YOUR PLACE ON OUR WEBSITE AND MAKE THE READING CONNECTION!

We've created a customized website just for our very special readers, where you can get the inside scoop on everything that's going on with Zebra, Pinnacle and Kensington books.

When you come online, you'll have the exciting opportunity to:

- View covers of upcoming books
- Read sample chapters
- Learn about our future publishing schedule (listed by publication month *and author*)
- Find out when your favorite authors will be visiting a city near you
- Search for and order backlist books from our online catalog
- Check out author bios and background information
- Send e-mail to your favorite authors
- Meet the Kensington staff online
- Join us in weekly chats with authors, readers and other guests
- Get writing guidelines
- AND MUCH MORE!

Visit our website at
http://www.kensingtonbooks.com

HOMETOWN KILLER

CAROL J. ROTHGEB

PINNACLE BOOKS
Kensington Publishing Corp.
http://www.kensingtonbooks.com

PINNACLE BOOKS are published by

Kensington Publishing Corp.
850 Third Avenue
New York, NY 10022

All Kensington Titles, Imprints, and Distributed Lines are available at special quantity discounts for bulk purchases for sales promotions, premiums, fund-raising, and educational or institutional use. Special book excerpts or customized printings can also be created to fit specific needs. For details, write or phone the office of the Kensington special sales manager: Kensington Publishing Corp., 850 Third Avenue, New York, NY 10022, attn: Special Sales Department, Phone: 1-800-221-2647.

Pinnacle and the P logo Reg. U.S. Pat. & TM Off.

First printing: April 2004
10 9 8 7 6

Printed in the United States of America

*This book is
dedicated to the
memory of the
victims and their families . . .*

*. . . and to Sergeant Al Graeber,
who died five hours after his retirement,
and before the conclusion of this case.
He dreamed of writing a book about it
and never got the chance.
I hope he would have approved of this one.*

ACKNOWLEDGEMENTS

I am so grateful to my family and my friends for their incredible support and encouragement (and patience) during the writing of this book—especially my children, Jeanne, David, and Dana, who never seemed to doubt that I could do it.

To my granddaughters—Mallory, Chelsea, Miranda, and Sarah: you can make your dreams come true.

Chief Steve Moody, Sergeant Barry Eggers, Sergeant Michael Haytas, and Captain Rapp became my heroes—and my friends—during this time. They seemed to recognize the sincerity and passion I had to complete this task, and they embraced me and opened their hearts and memories to me.

I deeply regret that I never had the chance to meet Sergeant Al Graeber, but through the eyes of others who were fortunate enough to know him, I can see that he, too, was a hero.

Steve Schumaker is a very interesting man. In fact, one of the most interesting I've ever met. He, too, was extremely helpful and forthcoming.

"I will be forever grateful to all of them" sounds like a cliché, but I mean every word of it.

To Rocky: thank you for encouraging me to "go for it."

To Artie, Lynn, Dave and Shirley, Dick and Dari: I thank you for being "family." And for being interested. And just for being there.

Thank you, Linda and Tammy, for your flexibility, making it possible for me to attend William Sapp's trial. And for your understanding and support.

To the "smoking room" at the *Springfield News-Sun:* I know there must have been times you got tired of listening, but you did anyway—and understood. Thank you for helping me through the "ups and downs."

And to all "the other people" at the *Springfield News-Sun:* thank you for your enthusiasm and support.

To Wes: thank you for keeping me informed of hearing and trial dates, etc., especially your phone call the night the jury recommendation came in.

To my agents—Ron and Mary Lee Laitsch of Authentic Creations Literary Agency: a standing ovation . . . you're the greatest!

To Ann LaFarge, my editor: Three cheers! I have truly enjoyed working with you!

And to the victims' family members: thank you. . . .

FOREWORD

The events of processing the crime scene behind 17 Penn Street are just as vivid to me today as they were then—over ten years ago. All the people involved in the case worked extremely hard to bring it to a successful closure. It was the most intensive and emotional case that I worked on during my career with the Springfield Police Division.

It began as a typical August day in Ohio—sunny, hot, and humid. I was floating in our swimming pool, seeking relief from the afternoon heat. I was enjoying my vacation and anticipating another few days home with my family.

What transpired next would shock the community and produce the largest criminal investigation in the history of the Springfield Police Division. That lazy Sunday afternoon was suddenly shattered by a single phone call. The evening-shift supervisor abruptly canceled my vacation: "We have a mess out here."

My unit, Crime Scene/Evidence Collection, was needed to process the scene.

I did not realize just how bad it would be until I arrived at the scene and saw it for myself. It was bad—real bad.

Captain David Walters informed me that two female bodies had been found on a small area of land adjacent to a small pond. They were, possibly, those of Phree Morrow and Martha Leach, two young girls who had gone missing the day before.

The missing girls happened to be the same age as my daughter, Heather, and I began to think, *How am I going to handle this?*

As the coroner's investigator and I waded across the pond

and approached the bodies, thoughts raced through my mind about the victims, their families, and my own daughter: What were the victims doing to get themselves in this situation and how were they murdered? The anguish and grief the family members must be feeling now—and of the days to come. The safety of my own daughter and of the other children of the community.

I put those thoughts behind me and began to process the scene—carefully, methodically, and with dignity for the victims.

As I was photographing the scene, I thought, *How can one person lure, control, and murder two girls? How did one person manage to spend so much time concealing their bodies? And yet, not be seen? How did one person dispose of all the evidence?*

It would take years of relentless investigation by the Crimes Against Persons Unit before I got my answers.

The hardest thing I had to deal with was removing the young girls' bodies from their positions, placing them in body bags, and carrying them through the pond to waiting officers. The vision of those girls is etched in my mind forever. What could these girls have done to be brutally murdered this way?

No parent should have to go through this ordeal. The scene was hard on all the officers who were there—but especially those who had children.

In all, over 450 items of evidence—and possible evidence— were collected. To this day, all the items collected are in the custody of the Springfield Police Department or the Clark County Common Pleas Court.

Over time—through other criminal investigations and the exhaustive work of the Crimes Against Persons Unit— the perpetrators of these murders were apprehended and charged. I cannot speak highly enough of the dedication these officers had in resolving this case and bringing those involved to justice.

I think about the girls' murders from time to time—and

how it changed my life. As my daughter was growing up, I kept an "extra eye out" for her safety and well-being. Today she is a grown woman and a young mother and I still have contact with her on a daily basis to check on her. I am sure other parents in this community have done the same—since the incident.

Whenever I drive by Penn Street, I have vivid memories of that day in August 1992—the scene, the girls, and all the lives that have been forever changed by the cruel actions of others.

Sergeant Michael J. Haytas (retired),
Springfield Police Division,
Crime Scene/Evidence Collection Unit

AUTHOR'S NOTE

The following story is true. I have tried to do my very best to tell it exactly the way it happened. My sources include written and taped statements, interoffice communications (police), inquests, newspaper accounts, tip sheets, property receipts, diagrams and narrative (crime scene), arrest reports, and letters.

I conducted personal interviews and was present in the courtroom for most of the arraignments, hearings, and trials.

When there were conflicting statements or time frames, I studied them closely and chose the most logical.

Most of the time real names are used, but at times I felt the need to use fictitious ones. There will be an asterisk beside the fictitious names the first time the name is used.

My goal has been to write this rather complicated and very controversial story as factually as humanly possible. I also endeavored to tell it in a straightforward manner that would be clear to the reader. To meet those goals is the fulfillment of a lifelong dream.

When I read *In Cold Blood* at the age of nineteen, a seed was planted. Over the years I have read dozens of true-crime books and somewhere, in the back of my mind, the seed was growing. I knew that I wanted to write a book "someday." Finally I came to believe that I could write a book—if I wanted to badly enough—and "someday" finally came.

Carol J. Rothgeb

Prologue

With clothes half torn from her body, the thin, pale woman ran for her life. She ran toward the highway—toward the sounds of cars and trucks—toward the hope that someone would save her. She stumbled and ran though the brush with blood and tears mixing together, streaming down her face and neck. She ran, with her head throbbing and her heart pounding, away from the terror. Was he following her? Was he right behind her? If he caught her, he would finish what he had started. She had fought him wildly and managed to escape his deadly grip, but she was bleeding profusely and she could feel herself growing weaker by the moment. She didn't have the strength to fight him a second time. She had to make it to the highway—or die.

Motorists traveling east on the interstate were shocked to see the bleeding, beaten woman emerge from the brush along the side of the road and collapse. Many of them pulled over and ran to the hysterical woman. One man didn't even bother to get out of his car. He got off at the next exit ramp, found the nearest phone, and dialed 911.

Within minutes the grateful motorists, who were trying desperately to stop the bleeding on the woman's face, could hear the wail of sirens in the distance. They assured her that help was on the way.

Part 1

The Murders

1

She didn't struggle. . . . She acquiesces . . . but Phree, I think, fought him a little bit. . . . But I think Martha was just . . . she didn't have a chance. . . . She just gave up. . . .

—Captain Steve Moody[†]

The bodies were almost completely hidden beneath the skids and the brush, but the boys could see patches of clothing and flesh as they circled around to the far side of the pile. After wading through the knee-deep water, and climbing ashore on the other side of the pond, they were met with the gruesome sight that would forever be burned into their memories.

As they inched closer through the thick brush, hoping against hope that some of their friends were playing a very cruel joke, they could see the blood-soaked hair of what appeared to be the body of a young girl, facedown. Next to her, their arms almost touching, was the body of another young girl. A huge rock was completely covering her head. She was also facedown.

They had no way of knowing that two girls about their age who lived in this neighborhood had been reported missing the night before. But the stillness—and the buzzing of the flies—

[†]Several investigators assigned to this lengthy case were promoted during this time period. The epigraphs reflect their title/rank at the time they were interviewed.

whispered to the boys that this was not a hoax. It was painfully real.

It was the last weekend of summer vacation—the last Sunday afternoon before homework and teachers and early bedtime. It was a perfect day for the two young brothers until they left a picnic at a nearby church and rode their bikes to the wooded area near the man-made pond behind the bakery, an amazingly secluded area only one short block from a busy street.

A small sign on a nearby tree read NO FISHING, but the boys just wanted to watch the goldfish in the tiny pond. They had been there many times before and they were curious when they saw two wooden pallets at the edge of the water on the other side. There were dozens of pallets on the loading dock of the redbrick warehouse next door, but these two were definitely out of place.

The L-shaped pond, which sits in an alcove with stone walls on both sides and a hill to the back, had been peaceful and serene earlier in the day. But then the boys discovered the terrifying secret.

Alarmed, the boys quickly made their way back to the other side of the pond and back to the church. They searched frantically for their father, but they couldn't find him, so the older boy—not knowing what else to do—coaxed a friend into going back to the pond with him. When they were almost there, they saw a fire truck up on the hill, past the warehouse. They left their bikes and ran up the very steep hill. By then, Keith was almost hysterical, but, with the help of his friend Jay, he managed to tell the firemen what he and his brother had seen.

The borrowed bicycle that the missing girls had been riding the previous afternoon had been found about two blocks from the pond in a sewer tunnel nicknamed the "Lion's Cage." The firefighters had been called to assist the police in retrieving it.

* * *

Springfield, Ohio, was once known as the "Rose Capital of the World." With a population of about seventy thousand, it is located in the southwestern quarter of the state, forty-five miles west of the state capital of Columbus.

In 1983, in the special anniversary issue of *Newsweek* magazine, Springfield, Ohio, was selected as the example of "the American Dream." According to the cover: "Our anniversary issue celebrates the men and women who live the news, the unsung people who make our country. . . . It is the true story of America."

Springfield is probably very much like most other Midwestern towns of its size. The old mixed with the new—and the good with the bad.

Nowhere in town is the mixture of old and new more obvious than in the center of town. The "old" consists of the post office, the courthouse, the county building, and the *News-Sun* building. The "new" includes city hall, the Clark County Library, the Springfield Inn, Kuss Auditorium, and the Public Safety Building, which also houses the new county jail.

Schuler's Bakery, "Home of the Homemade," is located a few blocks east of the center of town on the southwest corner of East Main Street and Penn Street. Everyone in town knows where it is, because they have the best doughnuts for miles around. The bakery is one of the "old, good" places in town.

Beside Schuler's Bakery, "Penn Street Hill" runs uphill south from East Main Street to East High Street. It is probably the steepest hill in town. A third of the way up the hill is Section Street, running east and west behind the bakery. Strahler's Food Warehouse is on the southwest corner of Penn Street and Section Street.

It was behind this warehouse, at the edge of the pond, that the search for Phree Morrow and Martha Leach ended. The tragedy and the heartache for their families and friends, and this town, had just begun.

* * *

At 3:27 P.M. on August 23, 1992, the chilling message went out over the police radios that two bodies had been found behind Schuler's Bakery. Although the crime scene was actually adjacent to Strahler's Food Warehouse, the bakery (the more familiar site) became an easy reference point.

Soon the wail of sirens filled the beautiful Sunday afternoon as emergency and law enforcement personnel converged on the area. Within minutes of being dispatched, Lieutenant John Schrader and Detective Al Graeber, from the Crimes Against Persons Unit, arrived on the scene.

Word spread quickly. Neighbors came. The concerned came. The curious came. And family members of the missing girls came, visibly anxious and distraught, and were kept at bay by the police officers.

The uncaring also came. As they mingled, they drank beer and laughed, caught up in the excitement. At one point Detective Graeber even saw a young man sitting on one of the police cars. He asked him to move.

Soon additional officers were needed at the top and the bottom of the hill. There were hundreds of people trying to find out what had happened.

Meanwhile, two blocks away, the police officers and firemen were finally able to retrieve the bicycle. They also recovered a pair of flowered shorts, a pair of cutoff blue jeans, and a silver hair barrette from the bottom of the Lion's Cage.

Sergeant Michael Haytas (head of the Crime Scene Unit) had been enjoying the last days of his vacation when he was called and asked to report back to work and process the scene behind Schuler's. To save time, he had brought his own camera and camcorder from home and had stopped at a drugstore to buy film.

At the pond, behind the yellow tape, the Crime Scene Unit prepared to preserve and record the crime scene. Sergeant Haytas and Debbie Schaffer (of the coroner's office) approached from the north side of the pond. From that vantage point, they could see nothing amiss, except some skids out of place. The bodies were not visible from that side of the pond—only the skids. As the boys had done earlier, they waded through the shallow water to the other side, careful not to contaminate or destroy any lingering evidence. Sergeant Haytas videotaped the area as they went. One of the first things they noticed was something on the bottom of the pond—a pair of underpants.

Upon reaching the other side, they were met with the same tragic sight that the boys had seen. They could see that the skids were covering only the lower half of the bodies. And through the brush they could see the hair of one of the victims, completely saturated with blood. She was wearing a pink T-shirt with striped sleeves.

A very large rock, with small patches of moss clinging to its surface, was covering the head of the other girl. She was wearing a dark T-shirt.

Sticks and twigs and small trees had been pushed and bent over in an attempt to conceal the bodies. One stick had been deliberately placed between two of the boards and was propped obscenely in the buttocks of one of the girls.

As the scene before him assaulted his eyes and his heart, Sergeant Haytas forced thoughts of his own young daughter from his mind. He had been investigating crime scenes since 1979, but he had never seen anything like this.

Debbie Schaffer made a cursory examination of the crime scene. Dr. Dirk Wood, Clark County coroner, approached the scene from the south. Sergeant Haytas photographed and videotaped the area, then carefully collected the panties from the water and handed them to Captain David Walters to be placed into evidence.

As they fought to keep their emotions in check and went about doing what they were trained to do, they were secretly relieved that they did not yet know the identity of the victims.

The body on the left (looking south) was labeled victim #1 and the body on the right was labeled victim #2.

The two skids and the brush were removed from each

victim, placed in clean sheets separately, and labeled. The bodies were side by side, facedown; victim #2's left hand was almost touching victim #1's back.

It appeared that someone had "posed" them in almost exactly the same position; each one was slightly on her right side, with her left knee drawn up, a familiar "sleeping" position.

Victim #1 was naked from the waist down, except for a shoe on her left foot. Her right shoe was lying next to her right foot. Victim #2 was also naked from the waist down, except for white socks. Both of her shoes were lying next to her left foot between the two girls.

Victim #2 was rolled over onto a body bag, but because of the blood and dirt that adhered to her skin, especially on her head and face, she could not be immediately identified.

When the large rock was removed from victim #1, they saw that her head was so embedded in the dirt that it was almost flush with the ground surrounding it. She also was rolled over onto a body bag.

A preliminary examination by Dr. Wood revealed that the obvious cause of death was severe head wounds. There were bluebottle-fly eggs present on the bodies, but since they were not hatched, it was determined that the two young females, who appeared to be in the early stages of puberty, had been dead for less than twenty-four hours.

Both bodies were transported to the morgue at Mercy Medical Center.

Even though it was not official at that time, the detectives knew that these were the bodies of Phree Morrow and Martha Leach, the two girls who had been reported missing at 2:08 that morning. Phree was barely twelve years old and Martha was only a few days from her twelfth birthday.

There can probably be no more difficult task, even for seasoned police officers, than investigating the murders of children. Many of them were family men with children of their own. And it was only a matter of time until they would have to notify the parents.

Earlier, while anxiously waiting with the gathering crowd, Bennie Morrow, Phree's father, collapsed and was transported to the same hospital where the girls' bodies were taken.

One of the transmissions over the police radio said it all: "This is a mess." And this was only the beginning.

As church bells rang in the distance and the birds sang in the nearby woods, Sergeant Haytas recorded the scene and the surrounding area on videotape. Dozens of still photographs were also taken.

On a large tree a few feet from the bodies, there was another sign. This one read, NO TRESPASSING OR DUMPING.

2

This really affected me because I had a daughter the same age . . . but I had to put that aside. . . . When I got home finally . . . I gave her an extra little hug and said, "I love you."

—Sergeant Michael Haytas

Although Phree Morrow and Martha Leach had only known each other a short time, they quickly became friends. The girls were almost exactly the same age and, like most adolescents, in too much of a rush to be grown up.

Martha lived with her mother, Jettie Willoughby, on Lagonda Avenue in an upper duplex, and Phree lived with her father in the south end of town. Phree's mother, Susan Palmer, lived around the corner from Martha, in a large double on East Main Street. Their backyards were adjacent to each other.

Recently Phree had been staying at her mother's house as much as possible. In fact, she was practically living there, and the main attraction seemed to be that her mother allowed her to do as she pleased.

Phree's father, Bennie Morrow, knew why she wanted to be there, and though he was concerned, he allowed her to go. Phree usually got her way with Bennie; she had him "wrapped around her little finger." Understandably so, since Phree had had a very rough start in life: she was born with a hole in her stomach and spent the first seven months of her life in and out of the hospital. Susan and Bennie were divorced when Phree was less than a year old and her father had had custody of her ever since.

Bennie went "through treatment" for alcohol abuse about the same time that Phree started her prolonged visits with her mother. Alcohol seemed to be an ongoing battle for Bennie and many times he lost. Susan had battled it for a while, but then it seemed that the fight was over, and the booze won.

Phree was Susan's only child by Bennie, but Susan had three older children: Phree's half brothers, Charles and Clarence, and her half sister, Dawn. On Bennie's side of the family, Phree was the middle child, with two half brothers, Kyle and Jason, and two half sisters, Candice and Casey. She was the only one who lived with her father.

Phree seemed to be pulled between two different lifestyles that summer. According to her father, when she was at home with him, she was not allowed "to run the streets," wear makeup, or have boyfriends. She went to church almost every Sunday. Outgoing and loving—and a "tomboy"—she had a black cocker spaniel named Shadow Baby.

Martha's parents were also divorced. She was the next to the oldest in a family of five children, which included an older sister, Tina, a younger half sister, Heather, and two younger half brothers. Raising her children as a single mom was a struggle for Jettie, but she was a strong woman, and she did the best that she could. Despite her large family, she kept her house as "neat as a pin."

The neighborhood where Jettie Willoughby and Susan Palmer lived is in a poor section of town that is known for the prostitutes who hang around on East Main Street after the sun goes down.

After the bodies were removed, the Crime Scene Unit began a thorough search of the crime scene, took additional measurements and more photographs. Later in the evening,

Box 27 of the Springfield Fire Division was called in to provide lighting so the officers could continue their work.

The firemen who were first on the scene after the boys informed them of their grisly discovery were called back to the area. Sergeant Haytas needed to examine the bottoms of their boots, and to find out where they had walked, so they could eliminate their footprints from any others that might be found at the crime scene.

Fire division personnel brought several large tarps to the area and the crime scene was covered to protect it from possible bad weather. The area was secured for the night at a little after 1:30 in the morning; Officer Brian Callahan took over at that time to make sure no one disturbed anything during the night.

The crime scene personnel returned to the police station and submitted the evidence they had collected to the lab. The film was also submitted for processing. Finally, about 3:30 A.M., they all went home.

Much of what they found would not be reported to the public: the fact that there were skids covering the bodies; the stick that was propped in the buttocks of victim #2; the fact that the girls were found facedown with their heads in somewhat of a "hole"; the huge rock that was found still on victim #1's head; the multicolored underpants in the bottom of the pond.

They also would not release the fact that the flowered shorts found at the Lion's Cage had been cut in a very unusual manner, probably with a knife. These facts, they hoped, would prove invaluable when it came time to question a suspect or suspects.

That sultry Sunday afternoon in August, Steve Moody was mowing his grass when his pager went off. When the handsome, young detective sergeant called police headquarters, he was told, mistakenly, that two little girls' bodies had been found in a sewer drain. Thinking that it had been an accidental drowning, he immediately went to the scene at the Lion's Cage, still dressed in his jeans and T-shirt.

There he was informed that two little girls were missing and that it was their bicycle that had been found. Originally it was thought that the girls had somehow managed to obtain entry to the sewer system and that perhaps they were caught inside. Personnel from the City Water and Sewer Division had been called and they began a thorough search of the sewer system—a search that continued until word was received that two bodies had been found behind the bakery.

Sergeant Moody and his partner, Detective Al Graeber, were about to go on a roller-coaster ride that would last for years. Many times they would slowly, hopefully, persistently, grind to the top, only to be dashed to the bottom again.

They had been uniformed patrolmen together and had been partners ever since. Al Graeber, the older of the two, was a Vietnam veteran who, according to Steve, tried to maintain a gruff exterior, but "wore his heart on his sleeve." He was a distinguished-looking man who wore a neatly trimmed mustache and had just the right amount of gray at his temples.

Steve Moody had originally planned to be a dentist, but he now believed that his vocation had picked him. He had followed in the footsteps of two of his beloved and much respected uncles and joined the police force and was now in charge of the Crimes Against Persons Unit.

Even though he was now Al Graeber's superior on the police force, these two men were partners in the truest sense of the word: They were friends and they learned from each other. And they were both dedicated to the same cause.

About 11:15 that evening, the heartbroken parents of both missing girls were asked to come to police headquarters. Sergeant Moody and Detective Robert Davidson gently interviewed Susan Palmer.

Susan told the detectives she had last seen Phree on Saturday about 4:30 P.M. when she asked to stay overnight at Martha's. She said that Phree was wearing a button-down black shirt with a pocket on the left side, light-colored blue jean shorts, and white canvas tennis shoes—no laces.

Detective Graeber and Detective Nathaniel Smoot, patiently and compassionately, questioned Jettie Willoughby and Martha's father, Noah Leach.

Jettie told them that she had last seen both girls when they asked if they could go to the bakery, between 5:00 and 5:30 P.M. Martha was wearing a pink T-shirt, black flowered shorts, and black tennis shoes. She said that Martha was also wearing a "gold, flat, glass necklace."

She added that Phree was wearing a black T-shirt and blue jean shorts and that she had her hair pulled back.

The detectives were not surprised that the description of the clothing that Phree and Martha had been wearing matched perfectly with the clothes found on the half-nude bodies and the shorts found at the Lion's Cage.

On Monday morning the headline in the local newspaper, the *Springfield News-Sun*, screamed: GIRLS FOUND SLAIN!

The Crime Scene Unit went back to work early that morning. In the area where the victims had been found, they painstakingly took soil samples, cuts from bushes, water samples, water vegetation samples, and more photographs.

They searched for evidence in the parking lot and in the pile of skids on the warehouse dock. They walked the wooded hill area on the south side of the pond.

They also searched the area around the Lion's Cage and photographed the graffiti on the walls that surrounded the metal cage.

They checked the storm drain that empties into Buck Creek at the Water Street Bridge a few blocks away; then they walked along Buck Creek to the Ohio Edison Dam on the western edge of town.

A police recruit class was dismissed so that the young men and women could walk the railroad tracks from the Lion's Cage area to Warder Street, several blocks away, looking for anything that might be considered evidence.

At a press conference, Police Chief Roger Evans promised to implement every available resource to find the person or persons responsible for this "tragic, gut-rending thing that shocks not only the community but also the police department." He also expressed his hope that the killings were an "isolated incident and not a series of incidents."

Dr. Robert Stewart (forensic pathologist) and Dr. Dirk Wood performed the autopsies on Monday morning at Mercy Medical Center. Dr. Stewart noted that both Phree and Martha had suffered severe skull fractures and bruising and abrasions around the face and forehead area. The girls had also suffered abrasions, contusions, and lacerations to various parts of their bodies. Both of the girls had been sexually assaulted and he was able to recover semen from each of the victims.

They found the cause of death for Phree Morrow and Martha Leach to be the skull fractures. The approximate time of death was placed between 7:00 and 9:00 P.M., Saturday, August 22, 1992.

It was also determined that the two girls had eaten a full meal sometime between when they disappeared and their deaths. Neither family had served an evening meal on Saturday.

Earlier on August 24, a fund had been set up at the Huntington National Bank for anyone wishing to make a donation to help with the funeral expenses for Phree and Martha.

The stunned and grief-stricken families were living through all parents' nightmare: making funeral arrangements for their child.

The services would be held at Richards, Raff & Dunbar Memorial Home, an impressive funeral home originally constructed to be the personal home of Ohio governor Asa S. Bushnell. It was completed in 1888 on a 3½-acre site. The mansion became a funeral home in 1939 and was placed on the National Register of Historic Places in 1980.

It was located within walking distance from where the bodies and the bicycle were found.

Sometime during August 24, a thirty-nine-year-old parolee named Willis Jordan* was brought to the police station on a parole violation after he told his parole officer that a young girl was "messing with him" and he was about to "go off on her." At 10:30 that night, Sergeant Moody questioned Jordan. Tom Sandy from the Adult Parole Authority was also present during the interview. During the questioning they noticed that Jordan had scratches on his hands and wrists, which he claimed were from playing with his niece's cat. He consented to having his blood drawn for testing and was photographed.

Also, that evening police officers found a transient by the name of Raymond Stone* eating his dinner in the area of the Lion's Cage. He was brought to headquarters and questioned. His fingerprints were taken and he also was photographed and voluntarily gave a specimen of his blood to be tested.

These two men became the first of many to have their blood drawn and tested. The hope was to match DNA from a suspect's blood with the DNA in the semen found inside the bodies of Phree and Martha.

Detective Barry Eggers reported that he had talked to a neighbor of Martha Leach's named Rhonda Sanchez* about the homicides of the two girls. Rhonda had been walking the streets, soliciting, on Friday, August 21, 1992, the night before Phree and Martha disappeared. A man in a maroon car, possibly a Camaro or a Pontiac, had picked her up. When Rhonda refused to have sex with the man, he started "punching" her. She told him it was okay, that she would have intercourse with him, but he continued to beat her, ramming her head into the car door window so many times that she almost passed out. Somehow she managed to escape. Although she was too afraid to look back, she felt that the man was chasing her on foot. She ran under the Spring Street Overpass (a few blocks from the bakery) and hid.

The petite brunette told Detective Eggers that the man was

*Asterisks throughout indicate fictitious names.

very quiet and that it was a little scary just being near him. She described him as a white male about thirty years old with shoulder-length, stringy auburn hair. He was approximately 5'10" tall and weighed about 185 pounds.

She remembered the car as being an older model with a lot of used Styrofoam coffee cups on the floor on the passenger side.

She felt that if she hadn't managed to escape from this man, he would have continued to pound her head against the window until she blacked out or died. It was her opinion that this could be the man who killed Phree and Martha.

Rhonda shared this information with the detective only after he assured her that she would not be charged with prostitution. She agreed that she would help in the future, if she could, because Martha was her neighbor.

Barry Eggers, a striking man with strawberry blond hair and mustache, had been an undercover officer in the Drug Unit for over four years and was "on loan" to the Property Unit when Phree and Martha's bodies were found. He was then brought into the Crimes Against Persons Unit to help investigate the murders of the two young girls.

He was originally from Portsmouth, Ohio, and joined the U.S. Navy right after his high-school graduation. He had worked as a prison guard at London (Ohio) Correctional Institution before becoming a police officer. He was the father of a three-year-old boy and an eleven-month-old girl.

3

*We had to return Martha's school clothes. . . . Couldn't
bring ourselves to return her Troll T-shirt.*

—Tina Leach, Martha's sister

Pat Gibson* had worked at the bakery since 1973 and
knew many of the customers by name. Martha Leach came in
nearly every day, so Pat knew her well, but she had just
started seeing Phree Morrow recently. She liked the girls,
even though there had been some problems with Martha earlier in the summer. On more than one occasion, Martha and
some other kids had stood outside the door of the bakery and
asked customers for money.

The two girls came in together on Friday afternoon, August
21, 1992, and bought a small chocolate cake. They asked
Nancy Gilmore*, the clerk, to write "We Love You" on the
cake. Pat watched as Nancy decorated the cake with a purple rose made out of icing, and she wondered why the young,
pretty girls would be wearing so much makeup.

Martha came in the bakery again the next day, late in the
afternoon, with a young man. The man told Martha she could
have whatever she wanted and she picked out nine doughnuts
and two "happy face" cookies. He handed Pat a $20 bill.

On this particular Saturday, Phree, with her dark auburn
hair pulled back in a ponytail, and Martha, with her curly
blond hair, were anxious for school to start the following
week. Phree liked school; music was her favorite subject and
she was learning to play the violin. She would be starting

the seventh grade at Franklin Middle School. Martha's twelfth birthday was only a few days away, and on Wednesday she would be starting classes at Schaefer Middle School. The only problem was, since they went to different schools, they wouldn't be able to spend as much time together.

Martha had stayed all night with Phree (at her father's house) on Friday night. It was the first time Bennie had seen his daughter's new friend—and, tragically, it would be the last. Martha was quiet, perhaps shy, in the presence of adults that she had just met. Bennie would later say that she seemed like "a nice kid—a good kid."

Early in the evening they had a cookout, and then he dropped the girls off at the roller-skating rink on the other side of town.

On Saturday morning, when Bennie took the girls to Susan's house, he warned Phree as she got out of the car: "This is it." She would not be spending so much time at her mother's—it was time to get serious about school starting the following week.

Another thing the girls had in common was that one of Susan Palmer's ex-boyfriends was Martha's uncle. Also, Deon Stevens, Martha's cousin, was one of Phree's "boyfriends." Tim Stevens, the uncle, and Deon were father and son. Phree's half sister Dawn Wilson was Jimmy Stevens's girlfriend. Jimmy and Deon are brothers.

Sometime in the afternoon, Susan sent Phree and Martha to the tavern down the street to get her some cigarettes. No one in Kinsler's Bar was surprised to see the young girls come in. Frequently Phree came in looking for her mother.

When they got back from the neighborhood bar, Susan asked Tammy Martin*, a sixteen-year-old girl who was staying with her, to walk with the girls to West North Street, the home of Tim Stevens's ex-wife, Tina—over sixteen blocks away. Susan had written a note for Phree to give to Tim.

Tina Stevens would later confirm that Phree had knocked on her door that afternoon and said that she was looking for Tim.

After the three girls stopped at the house on West North Street, they decided to walk over to the Dairy Mart on West Main Street. On the way they were shouting at guys in cars and asked one if he wanted a girlfriend. After leaving the convenience store, they headed back to West North Street to look for Tim Stevens. Shortly after that, a neighbor of Tina's gave the three girls a ride back to Susan Palmer's house.

Later that day, Susan, Dawn Wilson, Jimmy Stevens, and John Stevens (another of Martha's uncles) left to go swimming at Mad River. There wasn't enough room in the car for the girls and they really didn't want to go anyway. They asked if Phree could spend the night at Martha's house.

Soon after that, Deon and his best friend, Matthew Rude*, rode over to Martha's on their bicycles and the four of them sat around in the backyard, talking and laughing. The girls told Deon and Matthew that they were going to a party that night and then Martha started talking about getting some doughnuts.

She walked around the corner to the house where a twenty-three-year-old neighbor, Richard Patterson*, lived, and when she came back, she had $2 that Richard had given her for her birthday. Then Phree and Martha playfully persuaded Deon to lend them his bicycle so they could ride it to the bakery. The girls left together on Matthew's bike. (Deon came back later to get his bike, but the girls weren't back yet.)

Late that afternoon, Phree and Martha had asked Martha's mom if they could go to Schuler's Bakery. At first, Jettie wasn't too concerned when the girls didn't return right away. Kids get distracted sometimes. But then as afternoon slipped into evening, Jettie began to worry. The bakery was only a few blocks down the street and they had had more than enough time to get there and back. What was taking them so long? It would be getting dark soon.

Finally Jettie decided to walk around the neighborhood and look for the girls. She asked Tim Whitt, her boyfriend, to go with her.

Shortly after dark, Dawn Wilson and Jimmy Stevens left the house on Main Street to walk to the beverage dock on Lagonda Avenue. As they approached the corner of Main and Lagonda, they saw Jettie and Tim coming toward them.

Jettie fretfully told Dawn that the girls had gone to the bakery hours earlier and had not returned. They decided to ride around the neighborhood in Jettie's car to search for Phree and Martha. They even drove several blocks away to ask John Sargent*, one of Phree's boyfriends, if he had seen the girls, but he had not seen them at all that day.

By then, it was about 10:30 P.M. They drove over to Bennie Morrow's house in the south end of town.

Bennie and his girlfriend, Andria, were getting ready for bed when Dawn came to the door and told them that Phree and Martha were missing. Without even taking the time to put his shoes on, Bennie jumped into his car and drove to the house on East Main Street where his ex-wife lived. Jettie quickly followed. There he got into her car with the rest of the group and they continued the frenzied search.

Phree's mother had gone to Whitie's Tavern soon after returning from Mad River earlier in the day, so she was still unaware that her daughter could not be found.

When she came out of the bar, she was looking for a ride to another bar, the Key Lounge, where she was supposed to meet her boyfriend, David Atkins. By chance, Jettie drove by Whitie's at that time, saw Susan, stopped, and told her what was going on. Susan turned around and walked back into the bar.

Jettie was incredulous. She turned to Bennie and said, "Do you believe that?"

He replied, "That's the reason I have custody of Phree."

Shortly after that, a friend of Susan's drove her to the Key Lounge. She went in and told David that the girls were missing. He finished his beer. And then they also drove around searching for the two young girls.

After checking back several times, the group in Jettie's

black Nova eventually found Susan at home around midnight. The distressing news was traveling quickly throughout the family; Bennie's mother and one of his sisters were also there.

Several times during the evening, Bennie mentioned that he knew a place where Phree liked to play. After returning to his house to get his shoes and a flashlight, he took the same group that had been in the Nova to the area known as the Lion's Cage, which is part of the Mill Run Sewer System Collection Point. The "cage" is near the railroad tracks that run underneath the bridge on East High Street. East High Street runs parallel to East Main Street.

It is such a secluded area that it is difficult to imagine that they were only one block from this busy street. With the tall trees and the brush, they could barely see anything with only the small circles of light from their flashlights to guide them. As they approached the Lion's Cage, the sound of the rushing water obliterated the noise of the crickets playing their nighttime tunes and the sounds of the passing cars on the nearby street.

Meanwhile, Officer Keith Hopper of the Springfield Police Department had been dispatched to that area to check a suspicious vehicle at Penn and Railroad Streets. South of Railroad Street, a portion of Penn Street was closed off, with a guardrail blocking the way. As Officer Hopper walked back to his patrol car, he was surprised to see several people on the other side of the barrier walking toward him.

Some of them were carrying flashlights and one of the men appeared to be drinking a beer. One of them told the officer that they were looking for two missing girls.

Bennie told him that one of the girls was his daughter and then he started rambling about drinking, commenting that he hadn't had anything to drink for years until now. Bennie also told Officer Hopper that they couldn't find the bicycle that the girls had been riding and stated that "if they were alive," he wanted Phree taken to the juvenile detention home.

It appeared to the officer that everyone in the group was

intoxicated. While he was filling out the missing persons report on Phree, he was forced to call for assistance when, amazingly, a fight broke out between Jettie and Tim. Tim grabbed Jettie by the throat and forced her down on the hood of Bennie's Pontiac Grand Prix. After Tim let her go, they began yelling at each other and Jettie walked away.

When Officer David Marcum arrived to help, Officer Hopper called Jettie over to his patrol car and managed to fill out a missing persons report on Martha. Jettie repeatedly told him that it wasn't like Martha not to let her know where she was going and whom she was going to be with.

At 2:08 on the warm summer morning of Sunday, August 23, 1992, the missing persons reports were finally completed on both girls.

After the police officers left, Bennie told the others that he knew of another place where they could look for Phree and Martha. They drove across High Street, went down Penn Street Hill, and parked at the rear of Schuler's Bakery. Bennie, Jettie, and Tim walked behind Strahler's Food Warehouse to look around. Tim shone his flashlight on an area by an old gas pump while Bennie searched around a stack of pallets. Then Bennie walked back and forth on the wall at the edge of the pond, shining his light over the water, but he could only see some bushes and a tree on the small peninsula of land on the other side of the pond.

Jettie felt uneasy and said that she had an "eerie feeling" and wanted to leave. Without realizing how close they had come to finding Phree and Martha, they all left and went back to Susan's house on Main Street.

About 3:30 Sunday morning, Dawn Wilson asked Bennie to drive her to the home of Bobby Arthur* and Angie Sloan*. Dawn had baby-sat for them in the past and she thought maybe, while they were at Mad River swimming on Saturday afternoon, Bobby and Angie might have asked the girls to baby-sit. Dawn and Bennie drove over to Glenn Avenue and came back about ten minutes later with no news about Phree and Martha.

Susan told David and Jimmy that she had a feeling that the girls were "somewhere around water" and asked them to go back to Mad River and look in the area where they had been swimming.

By about 5:30 that morning, everyone had returned from their fruitless searching. After deciding there was nothing more they could do, they all went to bed.

They knew that Schuler's Bakery had been the girls' destination when they left on Saturday afternoon. The bakery was open until midnight, but according to Pat Gibson, not one of them had gone inside to ask if anyone had seen Phree and Martha.

4

*But Jesus said, "Suffer little children, and forbid them
not, to come unto me: for of such is the kingdom of
heaven."*

—Matthew 19:14

The morning after the all-night search was like all other
Sunday mornings at the bakery. Customers stood in line to
buy doughnuts for breakfast or after-church brunch and
desserts for their Sunday dinner. It was a beautiful summer
day.

Bennie returned to his house in the south end of town a little after 6:00 that morning, told Andria that they still had not
found Phree and Martha, and then went to bed. After tossing
and turning for quite some time, he finally fell into exhausted
sleep. Andria woke him up at about 8:30 and the two of them
went looking for the girls again, to no avail.

Finally they went back home and made arrangements to
meet the police at Susan's house. When they pulled up to the
curb, Jimmy Stevens came running out of the house and ex-
citedly told them that Tim Whitt had found the bike. He said
that he and Dawn had just gone in to wake David and Susan
to tell them that the bike had been found at the Lion's Cage.

What could it possibly mean? Only the bicycle was found?
Where were Phree and Martha?

They all went to the Lion's Cage to see for themselves,
but it was very difficult to see the bicycle lying in the bottom of the large cage. Some of them had to have it pointed

out; one of the tires was the only part that was visible. It seemed impossible that the bicycle could be in the water inside the steel cage. David thought that perhaps someone had put it down a sewer and it had washed into the cage.

When the police arrived, it was quickly decided that they needed help getting the bike out of the sewer tunnel. The fire division was dispatched to assist the police department. The firemen parked their truck on the bridge over the railroad tracks, on East High Street.

Deon Stevens was called and he came to identify the twenty-inch lavender bicycle.

When two of the firemen went back to their truck to get some tools, they saw two young boys running up the hill toward them. By the time Jay Martina* and Keith Casey* got to them, they were out of breath and Keith was almost hysterical. Captain Todd Bowser tried to calm the boys so he could understand what they were saying. Then it became all too clear.

Dawn Wilson was still at the Lion's Cage when she heard someone calling her name from up on the bridge. The person yelled to her that two dead girls had been found.

The bicycle and the girls' bodies had been found in two of the very same areas where the family members had been searching the night before.

The Crime Scene Unit returned to the murder scene about 8:00 Tuesday morning. With the assistance of the Springfield Sewer Division, they drained the water from the pond. Lieutenant James Keys and Officer Michael Beedy then crawled on their hands and knees in the drained pond searching for possible evidence.

The new police recruits—thirteen of them—were called upon to help with a search that ran west from Walnut Street to Spring Street and south from Buck Creek to the Conrail railroad tracks. They searched the woods and storm sewer catch basins, abandoned houses and buildings, abandoned and junked automobiles, fields, and along the railroad tracks and Buck Creek.

The crime scene was secured for another night at 5:00 that evening. Tarps and plastic sheets were used once again to protect the scene from possible bad weather. Uniformed police officers guarded the area.

Earlier in the day, the detectives learned from the two clerks at Schuler's that Martha Leach had been in the bakery the previous Saturday afternoon, August 22, with a young man. Pat Gibson and Nancy Gilmore differed slightly in their descriptions of the man, so they each provided information for composite sketches. The two sketches were released to the public that evening.

The white male was described as being approximately 5' 7", 120 pounds, very thin, and between seventeen and twenty years old, with a sandy-colored crew cut and hazel eyes. They also said his cheekbones "stuck out" and that he was very pale, "almost anemic," or "emaciated-looking." They both said that he wore a blue stud earring in his left ear.

Also, a woman named Marcy Lavelle* reported to the police that she was in the area of the murders around 3:30 Saturday afternoon. She said she saw an "old, dingy, trashy" bluish green van sitting on Penn Street and a man walking back and forth on the sidewalk. She also said she saw a second man who was "older, scummy-looking" get in the van with a box of doughnuts and then they just sat there.

Al Graeber's wife, Sharon, hadn't seen him to talk to him for three days. He had been home to grab a few hours of sleep here and there and then he was right back on the job. He took every case seriously—even personally—but this one preyed on his mind. The fact that he had a seven-year-old daughter added to his intense determination.

This case "hit home" with everyone who was closely involved in the investigation—almost all of them had at least one daughter. Al Graeber had three other daughters by his first wife, who lived in Indiana with their mother. Steve Moody was the father of two girls, eight and three, and a five-year-old boy.

At Dayton radio station WTUE, Steve Kerrigan asked for donations to a reward fund for information leading to the arrest and conviction of the person(s) responsible for the deaths of Phree Morrow and Martha Leach.

The Crime Scene Unit on Wednesday returned to the crime scene and searched the pond and island area for any evidence that might have been missed. With the help of the new recruits, another search was made of the same area that had been searched on Tuesday. Each officer searched in a different area than he had searched the day before, just in case he might spot something that another officer had missed.

The scene was secured with tarps and plastic sheets to protect it from possible bad weather at 3:30 that afternoon. Again it was guarded by uniformed patrolmen.

At 8:00 that evening, the area was opened and lab personnel "black-lighted" the scene to look for evidence. The whole area around the pond was sprayed with luminol, but no blood was found except in the spot where the bodies had been, which led the investigators to believe the girls were murdered right where their bodies were found.

Three hours later, the scene was again secured and guarded.

By late Wednesday afternoon, August 26, the police had received several dozen phone tips from the public regarding the composite drawings. They brought in extra personnel to help answer the telephones. They were determined to follow up on every possible lead.

A forensic artist worked with the bakery clerks to combine the two composite drawings into one single sketch of the man seen with Martha in the bakery on Saturday afternoon. Captain Richard O'Brien, the Public Information officer, stated that the artist was working with the witnesses to "come up with a more lifelike image."

There was a viewing at the funeral home for Martha Leach that evening. The funeral home had been wired with surveillance cameras in the event that the killer was bold enough to show up there. From the basement Detective Barry Eggers monitored persons coming into and going out of the funeral home. Also, from time to time, he walked around among the mourners inside and outside the building and even worked the door for a while as a greeter.

At some point, between 6:00 and 7:00 P.M., he noticed a young man outside in front of the building wearing a "cheap" light blue suit and a tie. Detective Eggers thought it was strange because he never did see the man enter the funeral home. The man had simply walked by the front door and looked in and then disappeared. And when the detective reviewed his tapes later, the young man's image had not been captured on any of the tapes.

Perhaps it didn't mean anything, but it was odd.

Later in the evening, a man showed up who had just recently had all his hair cut off, and a mob of family members and friends, thinking he may have had something to do with the murders, was about to attack him. At that point Detective Eggers—frustrated at having to make his presence known—rescued the startled young man from the crowd. It turned out that the reason for the new haircut was not to change his appearance—he had just joined the armed forces.

A very thorough Detective Eggers also asked an employee of the funeral home to make him a copy of the sign-in sheet in the guest book.

Reverend Forest Godin conducted the somber funeral service for Martha Leach on Thursday morning, August 27, 1992—two days after what would have been her twelfth birthday. There were about 130 mourners, including Martha's classmates, in attendance. A heart-shaped balloon floated near Martha's open casket. After they played one of Martha's favorite songs, "Wind Beneath My Wings," the minister tried, with his words, to comfort the brokenhearted family members and friends who had gathered.

Afterward, a procession of about fifty cars headed west on High Street toward Ferncliff Cemetery. They slowly passed between the two locations where the bodies and the bicycle had been found, less than a block in either direction.

By this time the crime scene personnel had already been back to work for several hours. They raked the island area and placed the debris in bags and took them to police headquarters. The pond was searched again. The overflow grates on the north wall of the pond were removed. They removed the debris, sifted it, and examined it for possible evidence.

The entire area was searched again: the stacks of wooden pallets, the parking lot, and the wooded area. Since this was considered a final search of the crime scene, all the tarps and plastic sheets that had been used to protect against bad weather were returned to their owners. At 6:00 that evening, Captain David Walters released the scene from further protection.

Sergeant Haytas remarked, "We did everything but bring the fish in from that pond."

Michael Haytas, a Vietnam veteran, had dreamed of being a police officer since he was a child. Originally from New Jersey, his tour of duty in the air force brought him to nearby Wright-Patterson Air Force Base. He liked the area and decided to stay.

His first attempt to join the Springfield Police Department was rejected because of a height requirement. Several months later, the department eliminated the stipulation and he was hired. He had a reputation for being thorough and meticulous.

Haytas was the father of two sons and a daughter. His daughter was twelve years old.

At 10:00 that night, the crime scene personnel returned to the Lion's Cage, where the bicycle had been found, to "black-light" the area to look for possible evidence. This area, too, was sprayed with luminol, but the results were negative.

More than two hundred people gathered at the same funeral home on Friday to mourn the loss of Phree Morrow. Even though it was late August, the temperature had dropped significantly and it was a cloudy, fall-like day.

Pastor Timothy Dotson, of the First Church of Christ in Christian Union, compassionately expressed a deep understanding of the overwhelming emotions present in the room. He told the Bible story in which the disciples tried to shoo the children away from Jesus.

Grief-stricken family members and friends filed through the alcove past the open, but white veiled, casket. A nearby table was covered with stuffed animals and an assortment of other gifts.

Afterward, a procession of fifty cars slowly headed east to Rose Hill Mausoleum. Away from the crime scene—away from where the bicycle was found. But they couldn't get away from the heartache and the pain, and, of course, the anger.

5

We were getting hundreds of little "tip slips" a day . . .
and they all were sending us in different directions.

—Sergeant Barry Eggers

Jamie was full of nervous excitement as he watched the activity around the warehouse. He had never seen so many police cars. He didn't have as good a view as he had had earlier because a detective had made him move. He knew he shouldn't be there. What if that detective found out that he had been there last night? But his curiosity would not let him stay away.

Within days Jamie Lee Turner had told several people that he had witnessed the rapes and murders of Phree Morrow and Martha Leach. On Thursday, August 27, 1992, Jamie was brought to police headquarters to be questioned about what he claimed he had seen.

The twenty-year-old mentally challenged man told Detective Al Graeber the same amazing story that he had told his friends. He claimed that he had been walking down Penn Street Hill when he saw a man having sex with a girl in the parking lot of the warehouse. He went away for a while, then returned and climbed up into a tree to watch.

According to Jamie, the man appeared to be "Chinese." From his perch in the tree, he then saw the "Chinese" man hit one of the girls in the head with a big rock. He said that he saw both of the girls' heads bleeding and that they were both naked, one faceup, the other facedown. He thought the girls were just "playing around."

Then while the "Chinese" man was covering the girls up with brush, Jamie threw a rock and hit the man in the head with it. Jamie claimed that he then heard gunshots and "got out of there."

Jamie also told the detective that he had seen a black pickup truck there. He stated that it was dark, but the light at the back of Strahler's Warehouse was "going off and on."

When Detective Graeber asked Jamie—a large man at 5'11" and two hundred pounds—how he got the bruises on his arms, he replied, "Run into a dresser or something getting up from bed."

While at police headquarters, at the request of Captain Terry Fisher, ten cc's of Jamie's blood were drawn for DNA analysis.

The next day, Detective Robert Davidson went to the Town and Country Day School to meet with its principal, Bernadine Delk, and Jamie's teacher, Mike Elfers. Town and Country is a school operated by the Clark County Board of Mental Retardation and Developmental Disabilities. Jamie Turner's IQ was approximately 50.

The principal and the teacher both told Detective Davidson that they were certain Jamie would not be capable of the degree of violence involved in the murders of Phree and Martha.

According to Davidson's written report about the conversation: "They did agree that Jamie would not be able to make up or catalog this if told by someone else the amount of information or details that he had. Jamie most likely could not have done this act but they were confident that he was probably present."

When Detective Davidson told them that Jamie had used the term "Chinese guy," they both said that Jamie would not have used that term. They explained that he would have described the man as a "guy with funny eyes" and that perhaps this was something that someone had told him to say. They added that if Jamie was with someone he feared, he most likely would do exactly as he was told.

Also, according to the report: "They are not confident of Jamie's ability to determine right from wrong. But they were very sure that Jamie would do nothing to 'bring blood' or injury to someone.

"Jamie, while in school, seemed to have an underlying need to be the center of attention. He was always playing the class clown to the point of getting himself in trouble and often he would elaborate on reality to capture attention."

Two days later, Sergeant Moody interviewed a man who knew Jamie "from church." Allen Tipton* told the detective that he got a phone call from Jamie about 6:00 P.M. on Saturday evening, August 22. He picked Jamie up at 6:15 P.M. and they went to the ball field on Mitchell Boulevard and watched some guys playing ball. While they were there, Jamie told Allen that he "had the prostitutes lined up."

When they got back in the car, Allen told Jamie that he "didn't want anything to do with this. They're all yours."

According to Mr. Tipton: "I dropped him off and told him he could have them." He "dropped him off" at Pleasant and Yellow Springs Streets.

He went on to say that he picked Jamie up again sometime Sunday afternoon and that Jamie was "real quiet" that day.

With the start of the school year—and still no arrest—parents became even more protective of their children. Instead of waiting alone in the morning for their school buses—as they may have done in years past—the children were now accompanied by their mothers and/or fathers. The ritual was then repeated in reverse in the afternoon.

The warning "Don't talk to strangers!" was repeated over and over.

According to Tina Leach, Martha's fourteen-year-old

sister, she and her siblings didn't start school that year until September 20. Her mother, in her grief, simply "forgot about school."

Unanswered questions—and much speculation—punctuated nearly every conversation in the community and the workplace: How had one man managed to control both girls? Did he force them to the pond area? Or lure them? How did this happen?

Physically Phree and Martha were the size of grown women, and the two of them together had been unable to fight off their attacker.

After the new composite drawing, a combination of the original two, appeared in the local newspaper, the police department was inundated with telephone calls. The citizens of Springfield seemed to see the suspect everywhere: in the face of a neighbor, or an acquaintance, or a stranger on the street, or even a family member. They had seen him at a party, at a discount store, a drugstore, everywhere.

The detectives were overwhelmed with hundreds of tips. They took each and every call seriously, no matter how outrageous or bizarre the information seemed to be; but, of course, they had to prioritize and follow up on the most promising leads first.

The contents of the tips revealed the paranoia that had spread throughout the city and even into neighboring towns and counties.

Several callers told the police about a man named "Sam" who lived in a house where they cared for mentally "retarded" people. It was not unusual to see "Sam" walking the streets of Springfield. Although he seemed to be harmless, a woman caller claimed that he had "flashed" her five years earlier.

An employee of a well-known fast-food restaurant called about a fellow employee and stated, "I just don't like him."

On Thursday morning, August 27, 1992, at 8:07, a woman named Donna Scott* reported to the police that a white male fitting the suspect's description "lives with his father just west of the Japanese Connection (auto repair shop) on East Main Street."

Thirteen minutes later, a man, who specifically asked that his name not be made public, telephoned to say that a "boy" matching the composite drawing lived in the second house west of Sycamore Street on East Main Street near the Japanese Connection. He stated that the "boy" wears glasses.

About 5:30 P.M. on the same day, Ellen Short* called and told them that the "suspect" mowed grass on East Main Street at Blessing Pump. She informed the police that he "looks just like the newest composite" and he had brown hair and was in his late teens or early twenties. She gave his name as "J.R." Lilly and said that he lived on East Main Street, just east of Dewine's Dairy Distributing.

That evening, August 27, 1992, a man walked into Whitacre's Drug Store on Lagonda Avenue, and when the cashier asked if she could help him, he said, "I'll sure be glad when they catch these child killers because they say I sure look a lot like him."

Laura Pace* was sure she recognized the man because they had filled prescriptions for him in the past. She called the police to report what she had heard and even gave the officer his name and address: Kessler Lilly lived on East Main Street, not far from Susan Palmer's house. She described him as being in his midtwenties, 5'7" to 5'9", 150 to 160 pounds, with "sandy" hair. She added that he wore glasses and had a "stubble" growth of beard.

The next day, Darlene Brooks*, a woman who had been a customer in the drugstore the evening before, called and told police that she had overheard a man talking about the murders. She reported that he said, "I hope the police catch the guy soon because I look like him." She said he was wearing jeans, a T-shirt, and white tennis shoes with gray trim. She added that it "looked like he had dried blood on his tennis shoes."

There was only one house between the Japanese Connection and Dewine's Dairy Distributing.

On Sunday, August 30, an unidentified caller told the police that they had overheard a conversation about a man who fit the description of the suspect and his brother who lived on East Main Street in the area of Schuler's Bakery.

The caller told them that the man's name was Bill Lilly and his brother's was J.R.

On Wednesday, September 2, a man named Eli Shaw*, who lived on East Main Street, informed the police that the "suspect's" name was Kessler Lilly Jr. and that he cut grass for Blessing Pump. He told them that J.R. matched the picture and that he had scratches on the left side of his face, a pierced ear, and tattoos on his arm.

Some of the investigators were familiar with J.R.; it wasn't unusual to see him riding his bicycle in the area, but they had never known him to be violent. However, Sergeant Moody and Detective Davidson did go to his home to question the mentally impaired young man and obtained a sample of his blood for DNA testing.

Even though, when the results came back, it did not match the DNA found in the semen in the girls, these tips would come back to haunt the detectives.

On Saturday morning, about 11:00, Sergeant Michael Haytas returned to the crime scene to check some measurements and to begin drawing detailed diagrams of the area.

6

I'm saying that somebody was sitting there watching me . . . and waiting for me to leave.

—Sergeant Michael Haytas

Incredible. Almost unbelievable. The pond had been drained. They had crawled on their hands and knees in the mud looking for anything that might help them solve these horrible murders. The rocks were not there. Now, seven days after the bodies had been discovered, two of the rocks had mysteriously reappeared. Who took them? Who brought them back? Why? Was someone watching?

Earlier in the week, Mrs. Strahler, whose family owned and operated Strahler's Warehouse, had reported to Sergeant Moody that there were three large lava rocks missing from the spot where the bodies had been found. They had been part of the landscape. She even had pictures of them.

The huge stone that had been left on Phree's head was not one of the lava rocks. Except for its enormous size, it was not unusual.

There was no doubt that the colorful lava rocks were missing. They had not been there when the crime scene was processed and did not show up in any of the many photographs taken. The area had been gone over with the proverbial fine-tooth comb.

Sergeant Moody was astonished when Mrs. Strahler called on Sunday afternoon and told him that she had just found two of the rocks in the pond. She had managed to get them out of the water with a rake.

This discovery was nothing less than eerie. In their original state these rocks had been embedded in the dirt. The killer had moved the rocks and then placed the victims' faces in the remaining "holes."

Sergeant Haytas had left the scene about one hour before Mrs. Strahler caught sight of them in the pond, just north of the place where Phree and Martha had been found. He had been there finishing his drawings and diagrams documenting the area and he was absolutely sure that the rocks were not there when he left. Between 1:00 and 2:00 P.M., a mere sixty minutes, the person(s) who had taken the rocks had returned them to within a few feet of where the girls' feet had been. Without being seen.

Had the killer taken them as a souvenir? Where was the third rock? Was the killer attempting to taunt the police officers? It was one of the most bizarre things any of them had ever heard of in all their combined years of investigative experiences.

They were, of course, aware that many serial killers do take a trophy, but there was no evidence at this time that these were serial killings. However, many killers, serial or otherwise, will return to the scene of a murder for various sick reasons. Was this one somehow trying to insert himself into the investigation by returning pieces of evidence?

After mysteriously reappearing and then being recovered by Mrs. Strahler, the two lava rocks were collected by Officers Lisa Westerheide and Linda Powell and submitted to the crime lab in the hope that the rocks would hold some sort of clue still clinging to their colorful surfaces. The investigators were not optimistic, however, since they had been found underwater. But they had to be sure.

Crime scene personnel returned to the pond area on Monday morning to make sure nothing else had been returned to the scene.

In the afternoon, with the assistance of the Springfield Sewer Division, they opened a nearby sewer manhole. Officer Beedy and two sewer workers searched the Mill Run sewer line for possible evidence.

A sewer suction truck was called to remove the debris from a storm catch basin on Lagonda Avenue, under the Route 40 overpass. The sludge was dumped at a site on Mitchell Boulevard, and Officer Beedy and Sergeant Haytas went through it, by hand, hoping to find something—anything—to help them with their investigation.

Over the next few days, several strange letters were received by the police department, the local newspaper, and members of the victims' families. They were all anonymous letters with many misspelled words and very little punctuation. The printing was childlike. The letter sent to Jettie Willoughby, Martha Leach's mother, read:

I don't want to hurt you But Thouh you should no
Dear MRS. Leach. my heart go out to the parents of
These 2 little grils But There is something you A MRS
Marrow Both Should no The police Dept is Saying your
grils were proistues That why they were there This is
The inside word They ARe Releasing iT To The pouple
They ARe also Blaming A encene person whom was
home Asleep at The Time

A similar letter was sent to Bennie Morrow, Phree's father. The letter to the *Springfield News-Sun* that was obviously written by the same person read:

The police DepT sTinks We are one of your best cus-
toms Here A inside scop if you want To prienT iT

To whom iT may concern Here is some inside info on
The 2 Little grils found They The police DepT or say-
ing The 2 grils wre prosiTues And They Are Trying To

frame A encene young man They have been Hassing
foR 2 nigHTs He cant even Ride Around wiThouT being
follow by The police They Have Retarted man qustion-
ing him. They Think He done The killing of The grils

And in the margin of the three-holed notebook paper, it read: "I hope To see part of this in you paper Anyway"

The police department received several letters containing "tips" about men that the writer considered suspicious, cars in the area, and asking if anyone had looked inside the warehouse.

In all, there were seven letters received by family members, the newspaper, and the police. Each and every one of them contained the misspelled word "grils" at least once.

The family members who had been out searching for Phree and Martha on the night of August 22 informed the detectives that Bennie Morrow had been the one to lead them to the Lion's Cage and the pond.

On September 9, 1992, Bennie submitted to having his blood drawn for DNA testing. When the results came back from the FBI, his DNA did not match the DNA in the semen found in the girls. It was just a very strange and eerie coincidence that he had led the group to the very area where the bike was found and to within feet of where the bodies were discovered.

A few weeks after the murders, in an effort to learn more about Phree's family life, Sergeant Steve Moody and Detective Robert Davidson interviewed Bennie's girlfriend, Andria Wells:

Davidson: Did you know both these girls? Or just Phree?

Andria: I spent the last seven years of her life with Phree. I had met Martha one night—and that was the night they went skating—that Friday night.

Davidson: Why don't you tell us how you felt about
   Phree? What did she like to do? What kind of kid
   was she?

Andria: Well, she was ornery—but what kid isn't
   ornery? She pulled the wool over her father's eyes
   lots of times. I caught her in different lies. But we
   had a pretty good relationship up until the time she
   was going to her mother's. There was different days
   that she went to her mom's to spend the night and, I
   don't know, it was like she was a completely different person after she went down there. She wasn't the
   same little girl.

Davidson: So, about three weeks previous to her being
   murdered, she started going down there a lot?

Andria: Yeah, and he went down to pick her up to
   make sure she was being fed.

According to Andria, Bennie worried about Phree's eating
habits at her mother's. Susan didn't always have enough
money to have supper on the table. Sometimes Bennie and
Andria would bring Phree home to eat supper with them and
then take her back to her mother's later in the evening or the
next day. But then Phree balked at having to leave her
mother's house even for that brief period of time, so they
would pick her up and take her out to eat and then take her
right back to Susan's house.

Davidson: How did he feel about Phree spending so
   much time with her mother?

Andria: He didn't like it. He didn't like it and then he
   got curious and was asking her why she had to be
   down there all the time. "What's drawing you down
   there?" And she nonchalantly wouldn't answer him.

Davidson: Do you have any idea what was drawing her
   down there?

Andria: Boys.

By the end of September, according to Captain Richard O'Brien, the police had spent "in excess of two thousand man-hours" on the case. They had received many hundreds of tips and had questioned more than two hundred people. But they still did not have a primary suspect.

It was mid-October before the police released to the public that Phree and Martha might have eaten a full meal between the time they disappeared and the time they were murdered. They thought it was possible that the girls had eaten in a restaurant.

It was also revealed that the girls were seen about 5:15 P.M. on Saturday, August 22, 1992, riding a boy's twenty-inch purple bicycle. Martha was riding on the handlebars while Phree pedaled the bike and they were going west on East Main Street.

They also said that Phree and Martha were wearing short-sleeved shirts and shorts and tennis shoes the day they were murdered.

Captain Richard O'Brien asked that anyone who may remember seeing the girls anytime on August 22 to please call the police with the information.

In December 1992 at least five concerned citizens called the police department and reported that they had seen, or were still in the possession of, a $1 bill with a message written on it: "Vance Brown* killed the two girls." Several of them turned the currency over to the authorities.

Brown was located and interviewed by Sergeant Moody and Detective Eggers. The middle-aged family man who had held the same job for twenty-seven years had obviously been the victim of a cruel hoax.

Six months after the brutal murders of Phree Morrow and Martha Leach, police revealed that they had two witnesses who had heard a child scream the night the girls disappeared. Sergeant Moody, along with Captain Walters and Lieutenant Schrader, was interviewed on a local radio station, WBLY, by talk show host Darryl Bauer.

Sergeant Moody explained that sometime within the previous month two men had come forward and reported that at about 11:00 on the night of August 22, 1992, they had heard a "bloodcurdling" scream coming from the area where Phree and Martha's bodies were later found.

Shortly after that, the same two men saw a burgundy Grand Prix with a white top leaving the same area. There were two men and a woman in the car. They said the car went west on Section Street, ran a stop sign, and sped away.

The two men knew the information was important, but they did not come forward sooner because they had been involved in illegal activity at the time and were afraid they would be blamed for the killings.

This new information was released to the public in the hope that even more people would come forward with important information.

By this time more than ten people had had their blood drawn for DNA testing.

7

That was kind of eerie . . . going up to her house but not being able to tell her, 'The guy living right next to you . . .'

—Sergeant Barry Eggers

The week after the detectives were guests on the radio talk show, they finally got a break in the case. Jamie Turner's mother informed them that Jamie had been having nightmares and she had heard him screaming the names of the two dead girls. Jamie's father had died and he and his mother lived together.

The investigators had talked to Jamie on several occasions since their first encounter with him. They had even taken him to the crime scene and had him "walk through" what he had seen on the night of the murders.

They had set the scene—as close as they could—to what the light, distance, etc., would have been, based on what Jamie had told them. According to Sergeant Haytas, "He's saying he saw all this in detail? You couldn't see your hand in front of your face. He had to be there or know what was going on. He didn't see it from that distance. He had to be involved in it. He's saying things that he saw that you couldn't see in the dark—not unless you were right up on it."

Another time they had even arranged for the chubby, unsophisticated man to be hypnotized, in the hope that they might learn more details—to no avail.

Jamie, wearing faded blue jeans and a turquoise striped

T-shirt, was brought in for questioning on the afternoon of March 1, 1993. During the interrogation Jamie, who had previously told the detectives that he saw a "Chinese guy" murder Phree Morrow and Martha Leach, implicated his cousin Alexander Boone*, someone named Damien, and someone named "Kevin."

> Graeber: Are you telling me he (Alexander Boone) is the one that killed the girls?
>
> Jamie (his voice husky, but his speech childlike): He didn't kill them. He watched.
>
> Graeber: Who killed them?
>
> Jamie: Kevin did.
>
> Graeber: Who had intercourse with the girls, Jamie?
>
> Jamie (briefly biting his lower lip before he answered): I didn't. Alex or Kevin—I ain't sure. They both did. Then I saw that guy kill the girls . . . Alex.
>
> Graeber: Whose idea was it to meet the girls?
>
> Jamie: It that Damien's.
>
> Graeber: Well, you told Allen—
>
> Jamie: Allen is full of shit I tell him.
>
> Graeber: And you told Chuck and Valerie.
>
> Jamie (pouting): They got me in lots of trouble.
>
> Graeber: You went down to the tree house, right?
>
> Jamie: Yeah, I went down there and nothing to do with this. They having sex with the girls . . . Kevin and Alex.
>
> (Jamie couldn't seem to sit still. He fidgeted with his hair, smoothing it down with the palm of his hand, and then tugged at his left ear.)
>
> Graeber: How did the girls get covered up?
>
> Jamie: They covered them up. They told me if I didn't help them, they'd kill me.
>
> Graeber: So what did you do?
>
> Jamie: Helped them.
>
> Graeber: Help?

Jamie (scowling at the detective): Yeah. I told you who fuckin' did it!

Graeber: Who had the rock?

Jamie: Damien.

Graeber: What did he do with the rock?

Jamie: Hit her head.

Graeber: Did they have their clothes on or not?

Jamie: No.

Graeber: What clothes didn't they have on?

Jamie: Their pants.

Graeber: Did they have any clothes on at all?

Jamie: Yeah, had shirts.

(Jamie told Detective Graeber that the blond-haired girl [Martha] slapped him.)

Graeber: Why did the girl slap you?

Jamie (running his hand over his face and then almost whispering): Because they say I'm ugly.

Graeber: You were holding the blond-haired girl because she slapped you, right? How were you holding her?

Jamie (biting his lip again): Was holding her behind her. Up by her neck. I wasn't doing nothing to her.

Graeber: And she was yelling at you, kicking you?

Jamie: Yeah.

Graeber: What did you do?

Jamie: Damien come down and punch her.

(Jamie told the detectives again that Alex watched while Damien hit the girls in the head. And then he told them that Damien was the one who had sex with them.)

Jamie: Damien keep hitting her with a stick. Blond-headed girl. Then Damien hit that one girl in the head with a rock—on the forehead. They take turns throwing rocks on their heads.

Graeber: Who took their clothes off?

Jamie: Damien—cut them off, I guess—cut it down
     here at the legs.

Graeber: How did they get the underwear off of her?

Jamie: Cut them off. Damien took off the underwear.

(Jamie told the detectives that Damien killed the girls
     and Alex had sex with one of them. They threw the
     clothes down the "sewer." Damien, Alex, and Jamie
     covered them up. Jamie said he helped because they
     threatened him. He said he just "got some weeds.")

Graeber: Then what was put on them?

Jamie: That big box or something. Some kind of two-
     by-fours—some kind of boards.

Graeber: Where did you get the boards?

Jamie: Over in that pile—just picked up one. I laid one
     on top—on the blonde.

(Jamie told them that he liked the blond-haired girl "be-
     cause she nice-looking.")

Graeber: Did you go back down there on Sunday?

Jamie (slouching down in his chair and yawning): No.
     I was home all day with my Mom.

Graeber (reminding Jamie): You were sitting on the
     hood of the captain's car.

Jamie: Yeah. Then I didn't go back down.

Graeber: Why did you go back down there?

Jamie: See if they still down there—I didn't know if
     they move them or not.

Before they questioned Jamie, they already knew from preliminary DNA tests that the semen found in Phree and
Martha was from one man. One man and only one man had
left his semen in both girls.

They also knew that Jamie was not that man.

Although Jamie was confused about who did what, there
was much truth in his statement. He knew about many things
that had never been released to the public. Jamie's mental
retardation was obvious, but he was also "street-smart."

The next day, Tuesday, March 2, 1993, Sergeant Moody and Detective Graeber questioned Alexander Boone, Jamie's twenty-seven-year-old cousin. Jamie's father and Alex's mother were siblings. Alex's mother was white and his father black. Tall and thin at 5'11" and 140 pounds, he had wild curly hair and a full mustache.

Alex was also mentally impaired, although not to the same degree as Jamie. He was what was commonly referred to as a "slow learner." Sergeant Moody and Detective Graeber had a very difficult time extracting information from him, but during the almost five hours they questioned him, he told them enough for them to suspect that he also was present during the murders of Phree and Martha.

As Alex fiddled with the collar of his gray pullover, he told them that he saw Damien hitting one of the girls "with a board or something."

Moody: You knew we would be coming eventually to talk to you, didn't you?

(Alex shook his head no.)

Moody: Why? Why didn't you think we would be coming to talk to you?

Alex: Because I didn't have nothing to do with this.

Moody (amazed): But you were there. If you didn't have anything to do with this and you were there, how come you didn't get ahold of one of us and tell us what had happened? Who had sex with the girls?

Alex: Damien.

Moody: What did you do?

Alex: Nothing. Leaving, trying to leave.

Moody: What did Jamie do?

Alex: Was helping.

Moody: Helping? What do you mean by that?

Alex: Well, he make love to them and Damien made love to them. And they said if I told, talked to you all, then he would have me killed. I don't know what else to tell you. I just seen them. Then they took advantage of them. They told me if I said anything that they was going to come after me.

Graeber: How was Damien taking advantage of the girls?

Alex (nervously running his fingers through his hair): After he was tossing them, whooping them around— after he hit the girl with the fist, he knocked her on the floor. Then he started ripping off her clothes.

Graeber (patiently): Let me interject something here, okay? Just so I can understand the story. Instead of knocking her "on the floor," let's say "knocked her on the ground."

Alex (a little confused, but agreeing): Oh, okay.

Graeber: Let's go from there.

Alex: Okay.

Graeber: I mean dirt ground—not wooden ground— dirt ground. Let's go through the story from there, okay?

Alex: Okay. After he knocked her on the ground, he took a stick and hit her upside the head with it on the other side. And that's just about . . . That's all. They left. And I came home.

It would be sometime before the detectives realized they had missed an important piece of information in this exchange with Alex: "knocked her on the floor." Sergeant Moody and Detective Graeber knew that the girls had been raped and murdered at the pond, so they were sure, when Alex said "floor," he actually meant "ground."

Much later in the statement, Alex said that they were in a house at first, but he couldn't tell them where the house was located, so this, too, was dismissed.

Moody: What happened to the two girls that we're talking about?

Alex: They got raped—beat up. Killed.

Graeber: Alex, who killed the girls?
Alex: Damien did. Stabbed—with a knife. Stabbed her
   in the stomach, hit her across the head with a stick,
   and hit her with a fist.
Moody: You saw what was going on, things were get-
   ting out of hand. These two little—little girls . . .
   Why wouldn't you do something to go get help?
Alex: Freaked out or something.
Graeber: Who hit them in the head with a rock?
Alex: Damien.

Although Alex's account was also confusing, he, too, told
the detectives many details, some that matched what Jamie
had told them and some that had never been made public. He
told them that Jamie and Damien set up the meeting with the
two girls and one had light-colored hair and the other had
dark hair. Jamie tried to kiss one of the girls and she slapped
him.

He also told them that they were all drinking beer. One of
them fell in the pond and got wet. Another one took a pair of
panties and put them in his pocket. He said that the heavyset
girl (Phree) was cussing and yelling.

And that the victims' bodies were side by side, both facedown, and positioned on an "island." Both victims were
partially clothed—tops on, pants off. One girl was cut in the
stomach area. One pair of shorts was cut and "pulled apart."

The girls were struck in the face and the head, and both
were sexually assaulted by one person. Even though he said
that Jamie and Damien both "made love" to the girls, when
he was asked who "had sex" with them, he said, "Damien."
Throughout this investigation it would become increasingly obvious that the idea of sexual intercourse varied
considerably among the mentally challenged.

Although neither girl was stabbed in the stomach, what
Alex most likely saw was her shorts being cut off with a
knife.

Moody: You said Damien had a knife. What did he do with the knife?

Alex: Well, at first I thought he cutted her with the knife. But I wasn't for sure.

Later that day, Jamie Turner was brought in for questioning again. Detective Graeber conducted the interview. Also present were Jamie's mother and Agent John Finnegan of the FBI.

After Detective Graeber read him his rights, Jamie removed his jacket and hung the dark windbreaker on the back of the chair, then asked: "Am I going to jail?"

Graeber: We can't answer that right now.

Finnegan: That's not up to us, Jamie.

Jamie: Who is it up to?

Finnegan: It's up to the prosecutor.

Jamie (whining): I have to go to jail for something I didn't do.

Graeber: Well, did we accuse you of doing anything?

Jamie: No.

Graeber (mildly exasperated): The only thing I've ever said is that you haven't always told me the truth. Isn't that what I've always said?

Jamie: Yeah. After we get done questioning, can I leave?

Detective Graeber (patiently explaining): Well, today we have to go through a whole bunch of people between me and you, okay? The prosecutor, the chief, the captain—

Jamie: I don't understand what he's saying.

Finnegan: It's not up to us.

Graeber: I've got to clear everything through them. Understand that?

Jamie (pleading): Yeah. After you do that, can I go home?

(Jamie would not admit that it was his idea to meet the girls, even though he had told several of his friends that he was meeting two girls that night.)

Graeber: You met the two girls downtown with them?

Jamie: Yeah.

Graeber: But you set it up.

Jamie: No, I did not. I swear to God I didn't set it up. They did. I swear to God, Al.

Finnegan: Who is "they," Jamie?

Jamie: Alex and Damien, they set it up. I didn't. I swear. You think I lying.

("Kevin" was never mentioned again.)

Graeber: Well, I don't know. It's like I said—there are some questions we've got to straighten out.

Jamie: I ain't lying to you, Al, you know that.

Finnegan: No, he doesn't, Jamie. He doesn't know that anymore.

Jamie (insisting he was not lying): I tell you square. That's a square answer.

Graeber (firmly): What did I tell you last night when you left? Didn't I tell you that we aren't done talking yet?

Jamie: Yeah.

Graeber: Didn't I tell you that you weren't the main player in this whole thing?

Jamie: Yeah. I ain't.

Graeber: And the best thing you can do is tell us everything. That's what we're doing here; we're finishing it up.

Jamie: Will you guys bug me no more?

Graeber: Jamie, that's up to you. Now I told you last night, you've got to clear everything up and don't leave any loose ends.

Finnegan: Jamie, do you want to sleep tonight?

Jamie: Yeah—at home.

(Jamie claimed that they stopped at Rally's on East

Main Street and got hamburgers, French fries, and drinks, then went to the pond to eat. He said he didn't get anything to eat because he was feeling sick.)

Finnegan: Jamie, they ate at the pond. Then they got doughnuts. Who got the doughnuts?

Jamie: Damien did.

Finnegan: He went into the bakery and got the doughnuts?

Jamie: Yeah.

(Agent Finnegan asked what time he thought it was by then.)

Jamie: About seven-thirty, something like that. I don't know, you know.

Finnegan: You weren't wearing a watch, were you?

Jamie (yawning and stretching his arms over his head): Huh-uh. I don't know how to tell time on a watch.

Finnegan: Was it still light out?

Jamie: Yeah.

Graeber: I'm saying that you were on the other side of the pond, the same side of the pond that Damien was on with the dark-haired girl. And you grabbed ahold of the blond-haired girl.

Jamie: I didn't kill her.

Graeber (his patience wearing a little thin): Did I say that? Did I say you killed her? Did I?

Jamie: No.

Graeber: I said you were over there and for six months you've been telling me this other bullshit that you weren't over there and that's exactly where you were.

Jamie: I wasn't doing nothing to her.

Graeber: That's where you were—you had your arm around her neck.

Jamie: I wasn't choking her.

Graeber: But you're rolling around on the ground with her.

Jamie: I wasn't choking her.

Graeber: Were you or were you not, did you or did you not, roll around on the ground with her?

Jamie: No, I wasn't rolling around with her.

Graeber: You were wrestling her on the ground.

Jamie: You act like you don't believe me no more.

Graeber: Hey, what did I tell you when we started out? Ninety percent of the stuff you told me last night was true, ten percent bullshit. This is part of the ten percent.

Jamie (sulking): I got them for you. What else do you want?

Graeber: You're damn right you did, which you could have done six months ago.

Jamie: I didn't kill her; you know that.

Graeber: Didn't say you did. I didn't say you did. But it took me six months to get you across this pond. Now what else aren't you telling me?

Jamie: I'm telling you everything.

Graeber: Jamie, you didn't tell me about being over here on the ground, holding her until Damien got over there.

Jamie (pouting): You didn't ask me.

Finnegan: All right, Jamie, you held her. You held the blond girl, Martha, and you are on the other side of the pond up where the pallets are in this picture.

Jamie: I didn't do nothing to her. I didn't beat her.

Finnegan: But you held her there.

Jamie: I didn't kill her, though.

Finnegan: You held her there for Damien. Is that true?

Jamie: Yeah, I didn't beat her, though.

Finnegan: You hit her. She hit you. Why did she hit you?

Jamie: Because I said something smart to her.

Finnegan: What did you say smart to her, Jamie?

Jamie (rubbing his eyes with the palm of his hand): I forget now.

Graeber: What did you say smart to her to make her
   slap you?
Jamie: I told you.
Finnegan: What did you say to her, Jamie? Jamie?
Jamie: I quit talking.
Finnegan: You quit talking? What does that mean?
Jamie (frowning): I finished.
Graeber: Well then, Jamie, I'm finished.

That night, about 9:30, Jamie Turner was arrested at his
home on Lagonda Avenue, next door to where Martha Leach
lived when she disappeared. He and his mother had moved
there about three months after the murders.

Jamie and his mother lived in an upper duplex, and Jettie
Willoughby, Martha's mother, still lived in the upper duplex
next door. The two houses were so close to each other that the
landings on the outside stairs almost touched each other.

About 10:00 that same night, Alexander Boone was arrested at police headquarters, where he had turned himself in.

Later that night, Damien Tyler* was arrested and questioned and then held on unrelated drug-trafficking charges at
the Clark County Juvenile Detention Center. He was fifteen
years old.

Alexander Boone and Damien Tyler both submitted to
having their blood drawn for DNA testing.

On Wednesday, March 3, 1993, Boone and Turner were arraigned and charged with two counts each of aggravated
murder. Their cash bond was set at $500,000 each.

The following Monday, the Clark County grand jury indicted Jamie Turner and Alexander Boone on thirteen counts
each: six counts of aggravated murder, two counts of rape,
two counts of kidnapping, one count of obstructing justice,
and two counts of abuse of a corpse.

The charge of aggravated murder carried death penalty
specifications. According to the law in the state of Ohio, com-

mitting murder with prior intent, or while committing rape, or while committing kidnapping, are considered separate offenses. Hence, since there were two victims, six counts each of aggravated murder.

That afternoon Jamie's distraught mother requested help from the police while, understandably, she moved away from her home on Lagonda Avenue. The uniformed officers stood watch while she moved her belongings, making sure that none of the neighbors bothered her. She claimed that some of them had been taunting her.

Detectives Eggers and Graeber had been to see Jettie several times over the months to keep her informed about the case, but because of the volatility of the situation, they knew they couldn't tell her that her next-door neighbor was a possible suspect.

With the arrests of Jamie Turner and Alexander Boone, the town breathed a collective sigh of relief. They thought it was over. They could stop viewing every stranger with suspicion. They could loosen their grip on their children—just a little. They thought they could go back to normal. They were wrong.

On Friday, March 5, twenty-three-year-old John Balser, another mentally impaired young man, came to police headquarters with information about the two murders. He and Jamie Turner had gone to school together at Town and Country. John would prove to be one of the biggest challenges to the detectives; his IQ was similar to Jamie's. He was a heavyset man at 5'7" and 180 pounds.

During this visit, in a very confusing statement, John claimed that Jamie had told him and several other people that he had been there when the girls were killed. John had tried to get Jamie to turn himself in and get help. John also told Detective Graeber and Sergeant Moody that Jamie told him a man named Lloyd Tyler* was with them that night. Lloyd was Damien's uncle and he also went to Town and Country Day School.

"I would get up in front of anyone and say Jamie didn't do it. I know . . . I know Jamie too well. I know Jamie would never hurt no one. Jamie's been with me almost since . . . I know Jamie all the way through school, never did nothing like this and all," John Balser stated.

But then John claimed that he heard Jamie say, "I killed both and raped both."

According to John Balser, John's stepdad, David Marciszewski, also heard Jamie say it.

John, however, did not believe Jamie. "I say it was Lloyd instead of Jamie. I don't think Jamie would do it," Balser maintained.

"Why do you say that, because Jamie's your best friend?" Graeber asked.

"No—no way. Me and Jamie got together always through school. Jamie never did nothing like that," Balser emphasized.

John told them the names of three other people who had heard Jamie talking about the murders. Besides his stepdad, John claimed that his three cousins had been present when Jamie was talking about the crime: Willie Jackson*, Robby Detwiler*, and Frank Fisher*.

He also claimed that Lloyd Tyler heard Jamie and told him to "shut up."

A few days later, Detective Graeber talked to Frank Fisher, a forty-year-old mentally retarded man. Frank verified that he was with John, Jamie, and the others when Lloyd Tyler told Jamie to shut up because he "did not want to hear no more." Frank could not or would not tell the detective what Jamie had said.

8

It was difficult with a lot of them because you didn't know whether you weren't getting the answers to your questions because they were being deceptive or if it was because their mental capacity just wouldn't allow it.

—Sergeant Barry Eggers

March 24, 1993, was an exhausting day for the determined investigators, as a number of interviews were conducted that day.

Sergeant Moody and Detective Eggers questioned thirteen-year-old Willie Jackson and fourteen-year-old Robby Detwiler, John Balser's cousins. Because the young boys had spent the weekend of August 22 and 23, 1992, at David and Wanda Marciszewski's house, the detectives thought they might have information pertinent to the investigation. John lived on South Light Street, with Wanda (his mother) and David (his stepfather). John's real father had died.

Willie, a thin, dark-haired boy, told the detectives that John Balser and Jamie Turner had been together the night of the murders. When John came into the house a little after 11:00, he asked Willie and Robby if they wanted a cookie. When they asked where he got them, he replied that he got them from "the bakery."

The detectives knew that the cookies that Willie described to them almost certainly came from Schuler's Bakery. These were soft chocolate-chip cookies, each wrapped individually in the cellophane that the bakery clerk used to pick them up gingerly and place them in a bag or a box.

But the cookies that John offered the boys weren't in a bag or a box—they were in his pants pockets. The two young cousins thought that he had stolen them, but they didn't ask because they "knew he'd get mad and start yelling."

Willie also told the detectives that when he saw Jamie a couple of days after the murders, Jamie had bruises on his arms. When Willie asked him what happened, Jamie claimed that he had wrecked his bicycle.

And, referring to John, Willie offered, "He kept coming up with details that wasn't on the news or nothing."

At 2:00 that afternoon Detectives Eggers and Graeber interviewed John Balser again. Even though it was early spring, John was bundled up in a bulky winter coat and sweatpants. John's very worried guardian, Joe Jackson*, accompanied him to the police station. Jackson was also John's uncle and Willie's father.

John Balser tried desperately to give Jamie Turner an alibi for the night of the murders. He gave a convoluted account of times, places, and people he had seen that day. His concept of time was questionable, so Joe Jackson tried to help the detectives interpret the series of events as John told them.

Joe knew that John had not been home all evening on the date in question because he had called the house several times to check on John, and neither John nor David Marciszewski was there. Wanda was at work, caring for an elderly lady who lived on Lagonda Avenue.

Eggers: From what I understand, John and Jamie were together from noon that day until ten-thirty that night.

Graeber: Here's the problem we got here—the way he's putting the times together, puts him right in the middle of the murder.

Jackson: That's what I'm afraid of.

Graeber: Believe me—putting him right in the middle of the murder.

Jackson: It worries me because when he came back home—he's been so upset. I don't know that he was there.

John (interjecting): I wasn't there when it happened.

Graeber: That's what he's doing, Joe. He's putting himself right in the middle. See, we know Jamie was there.

John (protesting): I know Jamie was with me at twelve.

Jackson: I know something happened that night that shouldn't have happened because John has been upset and his moods has changed terrible.

Graeber: Since that night?

Jackson: Real bad, yes. Well, he's so close to Jamie. Jamie graduated with him. We were there at the graduation. They were just like two brothers.

(The detectives talked to John for over two hours and got at least six different stories from him. At the end of the statement, John agreed to have his blood drawn for DNA testing.)

It had been a long day and it was far from being over. By the time Detectives Barry Eggers and Nathaniel Smoot interviewed David Marciszewski that evening, their patience was wearing a little thin. David was John's thirty-three-year-old stepfather and was also mentally impaired, although not as severely as John and Jamie. Unlike John, he was meek, mild-mannered, and soft-spoken. He wore slightly baggy blue jeans and a sport shirt.

Smoot: Tell us what John told you.

David: He was saying that Jamie and this other guy did have something to do with the murders.

Eggers (exasperated): What is that supposed to mean?

What exactly did he say? How did he put it? Did he
tell you that he was there? Now if somebody tells
you something like that—it's not going to be something you're going to have to sit here and think
about.

Smoot: Look at your face—we know the answer is
"yes"—but the thing is you know he told you that.

David (hanging his head): Yeah.

Smoot: John was there, wasn't he?

Eggers: He told you that, didn't he?

David: That's what he said. He said the girls was
raped and murdered. He told me that he was holding the girls down and he had something to do with
the murder of the girls.

David, a slight man at 5'5" and 130 pounds, became increasingly nervous and reluctant with his answers, but the
detectives persisted until they elicited the following information from him: "They stabbed them, after they raped
them. Beat them, really beat them—beat them to death too.
I think it was a board. Either a board or a lead pipe . . . I'm
not too sure what they beat them with. Jamie and that other
guy was with him. I think he said Lloyd. I think that's
what—I'm not sure about Lloyd. He did say there was
three or four of them. He said that they buried them with
leaves."

Eggers: Did John ever show you anything that belonged to those girls?

David (quickly and firmly): No, he didn't.

Smoot (to Detective Eggers): Did you see that?

Smoot (to David): Did John ever show you anything
that belonged to those girls?

David: No.

Smoot: But you answered that so fast.

David (insisting): No, he didn't show me nothing about that.

Smoot: You never answered a question like that—that fast before—all the time we've been sitting here.

Eggers: What did he do with the evidence?

David: I'm not sure what they said. I do know that he said that they buried something. I don't know what it was.

Eggers: Buried at the house?

David: Yeah. I don't know where at. It ain't in the house. Somewhere in the backyard, I think.

Eggers: This is your chance to prove to us what you've told us is the truth. . . .

David: About what?

Eggers: All that's happened here. So you tell us where the evidence is.

Smoot: Were you with him when these girls . . . ?

David (protesting): No, I wasn't. No, I wasn't. I was right there at the house. I was there at the house.

After a break to get some coffee, Sergeant Moody came into the room and read David Marciszewski his rights. He was firm with David, and to the point:

Moody: All right. You have big problems. Do you understand me? You are protecting someone that has committed a very serious crime.

David: Who? John?

Moody: I'm asking you.

David: I know it ain't me because I wasn't there.

Moody: If you have lied to these officers about your knowledge about any evidence that was disposed of, you're going to be arrested. Do you understand that?

David: Yes.

Moody: I want you to start at the beginning. How do you feel about John?

David: Love him. As a stepson—I am his stepdad. Even though him and I get into arguments at times, I still care. He needs help with his . . . his alcohol. He's got a problem with that.

Moody: What else does he need help about, David?

David: I guess about the girls. Because of what happened to them—they was murdered. He said that he held the girls down. That's what he told me. I don't know what to believe. If he didn't do it, he wouldn't say something like that.

Moody: Tell us what he told you, so we can get on with it.

David (hesitantly): He said that they had intercourse with the girls, him and Jamie and the other guy. I don't know who the other guy was. He did say that. And he turned around . . . Well, they turned around and murdered them somehow. But first they, they was holding them down to . . . I guess they took turns. He said that the girls were screaming and, uh, like I said, he said that he was holding the girls down and had . . . sex with them. That's what I was getting ready to say.

Moody: David, did you help him get rid of some things that they took from those girls?

David: No, I didn't.

Moody: Do you know where some of those things are?

David: No.

Moody: Now you told the detectives something else.

David: Wait a minute. At Leibold's (a junkyard across the street from Strahler's Warehouse), from what he was telling me.

Moody: All right. If we go to Leibold's and they're not there and we go to the house and we find them there, what do you think is going to happen to you?

David: I'll go to jail.

Moody: Why would you think that?

David: I don't know.

Moody: Yes, you do. You're not a dumb man. Why are you protecting him? Are you afraid of him? Or did you help kill those girls?

David: No, I didn't help kill them girls.

Moody: Were you there when it happened?

David: Huh-uh. No, I wasn't there.

Moody: Do you understand something? I want you to understand something here. You know we got John's blood today. John told you that, didn't he? He showed you where we took the blood out of his arm. You know it's just a matter of time; we're waiting for a phone call now. When that phone call comes in, we aren't going to be able to help anybody. Anyone that has knowledge of something in this crime . . . The arrests aren't over. The arrests haven't stopped with Jamie Turner or Alex Boone. This community wants everyone responsible punished, but this community also understands someone that is brave enough to come forward. Someone that is brave enough with some evidence to come forward. You can't help what happened to them, but you can do them some justice and do yourself some justice right now. It's the hardest thing in the world to tell on yourself. You tell me you weren't there, I believe you. You tell me that you didn't kill those girls, I believe you. But I don't believe you when you talk about the evidence.

David, I'm going to explain something to you right now. We know you're lying. I know you helped him hide it. Do you think John told you everything he told us today? No, he didn't. Why do you think you're sitting here? Because he told us what you did. Now it's your turn to tell the truth. Did you help him dispose of some evidence from the crime?

David (haltingly): Yes. Buried it—at the house—in the backyard. Down in some hole—I don't know how deep that hole is. Out in the field . . . really beside the house, toward back, more, you know, more toward back. You guys think I'm lying?

Moody: Why are you afraid of John?

David: He's a big man. I don't know where the stuff's at. All I know is—I'll probably go to jail. Panties . . . I don't know what they look like. You're looking for something.

Moody: That's pretty good. How do you know we're looking for panties? You know what I think? I think you're just as guilty as John is. I think you are just as guilty as Jamie Turner is and I think you are just as guilty as Alex Boone is. You're guilty of murder too, aren't you? Think you can survive in prison?

David: I don't know.

Moody: Think you're going to get to find out. Well, you aren't helping yourself any here, David. You tell me you think we're looking for panties, why? You helped kill them girls, didn't you? David?

David (insisting he was not there): I was at the house.

Moody: What is it you're afraid of, David?

David: I don't know.

Moody: What? Just go ahead and say it. Did you have sex with those girls?

David: No.

Moody: You willing to give us some of your blood?

(David nodded yes.)

Moody: Okay. Did you help him dispose of some things?

David (uneasiness apparent in his voice—and his manner—as he tried to convince the detectives): No. See I didn't even know . . . Let me put it this way— I knew they was going to Schuler's Bakery, okay. I was at the house, but I didn't know what happened. I wasn't there when all this was supposed to be taking place. I was not there. I don't know where the stuff is buried—'cause he didn't have nothing when he come in the house. All he said is, uh . . . that, uh, he had something to do with it. And, uh, like I told you first the other day, that one guy by the name of Lloyd turned around and told Jamie to shut up. I didn't help him with nothing. I didn't hide anything. I don't know where the stuff is at.

Moody: Okay, you stick with that. You understand what we told you, right? You understand that if you've done something wrong, you're going to be punished, right?

David: Yeah, but I ain't done nothing.

Moody: Okay, well, then, fine, you stick with that, all right. We're done talking.

At 11:42 that same night, Sergeant Moody and Detective Graeber interviewed John Balser again. This time Joe Jackson was not present. John was talkative and outgoing and there were never long silences when he was being questioned. He listened as Detective Graeber read him his rights again.

Graeber: Now what I want you to understand . . . You were home when they came up and got Dave, right?

John: Yeah.

Graeber: And we had a long talk with Dave, real long talk. And you and Dave are close. And you talk a lot.

John: Yeah.

Graeber: In other words, you tell Dave a lot of stuff. As a matter of fact, you tell Dave everything, don't you?

John: Yeah.

Graeber: Okay, so we're going back to what you told Dave about this night. Okay?

John: Okay.

Graeber: Okay, now you start and tell me the whole thing.

John: Okay, me and Jamie went after doughnuts like I told you and him. I took those back to Robby and Willie, like I said. Me and Jamie went our separate ways that night. I went home and Jamie went wherever with Lloyd. I don't stay in contact that night with those.

Graeber: What did you tell Dave you did that night?

John: I told him me and Jamie went after doughnuts. That's all I told Dave, Sergeant Mooo-nee. (John pronounced Moody as "Mooo-nee.")

Graeber: You told him you grabbed their arms, didn't you?

John: No, I didn't. I didn't say nothing like that, Mooo-nee. I didn't do nothing, Mooo-nee. If I did, I'd told you first beginning.

Moody: Were those girls mean to you?

John: No.

Moody: Did they say mean things to you?

John: No.

Moody: All right. Did they say mean things to Jamie?

John: Said it to Jamie.

Moody: What did Jamie do?

John: Jamie hit those. Me, Lloyd, and Jamie—

Moody: Lloyd wasn't there. We know Lloyd wasn't there.

John: Okay, me and Jamie. I didn't hurt those girls.

Graeber: We didn't say you hurt them, did we? But you did have sex with them, didn't you?

John: Yeah. I didn't mean . . . I didn't hurt those in no way.

Graeber: But you had sex with both of them?

John: Yeah. Jamie hold those down, sir, and Jamie did had sex.

Moody: No, Jamie didn't. Do you know why we know Jamie didn't have sex?

John: Why?

Moody: Because we have his blood too. And blood doesn't lie.

John: I didn't either, sir.

Moody: How come you lied to us about going down to the bakery with Jamie?

John explained: See, when my uncle was in here I didn't want to say nothing to him. I was wanting . . . talk to you guys by myself. You see my point. Okay, I did have sex with those. Me and Jamie met each other. Down at the bakery—in front of it.

Moody: Who else was there with you, John?

John: Another boy. Colored.

Moody: Do you know his name?

John: No, I don't. He was there before me and Jamie got there.

Graeber: Where did you guys meet the girls at?

John: Down in behind there. That bakery. Just a big wooded area, I think. A pond.

Moody: John, you lied to Detective Graeber earlier today.

John: I didn't want Joe to know.

Moody: Joe's not here now, John. Were you supposed to meet the girls down there?

John: Yeah. Those girls told Jamie. They said, "Bring one of your friends along." I told Jamie, I said, "Jamie, I don't want to go." I said I'd been drinking. I was drinking all day that day.

Moody: Did you hit one of the girls?

John: No. I wouldn't do that. I did try not [to] hurt those. I was so aggravated at what me and Jamie did. I wasn't aggravated at those girls. I was so far out on drinking I didn't know what I was doing.

(Finally John admitted hitting one of the girls with his hand, and then: "I broke a limb off and hit those by that. I didn't know nothing would happen like that.")

Moody: What did Jamie hit the girls with?

John: Same thing. I think Jamie hit those girls with a board. I tried to stop him. I tried to stop Jamie. He wouldn't listen to me.

Moody: Who took the girls' pants off?

John: Me and Jamie. Unbuttoned those—unzipped those—and pulled those off.

Moody: Did you have a weapon?

John: No. I didn't have none. I don't carry those. I didn't hurt those girls. I had my knife with me. I didn't . . . I didn't have it open. I use it to cut wires.

Graeber: Okay, what else are knives good for? They're good for cutting. What else?

John: Killing people. I didn't use it for that.

Graeber: Did you cut anyone?

John: I just cut her clothes.

Graeber: Did you guys already kill the girls when you cut her clothes?

John: Huh-uh.

Graeber: Was she still alive when you cut her clothes?

John: Yes. I didn't . . . I didn't cut the girls. What I mean . . . I wouldn't harm the girl like that. Okay, I did cut her pants. Cut it like this. Straight down. Across here. I was careful around that girl's—around her stomach. I didn't want to cut those.

Moody: Did you cut her a little?

John: I did it on accident.

Moody: What did you do with the panties?

John (giving several conflicting answers): Me and Jamie left those laying there. Me and Jamie throwed those away. They're laying up there still. Probably in my house—in my bedroom—in my drawer . . .

Moody: What did you guys throw away?

John: Her clothes. Me and Jamie kept some of it. Just those panties.

Graeber: Okay, now this is a big question, okay. Now I want you to give me a straight answer, okay? Was

it the girl you had sex with the first time or the second time, when you made this statement: "Kill the
tramp"?

John: I didn't call those "tramp." I didn't call her no
names.

Graeber: But you just said, "Kill her." Who were you
talking to?

John: I was talking to my own self.

Graeber: When you said, "Kill her" . . . What did
Jamie do?

John: Jamie did it.

Graeber: You told Jamie to kill the girl, right?

John: Yeah. I walked away. I said, "Jamie, I ain't hurt-
ing those." I said, "I'm too drunk to do anything, hurt
any girls."

Graeber: Hey, John, you're wandering again, buddy.
That's not the way that happened, was it?

John: I know that I was drinking that night. I wish . . .
I wish it never happened. They wasn't dead when I
left, sir.

Moody: Yes, they were. What did you do?

John: Cover those up—me and Jamie did—a bunch of
wood. That other guy killed that other girl—with a
board. Will I have to stay down here tonight? I was
wanting to go home. I'll lose my job.

After a break John told the detectives: "They said, 'Please
don't hurt me.' I said, 'I won't.' They was alive. That what I
can't get—me and Jamie didn't kill those. I don't know how
they was dead back there."

Moody: John, were they dead when you left them
there?

John: Huh-uh.

Moody: Were they talking?

John: Yeah. That one girl was.

Moody: You know they were both dead when you left them there. Don't you?

John: I thought they was alive. They was—dead. Me and Jamie only hit those once [with] our hands. The other guy, he did it with a pipe. Me and Jamie didn't want to hurt those, didn't want to kill those.

Moody: But you did, didn't you?

John: Yeah.

Graeber: Who all went back in there to throw that stuff in the Lion's Cage?

John: Me, Jamie and that other boy.

Graeber: Where's the bike at now?

John: Should be in water still. That all I know. Down where the ladder was at.

Moody: Who threw it down there, John?

John: I did.

Graeber: Why did you throw the shorts down in the water?

John: I just thought if I did it—me and Jamie stays out of trouble. I knowed sooner or later me and Jamie would got caught. All I took was those underwear.

Moody: Who took those rocks away from there?

John: What rocks?

Moody: The pretty rocks.

John: I didn't. I don't know nothing about pretty rocks.

Moody: There's no pretty rocks at your house?

John: No. I didn't take those. Jamie and that other boy . . . that other boy got those. In his—in his garage.

Graeber: Did you tell your mom you killed those girls?

John: No. And I didn't use my knife on those.

Moody: You used your knife to cut the pants?

John: Yeah . . . I didn't cut nothing else.

Graeber: Yes, you did. You cut a pair of underwear, didn't you?

John: No, I didn't. I am sure. I didn't cut no underwear.

Moody: What were the girls' names, John?

John: I don't know.

Moody: Do you care?

John: I care. I don't know their names.

Moody: Are you sorry for what you did, John? Are you sorry for raping and killing those girls?

John: See, when I come down, I said I didn't do it.

Moody: But you lied to us, didn't you?

John (denying everything he had just told them): I know that I didn't do it. I was at home at ten.

Moody: Are you telling us now that you didn't kill them?

John: I wasn't down there.

Moody: You're telling us now you didn't have sex with them?

John (agitated): I was never there! I didn't hurt no one. And I didn't kill those. I just . . . I just got . . . When I'm drinking, I don't know what I'm doing. I was drinking today when I come down.

Moody: Are you sorry for what happened to those girls, John?

John (insisting angrily): I didn't do it! I'm trying to tell you guys. Jamie and another boy . . . I wasn't in that that time. I gave you guys my blood.

Moody: Are you mad at us now, like you got mad at those girls?

John: No, I'm getting tired of getting accused down here. If I didn't do it!

Graeber: You were down there with the girls, the two little girls. . . .

John: No, I wasn't!

Graeber: Two little girls died.

John: No, I wasn't. I was at home at ten.

Graeber: Guess what, John? You could have been home at ten, okay?

John (his reasoning making no sense to anyone except him): And I didn't do it. I didn't hurt no one,

Mooo-nee. If I'm going to hurt someone, why I
didn't hit my uncle today?

Graeber: We said you were down there at the time
those girls died and you said you were and you
helped cover them up and you had sex with them.

John: That all I did. I had sex with . . .

Graeber: The girls died.

John: Jamie hit . . .

Graeber: They're dead.

John: With some pipes. . . .

Moody: The girls are dead.

Graeber: You hit them with a board.

John: I didn't hit those with no boards. I didn't hurt
those. I sat right here in front of you and Mooo-nee
and told my uncle. Why lie to my own uncle? I didn't
hurt those.

Graeber: But you were all messed up. Remember you
and Jamie were drinking all day?

John: Yeah, and I didn't go down. I went after my
doughnuts and cookies for Robby and Willie.

Moody: Did you go down when the police were down
there?

John: Yeah. I seen a bunch of cruisers.

Moody: Were you down there when we found the
girls?

John: No, I wasn't. I came down after I got off from
working on Linden [Avenue].

(As they continued to talk, John became more and
more agitated.)

Moody (finally): Let's take a break. You need to calm
down.

Graeber: Yeah, you do.

9

Now that it's all over . . . they were actually pretty smart. . . . They were street-smart.

—Sergeant Barry Eggers

On Saturday afternoon, March 27, 1993, John Balser and David Marciszewski, accompanied by Joe Jackson, went to police headquarters and stated that they had more information on the homicides of Phree Morrow and Martha Leach. Barry Eggers and Al Graeber questioned John Balser again, in the presence of Jackson, after reading him his rights.

Balser didn't seem to understand the seriousness of the situation.

> John: I want to get this behind me. I want to go back to work Monday.
>
> Graeber: Who all was with you?
>
> John: Me, Dave, and Jamie and Lloyd.
>
> Graeber: What about the other guy (Alex Boone) we already arrested?
>
> John: I couldn't see him. He stayed up in behind all that woods. I remember, when I turn around, someone did run. Lloyd stayed after that. Me, Jamie, and Dave all left together.

Essentially, it was the same interview they had had a few days earlier. John insisted that Lloyd was there and admitted that he didn't like Lloyd. And this time he implicated David

Marciszewski. But, as in the earlier interview, the "who, when, what, where, and how" kept changing.

John also insisted throughout the questioning that he tried to help Phree. Even though in the earlier interview he said he didn't know the girls' names, he now knew which one was which.

"I tried help Phree to live. Me and Jamie tried. I grabbed Lloyd and pulled Lloyd back off of Phree," Balser revealed.

He claimed that Phree told him to go find her dad: "I said, 'Phree, hang with me. . . . Tell me what you can. Tell me where your dad live at.' I couldn't get no address—nothing. I did hit her. I didn't have sex with her. I tried. . . . I didn't mean to hit Phree. I tried to hit Lloyd, get Lloyd off of her. Instead, Lloyd moved and I hit Phree. That made me mad. I said, 'Damn it, I didn't want to hit you, Phree. I wish you moved so I would hit him instead of you.' I hit Phree with a two-by-four. I didn't rape those."

> Graeber: Who did?
> John: Lloyd Tyler.
> Graeber: Who had sex with the girls, John? Serious. Now the truth—no bullshit—the truth. Who had sex with the girls?
> John: Boone.
> Eggers: Either you or Dave had sex with those girls.
> John: It wasn't me.
> Eggers: So it was Dave?
> John: Yeah, it wasn't me. I'm telling you the truth.
> Eggers (unwavering): We're telling you when the blood comes back, we're going to know.

The detectives moved John to Lieutenant Schrader's office so they could bring David into the interrogation room. Barry Eggers was joined by Steve Moody to interview Marciszewski, and David's rights were read to him.

Moody: Before when I asked you about getting blood from you, you told me we could have it. Is that still . . . ?

David: Yeah.

Moody: We can still get your blood?

David: Yeah, you sure can.

(According to David's statement, he, John, and Jamie walked to the bakery that evening. John and David went into the bakery, and when they came out, Jamie was gone.)

David: John and I was starting to walk home from the bakery. We heard screams, about three or four times. And we went back there . . . and that's when we seen Alex. We seen Alex there and we seen Lloyd there. Jamie was there too. They was raping the girls and beating them with the board. John tried to grab the board and, uh, Lloyd came back and tried to swing at John. And I hit Lloyd. Either Alex or Lloyd—one of them . . . and, uh, we was trying to help the girls. I'm not lying to you. I'm telling you the truth. Lloyd had the board in his hand. They was—all three of them was raping them.

Moody: We know that only one person had sex with those girls.

David: I didn't touch them.

Moody (very firmly): Who did? You know because you were there and you watched it. And you helped destroy the evidence. Didn't you? You may not have killed them, but you've got problems. You know you're going to be in trouble for destroying evidence, don't you? Yes or no?

David (softly): Yes—I didn't touch the panties.

Moody: You know who had sex with them and you watched it. So why don't you tell us. As soon as the blood comes back, we're going to know for sure who it was. Then we're going to know you lied to us. Who had sex with them, David?

David: John. I don't know about both, but I know he had the one. I think it was the dark-haired girl. She was trying to fight.

Moody: What's the other girl doing?

David (barely audible): Trying to help her friend.

Moody: You grabbed ahold of her, didn't you?

David: I did; I did grab the other girl, you know, not thinking. I don't know why I grabbed her. I was trying to, uh, trying to stop her from helping her friend. Just grabbed her, I didn't hit her. She is screaming.

Moody: You want her to shut up, right? Somebody's going to hear her, right?

David: I didn't hit her.

Moody: What did you do to stop her screaming, David?

David: Tried to put my hand over her mouth.

Moody: Did that work?

David: No. She started screaming again.

Eggers: How did you finally shut her up? You want to feel better? You've got to tell us then. What did you do to shut her up? She's screaming, you're scared, right? You've got to shut her up—now what did you do?

David: Okay. I did hit her. I did hit her with my hand, that's all (crying). . . . I guess the board made her quit screaming.

Eggers: The board that you hit her with?

David: Yes.

Eggers: Did she shut up then?

David: Yeah.

Eggers: Did she fall to the ground?

David: Yes. I didn't have sex with her. I didn't touch her. Just took her pants and panties off.

Moody: You kept them (the panties), didn't you? David?

David: Yes.

(Later he denied taking the panties. He also admitted to "having sex" with one of the girls, but would only say that he "played with her" with his fingers. He denied putting his penis in her.)

Eggers: How did you lay them?

David: Facedown.

Eggers: Which part of their body was closest to the water, David?

David: I'd say their feet.

Eggers: Were their shoes on?

David: No.

Eggers: What part of their clothes was on?

David: Their blouse.

Moody: Who else was there? Anybody else? You're lying about Lloyd, aren't you? Because you guys don't like Lloyd, do you? Was Lloyd there?

David: No.

Moody: Who all was down there with you guys? Name names.

David: Me, Jamie, Alex, and John.

(He told them that Jamie fell in the pond.)

About a half an hour after Detective Eggers and Sergeant Moody started questioning Marciszewski, Detective Graeber went into Lieutenant Schrader's office so he and the lieutenant could continue questioning John Balser.

Detective Graeber picked up the interrogation where he had left off earlier.

Graeber: Okay, but you hit her with a board?

John (admitting innocently): Yeah, on accident. I was trying to help Phree get loose of that rock. I couldn't get that rock loose. I didn't hit her hard. Then when

I tried [to] get that rock off, I use that board to get that rock loose.

Schrader: Dave's telling the truth. He's telling the truth and it isn't like what you're saying.

Graeber: John's coming around to it, aren't you?

Schrader: Is he getting closer to what Dave's saying?

Graeber: Yeah, he's getting closer.

Schrader (to Graeber): Did you find out who made the date with them before they went up there?

Graeber: He hasn't got into that yet.

John: Wasn't no date supposed to be set. Jamie said he got a couple friends going up there. Jamie knowed those. I knowed Phree longer than Jamie did. Phree lived next door to me. (Phree and John had been neighbors years earlier—not at the time of the murders.)

Schrader: Okay, so Jamie told you that those girls were going to be up there? How did he know that?

John (sounding bewildered): I don't know. That what I can't figure out to this day. I don't really know how in the world he knowed.

Graeber: What all did you take over to the Lion's Cage?

John: Someone took a big brick. When it all got out of control . . . None of us started about keeping nothing.

Schrader: Except the pants.

Graeber: Except the panties.

John: I don't know where those at. You was in my whole house.

Graeber: You told me they were in your top dresser drawer.

John: Yeah.

Graeber: Okay, when we got over there, they weren't in there.

John: Yeah, and I don't . . . I really don't know where they're at.

Schrader: Well, Dave says you do.
John: I don't. I never seen those.

The interrogation of David Marciszewski was still in progress.

Moody: When you were at the house before you and John and Jamie ever left that evening—did Jamie tell you that he had a date with two girls?
David: He said something about that. Said, "I got to go meet a couple of girls."
Moody: So you knew you were going to Schuler's to meet a couple of girls, didn't you?
David: Yeah.
Moody: Had Jamie or John been drinking?
David: I think they both were.
Moody: What else do you think we need to know about what happened? Did those girls slap you at all? Did they hit any of the other guys? Why do you think this all happened, Dave? Think it's just something that got out of control?
David: Yeah.
Moody: Why did you hit her with a board?
David (awkwardly explaining): 'Cause I wanted her to shut up. I didn't like the screaming. I probably wasn't, didn't really know what I was doing at that time. See, I wasn't drinking either. I don't drink at all. I ain't drinked in almost five years. Plus I had a headache on top of it that night—a bad one.
Moody: Who had the rock that night?
David: A rock? I didn't even know there was a rock involved with it. I knew about the board.
Moody: 'Cause someone said you hit them with a rock. Did you hit them with a rock?
David: No, all I hit them with was the board.

Moody: Did you see anybody hit the girls in the head when they were there by the pond? Did you hit them again when they were down there by the pond?

David: No, I didn't see anybody else hit them.

Moody: What did they get covered up with?

David: I thought they got covered up with branches, leaves, and skids.

Moody: How many skids?

David: I think there was two of them—I think.

Moody: Dave, did you guys all help cover the girls up?

David: Yeah.

Moody: Did you throw anything in the pond? Did you throw any article of clothing in the pond?

David: No. I laid them beside.

Moody: What did you lay beside?

David: Shoes.

Moody: You know when we found the girls that Sunday—remember when that all happened? Did you come back down there while all the crowd of people was down there?

David: No, I didn't go back down there. I was wanting to come down here and tell you guys about it. But I was scared.

Moody: Did you tell John that you wanted to come down and tell us about it?

David (softly): I did say something to him. He scared me.

Sergeant Moody and Detective Eggers once more read David Marciszewski his rights, at 10:45 that same night, and they asked him to go through his story again. It was the same story he had told them earlier, with some exceptions.

Moody: Were the girls hit one more time when they were there facedown? This is important, David. Was

there a discussion among you guys that you didn't
think they were dead yet? Did anybody say, "We
need to make sure that these girls are dead so they
can't tell on us"?

(There was a long silence before David finally whispered, "Somebody said it.")

Moody: So what did you guys do to make sure that
they couldn't tell on you? One last thing got done.
What was it? Come on, Dave. The hard part's done
with. Did you hit them one last time? David?

David: Yeah.

Moody: What did you hit them with? David? What did
you hit them with?

David: A rock.

Moody: A big rock?

David: Yeah.

Moody: Did you hit them both?

David: I think I only hit the one.

Moody: Why would you just hit the one, if you were
doing it to make sure they were dead? Did the one
make a noise or move or something that made you
think that she wasn't dead? Or did you hit them
both? David, we're almost done here, you need to
clean this up.

David (imploring): This is the last part of it?

Moody: Yep. This is basically the last thing we need to
know. You need to tell us. When the girls were facedown, did they get hit one more time? Before you
covered them up? Come on, Dave. You've already
said you hit the one with a rock. Did you hit the
other? With that same rock?

David: Yeah.

Moody: Where did you hit those girls with that rock?
The part of the body?

David: The head.

Moody: What part of the head?

David: It had to be the back of the head because they was facedown.

Moody: Where did you leave that rock when you were done with it?

David: I left it laying beside them, right there beside the girls.

Moody (emphatic): You left it on that girl's head. The last time you hit that little girl in the head, you left it on top of her head, didn't you? Now I sat here and told you we already been to the scene; we saw it. Why don't you tell us the truth? It's true, isn't it? The last time you hit her in the head, you just left it on her head, didn't you?

David (whispering): Yes.

Moody: David, are you sorry about what happened? Are you sorry about this?

David: Yes.

Moody: Why didn't you try to stop what happened? Was it exciting to you? I know you were scared, but was it exciting too?

David (his voice low): I was mainly scared.

(At the end of the interview, David Marciszewski submitted to having his blood drawn for DNA testing.)

Shortly after midnight on Sunday morning, March 28, 1993, John Balser and David Marciszewski were arrested and charged with two counts each of aggravated murder. The next day, both of the mentally challenged men were arraigned in Clark County Common Pleas Court and both pleaded innocent to the charges. They were held without bond in the Clark County Jail.

John and David both had told the detectives there could possibly be evidence in a "hole" in a field next to their house, but nothing of any evidentiary value was found. The hole turned out to be the basement of a house that had been torn down.

On Monday morning a woman named Sally Herman* came to police headquarters and asked to speak with someone about John Balser. Herman explained to Detectives Eggers and Graeber that she worked at the United Dairy Farmers Store on West Main Street. She knew John because he lived nearby and was a regular customer. She stated that John hung around the neighborhood with small children and on one occasion something had happened that frightened Sally's nine year-old daughter, Halley*. John had told the little girl that he would never hurt her—unless he was drunk or angry.

She also told the detectives that after Jamie Turner was arrested, John came in the store nearly every day and asked her to read the article in the newspaper to him about the investigation. When he asked her if the police were looking for additional suspects and she told him that they were, John became very nervous and upset.

According to Sally Herman, John always carried a cutoff two-by-four with him, with KILLEM printed on it. He told the kids in the area that it was his "equalizer."

When the grand jury met on Monday, April 5, 1993, they handed down thirteen indictments against John Balser: six counts of aggravated murder, two counts of rape, two counts of kidnapping, one count of tampering with evidence, and two counts of abuse of a corpse.

Fourteen counts were handed down against David Marciszewski: six counts of aggravated murder, two counts of rape, two counts of kidnapping, one count of tampering with evidence, two counts of abuse of a corpse, and one count of felonious sexual penetration. Marciszewski was also named as the principal offender.

When the DNA results came back negative on fifteen-year-old Damien Tyler, he was cleared as a suspect. His uncle Lloyd submitted to having his blood drawn for testing on March 30.

10

Nobody really doubted that there was involvement of some nature by these individuals and I had to make one of the most difficult decisions that I had to make in my prosecutorial career.

—Steve Schumaker

On Friday, April 16, 1993, common pleas court judge Douglas Geyer dismissed all the charges against Jamie Turner and Alexander Boone, at the request of Clark County prosecutor Stephen "Steve" Schumaker. The charges were dismissed "without prejudice," which meant that Boone and Turner could be reindicted at a later date.

Boone's trial had been set for May 6 and Turner's for May 25. In order to meet the requirements of the U.S. Constitution for a speedy trial, May 31 was the deadline to start the trials.

Schumaker stated that he would not have final results of DNA tests until mid or late June. He indicated that he would submit the evidence to the grand jury when it arrived from the FBI.

William West and Richard Mayhall, Alexander Boone's attorneys, objected to the dismissal without prejudice, to no avail. They contended that the only evidence against their client was the statement he made to the detectives.

According to their statement prepared for the court: "Had this case proceeded, we would have proven that Alex's statement was unreliable and, far from being evidence of guilt, actually proved that he had no independent knowledge of, or involvement in, these terrible crimes.

"The reason there is insufficient evidence is because Alex is not guilty."

Jamie Turner's court-appointed attorney, Noel Kaech, was pleased with the dismissal, but he was disappointed that it was without prejudice.

The final results of the DNA tests were received sooner than expected, and by the end of May, the investigators knew that not one of the four men who had been charged matched the DNA that was found in the semen in the bodies of Phree Morrow and Martha Leach. This did not prove that these men were innocent of the murders, but the question remained: Who raped the girls? And it raised new ones: Whom were the men protecting? A friend? Someone they were afraid of?

At the tender age of sixteen, while working part-time at his first job, in a dry-cleaning store, Steve Schumaker had been the victim of an armed robbery. The thief placed a gun between the slender teenager's eyes, demanded the money, and threatened to come back and kill him if he called the police.

Steve did call the police. A few weeks later, on a Saturday afternoon, the thief came back into the establishment, sat down, and stared at him.

"I did what every red-blooded American male does—I called my mother."

Within a very short period of time, Steve's father, a World War II veteran, "came roaring" into the store with a gun in his hand, told his son to get him a chair, and sat there with the gun at his side until the man left.

The man was caught, convicted, and sent to prison.

The experience of watching the case work its way through the court system sparked an interest in Steve, an interest that continued through college. While studying political science at nearby Wittenberg University, in his spare time he went to the courthouse and watched the trials and the lawyers in action.

He received his undergraduate degree in political science and went on to Ohio State Law School. After receiving his law degree and passing the bar exam, he returned to Springfield and served as the assistant prosecutor from 1978 to 1984. He became the Clark County prosecutor in January 1985.

He was the father of two young sons and a five-year-old daughter.

When Schumaker asked Judge Geyer to dismiss the charges against Jamie Turner and Alexander Boone, even though it was without prejudice, he realized that he was putting his job on the line.

He had had to make an extremely difficult decision in this high-profile case: whether to go forward—and, very likely, have Boone and Turner walk out of the courthouse permanently, as free individuals—or whether to dismiss the cases and "come back and fight another day."

On May 21, 1993, Detective Graeber interviewed John's young cousin Willie Jackson again. Willie's father, Joe Jackson, was present during the questioning, which mostly concerned the comings and goings of the people present at Wanda's house on Saturday, August 22, 1992.

A few days later, Detective Graeber questioned fourteen-year-old Robby Detwiler again. Robby, a thin boy with dishwater blond hair, was restless and uneasy throughout the interview. Typical for his age, his voice was changing. Mostly it sounded boyish, and then—midsentence—it would briefly crack with the fleeting promise of ensuing manhood.

Graeber: What time did John and Dave get back (the night of August 22, 1992)?

Robby: I think it was probably about ten-thirty at night.

Graeber: Those guys didn't tell you that night they were down to Schuler's?

Robby: Yeah, they said they stopped at Schuler's and got some doughnuts, but . . . I didn't even find out about it until a week later because I never watch TV or nothing. I mean, I watch TV—I don't read the paper and stuff.

Graeber: Willie knew about it. Willie said they told him about it.

Robby: They didn't tell me about it.

Graeber: Willie said you went down to Schuler's with them.

Robby (vigorously protesting): I didn't go down to Schuler's! I can swear on anything I didn't go down to Schuler's!

Graeber (firmly, but patiently): Let me tell you something. What did I tell you when we came down here?

Robby: "Don't lie," but I ain't lying!

Graeber: You'd better start talking to me. We're talking about four of your buddies killing somebody.

Robby: I know.

Graeber: Two somebodies. You never forget that.

Robby (insisting nervously): I didn't know they killed them. How was I supposed to know they killed them? I didn't go down to Schuler's. And I'll get him (Willie) in here and tell him to his face I didn't go to no Schuler's.

(After a break Sergeant Moody joined them in the interrogation room. But now Robby changed his whole story.)

Moody: I want you to calm down, okay. Are you saying that you weren't at Wanda's house that weekend?

Robby: I'm saying I was at my house. Wanda wouldn't let me come up.

(For the next several minutes, Robby tearfully insisted

that he had lied about being at Wanda's that weekend. He even claimed that Willie wasn't there either.)

Moody: Are you more scared of them or are you more
scared of the police?

Robby: Really I'd be more scared of them.

Moody: So you'd much quicker lie to us because you
know that policemen aren't going to hurt you.

Robby: I know.

Moody: Right. Why are you afraid of them?

Robby (incredulous): If they killed somebody, they're
going to kill again!

(Robby hesitantly admitted that he was at Wanda's that
night: "This is the truth.")

Moody: Did you walk down to Schuler's with them?

Robby: No. That's one thing I will not lie about. I
know I lied so many times, but I didn't walk down
there.

Moody: Are you willing to give us some of your blood?

Robby: Yeah.

When Sergeant Moody and Detective Graeber talked to
Wanda Marciszewski the next day, she told them that she had
been married to David for two years. She met him through
her son, John Balser. David and John knew each other
through mutual friends.

Heavyset at 5'2" and 172 pounds, Wanda had very long
salt-and-pepper hair, and was clad in dark polyester slacks
and a bright T-shirt. She was thirteen years older than her
husband, and she worked as a caretaker for an elderly woman.

Wanda was born and raised in southern Ohio and was the
youngest of sixteen children. She was not mentally retarded,
but the detectives soon came to believe that, at the very least,
she was mentally unbalanced.

She confirmed that Willie and Robby were at her house the
night of August 22 and she was angry with Dave because he

left them alone while she was at work. She called home every fifteen or twenty minutes, and when she got home about 10:00 P.M., Dave and John still weren't there.

Dave got home at 11:00 P.M.; about five or ten minutes later, John came home. She stated that she did not talk to either one of them because she was mad.

Dave told her, "I dirtied my pants." He threw his clothes away after he took a bath. Wanda claimed she never saw the clothes. When the detectives asked her about washing bloody clothes, she stated that John washed clothes also.

Wanda also claimed she didn't see any cookies. She said John told her he was just out walking around, and that after he came home he took a bath.

According to Wanda, Dave had not been drinking that night.

She told the detectives that Dave got quiet after Jamie was arrested and that John got angry.

John told his mother, "They're trying to pin a murder case on me." Dave would not discuss anything with her.

On May 26, 1993, John Balser's three cousins, Robby Detwiler, Willie Jackson, and Frank Fisher, submitted to having their blood drawn for DNA testing.

John Balser gave two more rambling statements to Sergeant Moody and Detective Graeber on May 27 and June 2. On May 27 John asked the deputy at the jail if he could do him a favor and get in touch with Sergeant Moody or "Sergeant" Graeber. Deputy Pat Ford asked if he wanted to let his attorney know that he was going to talk to Sergeant Moody. John replied, "Fuck the attorney—I want to talk with Sergeant Moody."

After John was brought over from the jail, Sergeant Graeber read him his rights.

Graeber: Who else was down there with you?

John: Was me, Jamie, Dave, and Frank. Willie, Robby, and Wanda wasn't with us. My mom was at work that night.

Graeber (frustrated): There had to be someone else too, John, because we know that none of those guys had sex with them. And we know you didn't have sex with them. Okay? Now who had sex with them? Straight up.

(John told them that it was Wade Aston*, an employee at the salvage yard across the street from Strahler's Warehouse.)

John (sounding puzzled): And something else been bugging me. Where I was painting at, on Linden Avenue . . . Dave's saying that was involved in that scene. That wasn't involved, Mooo-nee. That house wasn't involved that night. No. I one lock it up; I only one know how to lock it up.

Moody: When you got done painting, what did you do?

John: I went after doughnuts and cookies.

Moody: Did you ever go back home before that?

John: I went back home, got some money and all.

Moody: Did anyone take anything away from there that belonged to the girls?

John: Dave had those panties.

(John rambled aimlessly for several minutes and then said something about a bag.)

Moody: What bag you talking about, John?

John (stammering): Uh—uh—a bakery bag . . . I recognized it. Dave took it out of our house.

Moody: What was in the bakery bag?

John: Those panties. I'm telling you the honest-to-God truth.

Moody: Who had sex with them?

John: Dave, Frank, and Jamie.

Moody: All right, now, what do you mean by sex? What's sex, John, to you?

John (answering bluntly): Like people fucking, being plain out simple. I have sex with my girlfriend.

Graeber: What it boils down to, John, is who stuck their "thing" in the girls?

John: I didn't see who done it. If it be truthful, if you guys do a blood work on Frank, it come back, be him.

Moody: How come before you never told us that Frank was down there with you?

John: I didn't want to get Frank involved. Me and Frank go back a long ways. See, me and Frank [are] like brothers. I look out for Frank.

Moody: John, did anybody go back to the scene after the murders?

John: No . . . as far as I know.

Moody: Did your mom go down there?

John: No, I know she wouldn't. What I can't figure out, "Sergeant" Graeber, why keep on putting her through the hurt?

Moody: John, the next day after all this happened—it was a Sunday—what did you do that day?

John: I went over there and finished Linden up. Dave, me, both boys, and my mom. I stayed over there till I got it done.

Moody: Okay, when did you tell your mom what happened that night?

John: I told her like a week after that. I said, "Mom, it done time to tell you Dave did murder."

Moody: Now, your mom loves you, doesn't she?

John: Yeah, I'm trying to help her out too.

Moody: Listen to me a minute, because the guys in charge think that your . . . Since you told your mom so quick, what's the first thing she's going to do? She's going to try to help her son, right? And she's going to tell you what to do with it (evidence), or try to get rid of things for you. Now how else are we going to be able to tell that you're telling the truth, unless you tell us the truth about what you know and where the stuff went and where we can find it now?

John: Far as I know, it should've been right at the scene still.

Moody: No, now you know as well as I do, there was stuff taken away from there.

John: I didn't take nothing, Graeber. I'm telling you the truth.

Moody: And you've made the statement, and you know you did, that if we don't get that evidence we "ain't got nothing" on you. And, John, that's not true. We do. You're in jail, aren't you? And I know you're upset about your mom; I would be upset about my mom too. You love her. But you got to think now, because you know we talk to her. She calls me; I don't call her. She's worried about helping you.

(John continued to insist that he didn't know where "the stuff was at.")

John (exasperated): I told you guys the truth. I don't know what else to do. If I knowed, why in the world I ain't saying now?

On June 2, John Balser again asked the deputy on duty at the jail to get a message to Moody and Graeber. "I want to talk to those again," he said. "I want to talk to Moody or Graeber. Tell them today, not fucking tomorrow!"

They read him his rights again.

Graeber: Okay, the night . . . Who'd you take back down to the scene that night?

John: My mom. My mom couldn't believe it. She said, "Son, you been involved?" I said, "No, Mom, I didn't do nothing." She said, "Son, you did anything to them?" I said, "No." I said, "I didn't have sex [or] either rape those little children, Mom." She didn't believe it—about David would be that way.

Graeber: Did your mom scream when you took her down there?

John: My mom didn't do nothing, couldn't believe Dave did that.

(As the interview continued, John became furious with the detectives, yelling and screaming at them and denying that he had done anything.)

Moody: John, quit lying. That's it! Quit lying!

John: I ain't lying!

Moody: You told us earlier you hit Phree by accident.

John: Then you guys took another tape and I said No! I didn't hit her, Mooo-nee. I didn't hold her down. I didn't hold her down!

Moody: Well, I'm tired of you lying to us.

John (screaming and pounding the table): I didn't hold her down! I know a goddamn if I did or not! I know I didn't hit no one and I ain't been up there! I know I ain't been up there, man. Every time I come over here, say motherfuckin' bullshit!

Moody (calmly reminding him): You're the one that's wanting to come over.

On June 11, 1993, Judge Geyer dropped all charges against John Balser, also without prejudice, at the request of Schumaker.

Many people wondered how the prosecutor could let these "killers" back out on the streets. They did not understand how he could let these accused men go free.

Steve Schumaker firmly believed he had the best chance of obtaining a conviction against David Marciszewski; therefore, it was his intention to concentrate all his efforts, for now, on him. The hope was that he would plead guilty, cooperate, and lead the authorities to the elusive individual whose DNA had been found in the semen recovered from the bodies of Phree and Martha.

David Marciszewski remained in the Clark County Jail. James Doughty, his attorney, waived David's right to a speedy trial. His trial was set for January 18, 1994, after being postponed from June 8, 1993.

On Tuesday, August 3, 1993, Detective Barry Eggers and Sergeant Steve Moody talked to Wanda Marciszewski.

Moody: Joe Jackson indicated that you had some concerns over the weekend. What were those?

Wanda: John said, "Mom, I'm out of this mess, and if I get out freely, I will kill again. The first time was easy; the second time is going to be easier. I will kill again."

Eggers: You truly believe in your heart that that's going to happen?

Wanda: Yes, I do, because I'm scared about it. And he's doing weird things—I mean like masturbating.

Moody: Does he talk to you about the murders?

Wanda: He talks about them. He'll say, "Well, Mom, it's been almost a year. They're not going to find out nothing. The police are dumb."

Eggers: Well, Wanda, one night almost a year ago, you made a very terrible mistake.

Wanda: Of doing what?

Eggers: Of going down [there] with John. Now if you can clear that up for us once and for all tonight, then we can get John.

Wanda: If I was there, I do not know it, you know. I'll say it that way.

Moody: I mean, he may be your son, but you're sitting here telling us that you're terrified of him. And, you know, if you went back down there on the thought of helping them out, I understand it. You're a mother, but you need to let that go now.

Eggers: Who was covering them up? Let me ask you this—did you help?

Wanda: No.

Eggers: So you're standing there and they're doing what?

Wanda: Covering them up with leaves and stuff. They didn't touch them while I was there, you know. I screamed because I was panicky.

Eggers: And you're sure Boone drove you?

Wanda: Yes. They kept me there for a little bit. About an hour or something. I couldn't move because I was like I was froze. They're covering them like—covering them up with limbs and stuff, you know—getting ready to bury them because they said they had to bury them. They didn't say anything to me about having sex with the girls. They just said they had to die. That they had their own cemetery—that somebody had to die.

Eggers: Think real hard about this, and if you don't know, say so. At the scene you saw the two girls there. Could you see both of their heads?

Wanda: No. Because, huh-uh. 'Cause it looks like . . . 'cause . . . (crying) Oh, God!

Moody: Calm down, Wanda.

Eggers: I understand it's hard. Do you want a glass of water?

Wanda (hysterical): It looks like their heads is bashed in. I could see their heads. I could see the blood and I asked why they took the little girls' lives. I said, "Why did you murder?" And they said that "white honkeys had to die and they was tramps." And I said, "The girls is not tramps, you know. They've got a right to live here on this earth the same as any of us does." And they said that they "just had to die."

(After regaining her composure, Wanda continued: "It was already done before I got there, you know. The rape and stuff was already done.")

Eggers: So in your opinion, they were dead when you got there?

Wanda: Yes.

(Except for the fact that Alexander Boone's father was black, everyone else involved was white, including Wanda. Therefore, her claim that "they" said that "white honkeys had to die" did not make sense. Much of what she told the detectives was difficult to comprehend.

Wanda: Boone took us back to the house.

Eggers: Directly from there to the house?

Moody: You didn't go anywhere else? Now, this is important.

Wanda: No, I didn't. I went home because I was upset. I mean, I didn't want to go no more. Dave just told me that he wouldn't tell me nothing. 'Cause he told me I had to go to bed because I had to go to work the next morning.

Moody: Why . . . I guess, Wanda . . . Why didn't you turn them in?

Wanda: Because I was too upset and, you know, I just tried to more or less block it out. I just wanted to forget it.

Moody: Wanda, are you telling us the truth?

Wanda: Yes, I am.

Moody: Did you go down there?

Wanda: Yes, I did.

Eggers: Have you told anybody else this?

Wanda: No. I just more or less wanted to keep it to myself, keep it blocked out. That's why I ask you to rearrest him because I am scared of him, you know. Because once he knows that I turned it in, then he's gonna be mad at me again.

Eggers: Has John ever told you that there is anybody else involved in this?

Wanda: No, he just said there was five of them, but I

can't believe about Frank. I mean, I cannot believe
about that boy.

Eggers: And Frank wasn't with you when you went
down there?

Wanda: No, he was not. He was not with me.

Eggers: This is important, Wanda. There are people
telling us that Saturday afternoon, they saw David
and John down there at the bakery in a van—a bluish
green window van with a bunch of trash in it. Any
idea who that could be?

Wanda: I don't know who it could be. That's what
Moody asked me and I said I didn't know, you
know.

Eggers: Did you help them in any way?

Wanda: No.

Eggers: For your son's sake—for your husband's
sake . . .

Wanda: No, I would not touch a body.

Eggers: Well, I'm saying that somebody there was
smart enough to get rid of all the evidence.

Wanda: No, I did not get rid of nothing.

Moody: Did you tell them that they needed to?

Wanda: No, I did not.

Eggers: The following day after everything happened,
did anybody go down there again?

Wanda: No.

Eggers: What was the next day like?

Wanda: To me, it was like hell.

Two days later, on August 5, 1993, John Balser told
Sergeant Moody and Detective Graeber that his "best friend,"
Jason Holmes*, was the one who raped Martha and Phree.
And he now claimed that the initial attack had taken place at
the house on Linden Avenue.

John: And I seen Jason rape those on Linden and that
  scene, Mooo-nee. Jason was already up on Linden.
  That when I heared [sic] those girls. When girls came
  up with Jamie and Boone, they went on upstairs. I
  heared someone screaming. I seen someone up in the
  attic. Jason Holmes . . . Jamie Turner and Boone.

Graeber: Where were the girls?

John: Up there with Jason, Boone, and Jamie. I'll be
  straight out, Mooo-nee—raping those. After those
  got done, Mooo-nee, they put something in her
  mouth [so] she couldn't scream, and covered those
  up. I don't know where blankets come from. They
  put blankets over those girls. They went down and
  behind the scene where you guys found . . . and those
  have sex again. Jason—just Jason Holmes—no one
  else. Have it with both girls and I seen Dave have a
  stick, Mooo-nee. Dave stuck it up that girl's thing.

Graeber: How did you guys get from the house on
  Linden to the pond?

John: That black truck—Boone's. They laid those girls
  down in bed (of truck). I tried talk them into not hurt-
  ing those. They wouldn't listen to me, Mooo-nee.

Graeber: Where did you go from Linden Avenue?

John: To that scene where those girls met death (at the
  pond).

Moody: Did you help carry them from the truck to the
  pond?

John: I carried Phree . . . and laid her down.

Graeber: Let me ask you something, John. If we told
  you that Jason Holmes didn't have sex with the girls,
  who would it be then?

John: I don't know, Graeber. I don't know, [to] be truthful with you. I'm being straight up. I don't really
  know.

* * *

Every time John gave them a new name, there was more DNA testing, always with the hope that this time he was telling the truth.

Jason Holmes no longer lived in Springfield; he had since moved to South Carolina. So Sergeant Moody and Detective Graeber made the long, time-consuming drive south to collect a sample of Jason's blood. They placed it in a cooler and iced it down for the trip home, only to find out later that, once again, John Balser had lied to them.

11

We knew. . . . We just looked at each other. . . . "He's still out there. . . . He's still here."

—Captain Steve Moody

Even though the police did not want to take the report, her family knew that Belinda was missing. The officer said she would probably show up in a few days, but her worried family members insisted on filing a missing persons report. There was "no way" she would stay away this long without calling.

Belinda Anderson, thirty-one, had moved from Springfield to Bellefontaine, Ohio, to stay with her brother and sister-in-law, Richard and Karlene Anderson, five months before she disappeared. She loved animals and had been working as a dog groomer in a pet shop several miles away in West Liberty. She was the next to the youngest in a family of five children. She was also the mother of two little girls: eight-year-old Kimberly and eleven-year-old Stephney.

Sadly, Belinda was addicted to crack cocaine, but, as far as her family knew, she was trying to stay clean during the time she was living with Richard and Karlene.

In March 1993 a friend of Belinda's had borrowed a car from her boyfriend, and when she was gone longer than he thought she should be, he reported the car stolen. The friend had asked Belinda to drive, and when they were pulled over by the police, Belinda was charged with "receiving stolen property." She was to appear in court on Thursday, September 9, 1993, to have the charges formally dropped.

The weekend before her scheduled court appearance, she returned to Springfield to spend some time with Deborah Anderson, one of her sisters. On Tuesday evening, September 7, they decided to have steaks for dinner and Deborah went to the grocery store to get what they needed. When Deborah returned from the store, she found a note from Belinda saying that she would be back in a few minutes; she had gone to make a call from a pay phone at a nearby gas station on South Limestone Street.

She never came back.

When she did not appear in court on Thursday, her mother, Christine Anderson, knew there was something terribly wrong. Taking a picture of Belinda with her, she started going door-to-door in the neighborhood where Belinda had disappeared, but could not find anyone who had seen her.

The area was made up of large, old houses that many years ago had been fine single-family homes. Now most of them had been divided up into small apartments. Some of them were well kept, but many were in bad repair. A few were vacant with their windows boarded up.

Finally Christine, accompanied by Karlene, went to the police station to report Belinda missing. The officer on duty reluctantly filled out the report and informed the distraught family members that "the police would not be out looking for her."

The authorities were familiar with Belinda Anderson because of her criminal record. In 1992 and 1993 she had been arrested on a variety of charges, including failure to register a dog, criminal trespassing, drug paraphernalia, and several times for passing bad checks. The officer was sure she was just "shacking up" with someone for a few days and would be home soon enough.

The days, weeks, and months dragged by with no word from Belinda. Slowly, agonizingly, Belinda's parents, siblings, and two young daughters felt hope slip away that they would ever see her alive again. Their hope never completely vanished, but it was like trying to hold on to a whisper, and in their hearts, they knew.

Heartache and pain were not strangers to this close-knit family, but now it came to live with them indefinitely. None of them would ever be the same again.

In the wee hours of the morning of October 22, 1993, a man was driving down East Main Street near Schuler's Bakery when he saw a woman who obviously needed help on the corner of Main and Sycamore Streets. He stopped and managed to get her into his car and quickly took her to the emergency room at Mercy Medical Center.

Twenty-eight-year-old Caitlin Levalley* had been severely beaten and was in serious condition. When the detectives talked to her in the intensive care unit, she told them that she had been walking on Main Street about 10:00 the night before. A man approached her and forced her to go with him behind a building on Penn Street.

Once there, he started beating her with a pipe until she somehow managed to grab it away from him and hit him with it. Her attacker fled and she was barely able to make it back to Main Street. Despite her injuries, she slowly started walking east and then the Good Samaritan picked her up about 12:30 A.M. and brought her to the hospital.

She was moved out of the intensive care unit on Saturday, October 23, and her condition was upgraded to stable.

The area where she had been attacked was across the street from where Phree Morrow and Martha Leach's bodies had been found.

On November 30, 1993, Sergeant Moody and Detective Eggers interviewed Wanda Marciszewski again. She told them that she was at work on the night in question. When she got off work, she went home and then Dave, John, Alex, and Jamie came in the truck and told her, "You have to see something."

They took her to the crime scene and showed her the girls. Wanda claimed that Phree screamed, "Go get my daddy!" Then David hit her in the head with the rock. Jamie Turner started jumping up and down in the pond. John Balser hit Martha in the head with the rock.

She also told them that she took the girls' pulses and they had none: "I remember I was the only one that could take the pulse."

She said the name Jake Campbell* "came in my mind." She claimed that he was "in the background" at the crime scene.

On Wednesday morning, December 8, 1993, a woman was found savagely beaten behind the YMCA near downtown Springfield. When two employees of a nearby business looked out a window, they saw her propped up on one of the "islands" in the parking lot of Clark State Community College.

She had been beaten so brutally, and was so close to the railroad tracks, that their first thought was that maybe she had been hit by a train.

Her face was horribly bruised and swollen and she was naked from the waist down. With tears in her eyes, and despite her massive wounds, she begged them, "Help me." After calling the police, the men stayed with her until help arrived. While they anxiously waited, one of them gently asked if she had been raped and she nodded yes.

Sergeant Moody and Detective Eggers heard the call on the radio to uniformed officers that there was a woman who was seriously injured near the railroad tracks behind the YMCA. Since they were already in their vehicle, they proceeded to the area and were the first ones on the scene.

There they found thirty-eight-year-old Helen Preston*, sitting on top of her pants, in the grassy area near a loading dock. At first, they weren't even sure what race she was because the blood from her wounds had dried and it was in her hair and covered her face. And, of course, because of the bruises.

They finally determined that she was Caucasian.

When the emergency squad arrived, the paramedics carefully lifted her up to put her on the gurney. When they started to lay her down, she made a whimpering sound, and that's when they saw that her throat had been cut. They were so certain that she wouldn't survive that Detective Eggers rode in the ambulance with her to the hospital and started interviewing her right away.

It was tremendously difficult for him to understand what she was saying. She slipped in and out of consciousness, so he was only able to obtain a small amount of information from her. But he did manage to get a very general description of her attacker: a white male in his midtwenties wearing a white T-shirt and blue jeans with long, curly hair. Also, despite her condition, she kept holding her hands up to her eyes as if she were looking through binoculars. Detective Eggers believed she was trying to tell him that the man wore glasses. It wasn't much, but at least they had something.

When they arrived at Community Hospital, she was rushed into surgery. Her condition was extremely critical. In addition to the five-inch slash across her throat, so deep that her trachea was exposed, she had been stabbed in the abdomen.

However, the worst injuries were to her head and face. Her skull was fractured and her cheekbones were so badly broken that they were no longer connected. Also, her jawbone was broken in several places.

Because she had been exposed to freezing temperatures for a number of hours, several of her toes had to be amputated because of frostbite. Ironically, the low temperature probably saved her life. She was very close to death when she was found; her body temperature was only 94 degrees.

Helen's condition demanded that the doctors move quickly, and in the rush to save her life, a rape kit was not done on her. Perhaps she didn't understand when the doctor asked if she had been raped because she told him she had not been. There was no time to investigate, so they cleaned her vaginal area and inserted a catheter.

Even though he understood that the doctor did what he had to do, Sergeant Moody was very upset when he learned about this. He knew she had been raped, and he was sure that the person who raped Helen had also raped and murdered Phree and Martha. But now he couldn't prove it.

He knew because the jeans that Helen had been wearing were found at the crime scene. They had been cut off in the same manner that the investigators had seen one other time.

Even after Helen's condition miraculously improved, she was able to tell the detectives very little about the night she was attacked and, no doubt, left for dead. She told them that she had been in John's Bar with her boyfriend and they had gotten into an argument and she had left. The next thing she remembered was crawling over to the railroad tracks by the YMCA after the attack. The only thing she recalled about the attack itself was that the man wore glasses.

Soon after that, she remembered a man who had been at a family gathering a few weeks earlier. He was a distant relative of Helen's and wore glasses. She became convinced that he was the man who had viciously assaulted her.

Detective Eggers and Sergeant Moody were able to locate the man and brought him in for questioning. Besides the fact that Michael Cross* was able to account for his whereabouts during the time Helen was attacked, both detectives felt that he was being truthful and neither could detect any attempt at deception.

Only the scantest of details were released to the public. The police did not reveal that they knew where Helen had been before the attack or about the fight with her boyfriend. Or that her attacker wore glasses. And, of course, they did not reveal the fact that Helen's jeans had been cut.

The public still didn't know at this point that the flowered shorts found at the Lion's Cage had been cut. Therefore, they did not realize there was a connection between these horrible crimes.

Years later, Barry Eggers would tell this author: "I've been doing this for sixteen years and she was beaten probably the worst I've ever seen and still survive."

A day or so later, Sergeant Moody and Detective Eggers were canvassing the old neighborhood around South Limestone Street, where Helen lived, to see if anyone had noticed anything unusual the night she was attacked. Around the corner from Helen's house, in a large Victorian-style house on Miller Street, they interviewed Bill and Karen Sapp.

As they entered the upstairs apartment, they couldn't help but notice that everywhere they looked there were birds in cages and dozens of knickknacks. The apartment was fairly well kept, but crowded—the home of a low-income family making the best of what they had. There were signs that a small child lived there: a few toys scattered about, a colorful cartoon-character drinking glass, and a tiny, frayed winter jacket hanging on the back of a chair. But the child was nowhere in sight, probably because it was early afternoon—naptime.

Bill, whose head had recently been shaved, was standing at the stove, frying bologna. His wife, Karen, claimed that she had seen a man in the neighborhood who was looking for Helen, earlier in the day, before she was attacked. Karen readily agreed to help with a composite drawing: "There's obviously a sicko around the neighborhood. Let's get him!"

Karen Sapp was very helpful and told the detectives: "Any time of the day or night you need anything, feel free to drop by."

The same day Helen was found, Bill Sapp had reported that he was assaulted at the corner of Fountain Avenue and Miller Street. Miller Street is only one block long and runs between Limestone and Fountain.

* * *

On February 9, 1994, Shelby Boone* decided it was time to report her beautiful thirty-seven-year-old daughter missing. No one had seen her since February 2, at a grocery store on South Limestone Street.

Ten days later, some children playing in a wooded area on East Pleasant Street found the frozen body of a light-skinned black woman. It was reported to the police at 6:20 P.M.

The investigators, including prosecutor Stephen Schumaker and Clark County coroner Dirk Wood, were at the scene until after 11:00 that night. Detectives used flashlights to search the wooded area diligently and lights were set up to illuminate the crime scene.

A few days later, the victim was finally identified, through fingerprints, as Gloria Jean White, Shelby Boone's missing daughter.

Dr. Dirk Wood estimated that Gloria Jean had been dead for at least two weeks before her body was found. The cause of death was determined to be a hemorrhage that resulted from skull fractures. She had been struck repeatedly on the head and also on her legs.

The coroner's office also reported that she died, if not immediately, then within a few minutes of the attack. Preliminary toxicology tests indicated that cocaine was present in her body.

Besides her parents, she was survived by two sisters, a brother, a son and a daughter.

Visitation for Gloria Jean White was on the afternoon of February 24 at Dennis L. Porter Funeral Home. That evening, services were held at Second Missionary Baptist Church. Because of the severity of her injuries, her casket had to remain closed. She was buried in Ferncliff Cemetery the next morning.

Gloria Jean White was Alexander Boone's cousin.

* * *

On February 10, 1994, Wanda Marciszewski called Detective Graeber and told him that she needed to see him. Wanda had moved into a large duplex on Lagonda Avenue, upstairs from Eleanor, her elderly employer.

When Al Graeber went to see her, Wanda informed him that she had been at the crime scene twice on the night of August 22, 1992. The first time was after John called her at Eleanor's and she met him on Main Street and he took her to where the girls were, still alive. The second time was after Joe Jackson picked her up at Eleanor's and took her home to Light Street. She claimed that John, David, Jamie, and Alex then came to get her to take her back to the crime scene.

The picture became a little clearer. She had told the detectives about both trips to the crime scene, but previously it seemed that she was telling different versions of the same story.

Each time they talked to her, they obtained a little more information about what had happened that night.

Several days later, on February 16, John Balser called and wanted to talk to the detectives again, so Al Graeber picked him up at his house and drove him to police headquarters. Once again, it was a long, rambling, convoluted statement sprinkled with the truth.

Sergeant Moody spent several minutes reading John his rights and explaining them to him.

Moody: Your mother came in here and told us that she did go back down there, after everyone had been down there.

John: Yeah.

Moody: Now I guess my question to you is—if you want to answer it—were those girls still alive when your mom got there?

John: Yes. Those was alive after I left and I don't know who killed those.

Moody: Well, now you said . . .

John: I admit to my part.

Moody: And what is your part, John?

John: I did drop the rock and it didn't hit Phree.

Moody: Well, now that's . . . You're kind of hedging now, because that's not what you told Al on the way in.

John: Okay. It did hit her and it didn't hurt her. I couldn't hurt kids, Mooo-nee.

Moody: John, I know you think a lot about kids, but sometimes, partner, things happen that are beyond our control.

John: Yeah. That's what I told all of us. I said that did get out of control on me on Linden. See on Linden—wasn't nothing supposed to went down—and Jamie Turner brung these girls in the house. And Jamie and Dave and Jake Campbell all went upstairs and I couldn't find those right away until I heared Phree screaming.

Moody: So who went upstairs?

John: Dave, Jamie, and Jake . . . Jake Campbell. And I got Jason Holmes mixed up with Jake Campbell. Both of them has got the same color hair.

Moody: What was Jake driving then, John?

John: His van.

Graeber: You were seen getting in a blue van at Schuler's, putting some doughnuts in there, okay? And it was blue.

John: Okay, Jake did have it blue, then he took it to—

Graeber: And then he had it painted black.

John: Yeah.

Graeber: What color was it the day the girls got killed?

John: Blue.

Moody: See, I want to tell you something, John. We've got two witnesses and they've got nothing to do with nothing—none of this—that saw you walk over to the van and saw David standing right on the sidewalk next to Schuler's.

John: I did get in the van, Mooo-nee.

Moody: How did the girls get from Linden Avenue down to Schuler's, John?

John: Jake took those.

Graeber: Well, let me ask you something: did they walk out to the van or did something else happen to get them out in the van?

John: Jamie hit those, that's the truth.

Moody: So how did the girls get from the house to the van, John?

John: Jamie and Jake pack those.

Moody: Did they cover them up?

John: Yes. A sheet . . . and I don't know where that stuff at Mooo-nee. The sheets and all . . .

Moody: Now I want to ask you something—the truth: When you went in and got those doughnuts and came back out to the van, were those girls in that van?

John: They was in the van first, beginning—

Graeber: Hey, John. When the girls were packed out to the van (on Linden), were they awake or were they knocked out?

John: Jamie knocked those out.

Graeber: Okay, Jake drove the girls over to the pond in the van, right?

John: Yeah.

Graeber: Okay, your mom also told us who dropped the rock on them. She told us exactly what she saw. Now, what did she see, John? The truth now, buddy.

John: I didn't drop the rock.

Graeber: Now wait a minute, wait a minute. What did your mom see?

John: See, Mommy said [she] see me drop it and I didn't drop it, Graeber.

Graeber: Your mom says you dropped a rock.

John: Not kill those, I didn't.

Graeber: Who did you drop the rock on? Now remember what she said.

John: I drop it on Phree. That all I did. No one supposed to got hurt.

Graeber: You brought Wanda back down there. What happened then? What did Wanda do?

John: She took pulse on those. She said those girls dead.

Graeber: When did she take the pulse on them?

John: After I hit Phree. And that all she did.

By combining John's sprinkles of truth with what the detectives had learned from other witnesses, the logical conclusion was that Phree and Martha had gotten into the van at Schuler's Bakery, either voluntarily or forced, and were taken to the house on Linden Avenue. The initial attack had taken place there, resulting in the girls being knocked unconscious. John and the others then "packed" them out to the van and went to the pond area behind Schuler's, where their bodies were found the next day.

On the morning of March 14, 1994, Wanda contacted Detective Eggers and told him that she needed to talk to the detectives again. When she came to police headquarters, she was taken to an interrogation room and Sergeant Moody read her rights to her.

Crying the whole time, Wanda told Sergeant Moody and Detective Eggers again about meeting John on Main Street: "He just told me that I had to go with him. And when I walked with him, he took me in back of the bakery. And that's when I seen the girls. And I . . . I just stood there and you know . . . They had my hands—I believe it was John, because John knew that I would try to do something if they didn't get my hands behind me."

Moody: Who else was there, Wanda?

Wanda: John, Turner, Boone and uh . . . that one boy, I can't think of his name.

Moody: Was David there?

Wanda: Yes, David was there.

Moody: And another guy . . . you don't know his name?

Wanda: I don't know his name. He was white. It was that Jake Campbell.

Moody: Did you know who it was at the time?

Wanda: No, I didn't know.

Moody: How do you know it's Jake Campbell now, Wanda?

Wanda: Because they told me. John told me. He says, "Mom, you're stupid, that was Jake." He said, "You have seen him a lot." And I says, "John, I don't even know the guy."

Eggers: Well, you've seen his picture since?

Wanda: Yes, I did. Yes, it is him. And everything I am telling today is the God's truth. I was standing on the other side of the girls—across from where the girls was laying—the first time. It was still light, the first time. Martha did not say nothing, but Phree told me to go get her daddy and I couldn't do it. When I went back the second time, the girls were dead. They just told me that the little white trash had to die. They said, "The white trash has to die." (Once again, as with "white honkeys," Wanda's reference to "white trash" makes no sense.)

Eggers: Do you think Phree was still alive the second time you were there?

Wanda: No, Phree was dead the second time that I was there.

Eggers: John hit her in the head with the rock anyway?

Wanda (sobbing): Yes!

Eggers: Did David also pick up a rock and do the same? Did he?

Wanda: Yes. Oh, God!

Eggers: Where was Jake Campbell?

Wanda: I don't know. He wasn't . . . He wasn't in the

truck with us. He was there at the scene the second time.

Eggers: So he was down there waiting for you?

Wanda: Yes. It was dark when I went back the second time.

Moody: Wanda, why didn't you go dial 911?

Wanda (whining): I couldn't . . . I couldn't because I was . . . I was just so scared.

Moody: Did you tell those guys that they had to hide the stuff?

Wanda: No, I did not tell them.

Moody: Did you tell them that they had to do something with the girls because they had problems?

Wanda: No, I did not tell them nothing like that.

Moody: Well, why—if you were so upset about this— why wouldn't you call the police?

Wanda (voice becoming increasingly shrill): Because Dave and them told me that if I told . . . They said it will happen again and again and again! John just tells me, he says, "Mom, the police is stupid. They're dumb. You're dumb." He says, "You're gonna see the same thing over again." And I says, "Not me. John, don't call me if you guys do this again. Just leave me alone, leave me out of it. I can't take no more." And I can't.

Moody: Wanda, I'm going to ask you one more time: Did you—after being coerced—forced by them— help them dispose of any of the evidence?

Wanda: No, I did not.

Moody: Did you help cover those girls up?

Wanda: No.

Moody: Did you tell them, "You better make sure that they're dead?"

Wanda: No, I did not.

Moody: Why would John tell us that?

Wanda: I don't know. John is lying, because I did not say a word like that.

Moody: Well, there's been . . . There's been a whole lot of lying going on.

Wanda: Yeah. But I did not say nothing like that.

Eggers: Every three months you come down here and you got just a little bit more.

Wanda: Yeah, but this is all I've got to say. Just like I told John, I don't want it to happen again.

Eggers: We don't know what's the truth and what's not anymore. You've lied to us so much.

Wanda: Well, this here I am telling is the God's truth.

Moody: It's not just you, you know. John's lied to us. Dave's lied to us. Turner's lied to us. Mr. Boone has lied to us.

Wanda: Yeah, but everything I have told today is the truth, you know. I have no more to say.

Moody: Do you think you should be punished?

Wanda: Yes, for what I did.

Moody: For what? What'd you do?

Wanda: For not telling the truth.

Eggers: Do you think that the first time that you went down there and Phree asked for her daddy that if you went to a phone and called, she'd still be alive today?

Wanda: I don't know. I really don't, because I didn't know what to do, or nothing.

Eggers: If you ran directly from that pond across the street where there's a phone . . .

Wanda (whining again): I didn't have no money.

Moody: 9-1-1 doesn't cost you anything, Wanda. You know that.

Wanda: But see, they kept telling me that . . . I couldn't call nobody, you know.

Eggers: How many times have we heard the "truth"?

Wanda: But this is the truth. I mean . . . I don't want it to happen again.

Eggers: You think we ought to just get up and go lock John up?

Wanda: I think so, because if it happens again . . .

Eggers: What do you propose we lock him up for?

Wanda (voice like fingernails on a blackboard): I know he done the murder! That's what I'm trying to tell you guys! He done it and he's gonna do it again! And you guys is gonna start the same thing all over again and again and again and it will never be solved!

Eggers: Has John killed anybody since these two little girls?

Wanda: No, but he is so mean, he . . . God, he's so mean, but I can't get anybody to believe me. I'm just like I'm nuts or something.

(As Wanda became more and more emotional, Sergeant Moody tried to reason with her.)

Moody: We're not saying that at all, Wanda.

Wanda: That's what I have been told. I'm nuts, keep my mouth shut.

Moody: Who's told you that?

Wanda (crying again): John did. He says, "Keep your mouth shut, Mom, you're nuts. You know you're nuts." I am believing that I am nuts.

Moody: You're not nuts, Wanda.

Wanda: God, why didn't . . . I wished I would have been laying there with the girls.

Moody: Why?

Wanda: Because it would have been over.

Moody: What's that going to accomplish?

Wanda: It would have been over. . . . It would have been over! Oh, God! Oh, God! Can I go home?

Moody: Yeah!

(They ended the interview immediately, but Detective Eggers persuaded Wanda to sit there for a few minutes and calm down before she left.)

* * *

On April 13, 1994, Wanda Marciszewski called police headquarters to talk to Detective Graeber, but he was out, so Detective Eggers took the call.

Wanda: I'm just wondering now if there was even a rapist involved.

Eggers (incredulous): You say that you wonder if there was even a rapist? But there's semen. . . .

Wanda (explaining her reasoning): Yeah, but . . . I just came up with that, you know. I just came up with that myself, okay. They can't, you know, really find the rapist. . . . They don't know who the rapist is, right? Okay. If nobody knows who the rapist is and won't tell who he is, well, how is anybody ever gonna find out who this guy is?

Eggers: Do you think that the guys know who the rapist is?

Wanda: I think they do.

Eggers: Well, hasn't John told you that he knows who the guy is, but he's never going to tell?

Wanda: He told me . . . he says, "Mom, I know the guy." And he says, "The guy will never be told." He says, "You will never know this man." But he keeps repeating this same guy that I turned in (Jake Campbell) that was there at the scene. But he says, "Mom, I will not tell. Nobody can make me tell."

In April 1994 a fisherman found the lower torso of a woman on the bank of a stream in neighboring Miami County. Two weeks later, the dismembered legs of the same woman were found a few miles to the east, in Clark County. Springfield is the county seat of Clark County.

Land surveyors found the right leg about a quarter mile

away from a country road. Authorities from both counties thoroughly searched the area and Miami County sheriff Charles Cox found the left leg in a nearby ditch, in a plastic bag. It was believed that someone threw the legs, both in the plastic bag, from a vehicle traveling on Ballentine Pike and that an animal had dragged the right leg into the woods, where the surveyors later discovered it.

Belinda Anderson's family anxiously held their breath and braced themselves. The only information they had was that the body parts belonged to a white woman. Belinda had been missing for over seven months and the torso and legs were well preserved. It was possible that whoever was responsible for the murder of the unknown victim had kept the parts in a freezer until deciding to dispose of them.

Three days later, a woman's severed head was discovered in Champaign County, Clark County's neighbor to the north. The location of the grisly discovery was only about a half mile from where the legs had been found. A couple traveling in a car on Cow Path Road had spotted a plastic bag in a ditch and notified the sheriff's department.

Officials described the unidentified woman as having brown hair tinted blond on the ends, possibly brown eyes, and that she may have been in her early to middle thirties. They said she was probably 5'3" to 5'5" and weighed between 125 and 135 pounds.

Belinda, thirty-one, had blond hair and green eyes, was 5'5", and weighed 125 pounds.

Two days later, the victim was identified as Peggy Casey, thirty-seven, of Latonia, Kentucky. That same day, her arms and hands were found in a wooded area close to Ballentine Pike, not far from where her legs had been discovered.

Although their hearts ached for Peggy Casey's family, Belinda's loved ones could breathe a little easier again and continue to hope against hope that Belinda was still alive somewhere—somehow.

12

He was a follower . . . but he had the opportunity to stop it. . . . Wanda controlled David. . . . Wanda called the shots on David . . .

—Captain Steve Moody

In June 1994, at a hearing held in Judge Douglas Geyer's courtroom, David Marciszewski's attorneys, James and Jon Doughty, argued that David's statements to the detectives should be suppressed because they were obtained by threats and coercion. Even though the detectives had explained David's rights to him and he had signed a waiver, his attorneys questioned whether or not he really understood what he was doing.

On the first day of the hearing, the taped statements from March 24 and March 27, 1993, were played in court:

Moody: David, it's very important you tell us the truth, because I'm going to tell you something. If you're protecting somebody, you're going to burn in hell for it. God is not going to forgive you, so don't lie to me now.

David: I'm not lying to you.

Moody: Because, you better understand something, here on earth policemen are God's angels.

David: I'm not lying to you. I'm telling you the truth.

Moody: You understand that you may burn in hell for this?

David: Yes, I do understand.

Moody: Tell me the truth now.

David: I am telling the truth.

Moody: If you lie about someone that was there, and wasn't there, you're going to burn in hell for it.

David: I am telling you the truth.

Moody: All right, now I'm going to explain something to you. Better think about something here real hard. Remember that light that kept coming on by the loading dock? Remember when you walk over toward the loading dock across from the pond and that light comes on? Remember that? You know that there were security cameras down there and we know exactly what everybody did. No one knew that until now. John knew about the security cameras in Schuler's because we told him. Now you better start telling the truth. We knew you hit her in the head with a board. We've known every time you've lied to us. We've just been biding our time. Now, what happened after you hit her with a board? Huh? Come on, David, time's running out, buddy.

David: She quit screaming.

Moody: Then you need to tell—I told you we know the truth about questions when we ask them. And you lied to us. That doesn't appear to be somebody who wants forgiveness. Do you believe in God? Huh?

David: Yes.

Moody: You go to church, don't you?

David: I used to—I don't now.

Moody: Well, you want to go back and have Jesus in your heart? Huh?

David: Yeah.

Moody: Well, then, what are you going to do? You have to start by asking for forgiveness right now. And part of that forgiveness is saying what you've done, asking for help. Now did you take the pants and panties off one of the girls? David, answer my ques-

tion, please. Answer my question, please. Did you or
didn't you?
David: Yeah.

Then later, an exchange between Marciszewski and Detective Eggers:

David: I don't understand the question.
Eggers: That's bullshit. You're going to have to quit
    jerking us around. You're not as stupid as you're act-
    ing. Was he there when this happened to these girls?
    David, was he or wasn't he? Huh? Was he or wasn't
    he? Were you there? Huh? That's it. That—is—it!
Moody: You're gonna fry.

When Sergeant Moody took the witness stand the next day,
James Doughty pointed out that some of the questioning of
David sounded like threats. Moody replied that they were
intended to get Marciszewski "out of the denial stage."
Moody defended the detectives' statements and the ploys that
were used as being "in pursuit of the truth."

Sergeant Moody explained that Marciszewski showed visible signs that something was bothering him and that the
detectives had already obtained information about his involvement in the murders of Phree Morrow and Martha Leach.

Doughty: How do you know God is not going to forgive
    him?
Moody: This is just something said to appeal to his
    moral sense of decency.
(Doughty pointed out that when the detectives ques-
    tioned David, they told him that there were security
    cameras outside near the crime scene, and that this

was a lie. Sergeant Moody replied that it was a ploy
used as an interrogation technique.)

Doughty: Are all confessions similar to this one?

Moody: No.

Doughty: What did you mean when you told Marciszewski that police officers were "God's angels"
on earth?

Moody: I don't take myself literally as an angel. I was
trying to get across that we're duty bound to protect.

Doughty: Do you tell everyone that police are "God's
angels"?

Moody: No.

(Sergeant Moody explained that he didn't learn this at
any seminar and that each officer develops an individual style.)

Doughty: You had him admit to everything you asked
him.

Moody: He made statements about the murders containing information that only someone at the crime
scene would have known.

(When asked about Marciszewski's mental capacities,
Moody replied: He appeared "street-smart." If he
didn't understand, he'd ask.)

On the third day of the hearing, Dr. Erhard Eimer, a pro-
fessor of psychology at Wittenberg University, testified
that fear and coercion were used by the detectives in the
interrogation of David Marciszewski. He said that the combination affected Marciszewski's statements. He claimed
that when the detectives told David that he would "burn in
hell" if he didn't cooperate and that he was going to "fry,"
it amounted to "spiritual coercion."

Dr. Eimer, who had interviewed Marciszewski, said that
David had an IQ of 74. Therefore, David interpreted the detectives' comments literally, and some of their statements would

be considered physical threats. Eimer went on to say that the confession was not an exercise in free will and that Marciszewski would give answers he thought were expected of him.

Dr. Eimer also told Judge Geyer that psychological tests indicated that Marciszewski had very little moral standards and that he had to rely on his environment and the people around him to know what was acceptable: "It is very important for him to gain the approval of others."

Very early on the morning of August 16, 1994, there was a horrible fire at a house on Miller Street. A four-year-old boy named Avery Bailum died from smoke inhalation.

His mother's boyfriend, Donald Mosier*, had tried to go down the stairs, but the lower floor was engulfed in flames. Desperate, he gathered the large family at a second-floor window; there he jumped out first and, along with neighbors, caught four of Me-Chelle Bailum's children as she dropped them, saving their lives.

But when Me-Chelle turned to pick up Avery, he ran away from the window into the burning house. She searched frantically but could not find him in the smoke-filled rooms. When her own clothing caught on fire, she finally jumped out the window.

Me-Chelle's mother lived on the other side of the large double house, and after she made it safely out of the burning building and realized the horror of what was happening, she grabbed a garden hose with the intention of going in to save her young grandson. The firefighters, who arrived within minutes of the alarm, would not allow her to enter the house.

Avery's body was later found under the bed in his bedroom, where he apparently had gone to hide.

It was determined that a large amount of gasoline had been poured onto the front porch and ignited.

* * *

On October 31, 1994, John Balser went to police head-quarters and talked to Detectives Eggers and Graeber again. During the course of another long, rambling statement, he gave them at least three more names of men who were supposedly at the crime scene the night Phree and Martha were murdered. More DNA testing followed.

As it turned out, a decision never had to be made concerning the suppression of David Marciszewski's statements to the detectives or about his competency. In November 1994 David Marciszewski agreed to testify before the grand jury and to assist in the investigation as part of a plea agreement.

He pleaded guilty to two counts of aggravated murder. Prosecutor Stephen Schumaker dismissed four counts of aggravated murder, two counts of rape, two counts of kidnapping, one count of tampering with evidence, two counts of abuse of a corpse, and one count of felonious sexual penetration.

According to the agreement, common pleas judge Douglas Geyer sentenced Marciszewski to life in prison, with a chance for parole no sooner than 2014. He was spared the possibility of facing the death penalty.

The plea agreement was signed in Judge Geyer's court-room on November 7, 1994.

The next morning, Sergeant Moody and Detective Graeber interviewed Robby Detwiler again.

Robby told them again about staying at Wanda's house the weekend of August 22 and 23, 1992. He said that he, John Balser, David and Wanda Marciszewski, and Willie were at a house on Linden Avenue painting earlier in the day on Saturday, August 22. Then Wanda left for work. The rest of them went to Wanda's house on Light Street.

Frank Fisher came over and the three of them were in the basement drinking beer. Later in the day, everyone else left and he and Willie were there by themselves for about four hours.

Moody: So, who's the next person to come home?

Robby: Wanda—asked where Dave and them was. She just sat down and then when they came back . . . Dave, John, and I don't know the other guy. Like kind of tall, like blond hair, maybe—dirty blond. She asked them where they was and John told her to come with him. She told me to come on.

Moody: Where was Willie?

Robby: The front room.

Moody: Okay, but he didn't go?

Robby: Huh-uh.

Moody: And how did you leave there? What were you in?

Robby: Car. Kind of an old one—I don't know—the color was like off-red maybe.

Moody: Who was driving it?

Robby: A guy. I don't know who it was.

Moody: Who's in the car?

Robby: Jamie. Me, Dave, John, and Wanda.

Moody: And this guy?

Robby: Yeah.

Moody: Nobody else is in the car?

Robby: Boone.

Moody: Who's driving the car, Robby?

Robby: I don't know. I don't know him.

Moody: Do you know him or you just don't want to tell us?

Robby: I don't know him. When we got out of the car, John went over to the girl. Everybody else was standing, and he was saying . . . yelling about something . . . Phree . . . Wanda goes over there. . . . (Robby speaks haltingly.)

Moody (coaxing): Just let it go, Robby. Just tell us what happened.

Graeber: Wanda goes over there and what?

Robby: She checks her pulse. She comes back. And

she looked at John and told him to kill them. She said, "Kill them."

Moody: What did Wanda tell you, Robby?

Robby: That if I ever told anybody, they'd kill me.

Graeber: Had you ever seen that guy before? First time you'd ever seen him?

Robby: Uh-huh.

Moody: Have you seen him since then? I mean, this guy comes into your life for an hour, you know, two years ago and you've never seen him again?

Robby: Uh . . .

Moody: Don't make something up.

Graeber (reassuringly): If you know who it is, it isn't going to hurt you. No one's going to hurt you.

Moody: Robby, I tried to tell you, buddy, this is over with and the only way it's over with is if you tell the whole truth. So if you lie to us about something now, you're not relieving yourself of it, okay. You're not helping yourself forget about this. You're not putting it behind you. So you need to be honest with us about what went on down there at the scene and who this other guy was, if there was another guy. You need to tell us the truth. Now, some of this stuff I know that you're telling is the truth. Other stuff I know that you're not. You got to tell it all. I mean that's just—

Robby: Can I use the bathroom? Skip . . . I don't know the name. I think that's what they call him.

Moody: How do you feel about all this? How do you feel about these girls?

Robby (hanging his head): I feel like I should have done something.

Moody: Well, and that's exactly right. But look at me . . . how old were you?

Robby: Fourteen.

Moody: Okay. What are you going to be able to do?

Robby: Pick something up and hit them.

Moody: All of them? Are you going to be able to take them all out?

Robby (softly): Should have tried.

Moody: What do you think would have happened to you if you would have tried to beat them off?

Robby: Got killed.

Moody: Did you help cover them up?

Robby: Yeah. Leaves . . .

Graeber: Which one of these girls did you help carry over there?

Robby: The blonde—John helped me.

Graeber: Who carried the dark-haired girl over?

Robby: Wanda and Dave.

Moody: So you tell me who this other guy is.

Robby: I don't know his name.

Moody: Robby . . .

Robby (insisting): I don't know his name.

Moody: Well, let me point something out to you here, okay. When we first started out here—you didn't have anything to do with this. You didn't even go down there. But we all know now that wasn't true. And when we first started out here, you didn't have anything to do with covering the girls up. And now we know that you had something to do with that too. But you're not responsible for this because you're a juvenile. Do you hear what I'm saying?

Robby: Yeah.

Moody: You're just a kid. And before—you didn't even touch the girls. So, now you're helping John carry one of the—the blonde over. And you're there helping them cover them up. Okay, and then you're telling us that you didn't have anything to do with all this stuff, but now you're trying to get rid of—how you feel. Right?

Robby: Uh-huh.

Moody: Okay, and then you're telling me now you

don't know who drove you down there. Now I want to tell you something. You know how we know you're telling the truth about Wanda being there? Because someone heard her scream. And someone saw that red car driving away from there. Now you can't tell me that you don't know who was driving that car. I don't want you to lie anymore. You need to let it go. There is no one that is going to hurt you. We are not going to let anyone hurt you. Carrying this around inside of you, Robby, has wrecked you. We can see it physically on you over the last two years. I told you that. We can see how it's affected you. You don't even hang with Willie that much, do you?

Robby: No.

Moody: Well, it's time to let go of this. You have admitted what's going on here, Robby. You couldn't control it. You've got to let it go. There was nothing you could do for those girls. If you had tried to do something, you'd have been there right beside them. You know that and I know it. And these people are supposed to be your friends? You knew in your heart that they'd kill you just as quick as they could if they thought that you'd betrayed them.

Robby: Uh-huh.

Moody: Well, those days are gone, Robby. Dave understands it. He's gone. You don't have to worry about him. But Dave was never really a threat to you, was he?

Robby: No.

Moody: Okay, who is? Who are you scared of the most? Or are you scared of anybody right now?

Robby (with more bravado than he actually felt): I ain't scared of them.

Graeber: Who worries you the most, Robby?

Robby: The guy that was driving. Everybody said he's mean.

Moody: Who was driving the car?

Robby: I don't know his name. I've seen him a couple times. Wanda's . . .

Moody: And this was after everything happened?

Robby: Yeah.

Moody: When was the last time you saw this guy, Robby?

Robby: A pretty long time ago.

Moody: Did he ever threaten you?

Robby: Huh-uh.

Moody: Well, then, what are you afraid of him for?

Robby: I ain't.

Moody: Who are you afraid of?

Robby: John.

Moody: Are you afraid of Wanda?

Robby: Not really.

Moody: She threatened you anymore?

Robby: Not since it happened.

Moody (slightly annoyed): Robby, you can't lie to us about things now, do you understand me? I've tried to tell you. I don't know what else to do. If you're making this guy up, you've got to . . . You know what I'm saying. Are you telling us the truth?

Robby: No.

Moody: What? What aren't you telling us the truth about? Right now, let's get it over with.

Robby: About the guy. Weren't never there.

Moody: So why would you make that up?

Graeber: You're protecting someone, aren't you?

Robby: Boone. I'm afraid of Boone.

(Robby changed his story and insisted, repeatedly, to the frustrated detectives that Alex Boone was the one driving the car.)

Moody: Did they ever talk about getting rid of evidence in front of you? John or Dave?

Robby: No, but they made us move boards—into that

hole—over by the house. Made us throw boards and stuff away.

Graeber: Was there any blood on them?

Robby: Yeah. I mean you couldn't tell it was blood. It was stained.

Graeber: What else did you throw down in the hole?

Robby: Sack. Wanda went and got it for us. Told us to throw it down there.

Graeber: Who brought the sack home?

Robby: Dave had it in his hand.

Moody: What was in it? Robby, what was in it?

Robby (whispering): Girls' panties.

Graeber: Did you see them?

Robby: No, but that's what Dave said was in it.

Graeber: What kind of stories did Wanda and John tell you to tell us?

Robby: To tell you that I don't know nothing.

Sergeant Moody and Detective Graeber interviewed Wanda Marciszewski that afternoon. Al Graeber dreamed of the day they would be able to put handcuffs on her and take her to jail.

Moody: Well, I want you to understand something. David has testified in front of the grand jury. He has testified to the truth of what happened down there. Do you understand that?

Wanda: Yeah.

Moody: That's why he pled guilty to two counts of murder and that's why he's going for the rest of his life.

Wanda: Yeah.

Moody: Okay, so when you got down there and you saw what they had done and you checked their pulse and found out that they were still alive—I want to know why . . .

Wanda: That I didn't go for help.

Moody: No, I want to know why you said, "You've got to kill them."

Wanda: I did not say that.

Moody: Well, I'm going to explain something to you. Mr. Marciszewski testified to the grand jury, and other people that were there have told us that you said that.

Wanda: No, I did not say that. That is a lie.

Moody (keeping sarcasm out of his voice, barely): Oh, is it? And I want to tell you something, Wanda. You haven't lied to us at all, have you?

Wanda: I know some of it I have told you fibs on. Everything I have told you today is the God's truth. I mean . . . I wish to God . . .

Graeber: We've got four people that have testified that you told them to kill the girls and clean the area up.

Wanda: I did not tell them guys to kill the girls. I would never tell anybody to hurt any kids because I love kids myself.

Moody: You love your son, don't you?

Wanda: I love my son. I love any kid.

Moody (trying to reason with her): This is your baby. This is somebody you've tried to raise, tried to raise right, tried to do the best job you can under the hardest circumstances. People have made fun of him. Made life hard for him. Sometimes he gets angry; he's hard to control, but you still love him. He's still a part of you. And all you could think about, you know—not only are you going to lose your husband, but also you're going to lose your son.

Wanda: But I love kids. I mean, I've been around kids all my life. I mean babies; I hold babies in my arms constantly. So if I was going to say something like that . . . why would I want to hold babies? Why would I want to be around kids?

Moody: Why wouldn't you go and dial 911?

Wanda: I don't know.

Moody: Because you love your son. And you didn't want your son to be in trouble that night. Now it has come down to trying to save yourself. And you don't feel guilty about anything, huh?

Wanda: I feel guilty for taking their pulse and not going and getting the police or not going and getting Bennie. I feel guilty about that, yeah. That was my mistake. I should have did it, but I didn't. I was just froze.

Moody: Wanda, I want to tell you something. You have not to this day, nor will you ever take responsibility for what you were involved in. And you have lied to us all the time and you just keep minimizing it. And you tell us how much you love children and everything else, but the bottom line here is you were protecting your son.

Wanda: Let me tell you this. . . . If I am guilty, then why don't they put me in the chair tomorrow and get rid of me?

Graeber (attempting to keep sarcasm at bay): Takes longer than that.

Moody: Wanda, who is Skip? Do you know anybody named Skip?

Wanda: I don't know anybody with the name Skip, I don't. They keep coming off with different names and things. I just wish that it never happened. I wish that I would have called the police. See I had lost seven kids in miscarriages. And I swore, I said, "God, if you only let me have one, I will be the best mother that ever walked." You know, God let me have him. And I thought that I was the perfect parent. But I see now that I wasn't.

Moody: Well, let me explain something to you. You go back down there and you see what's going on. You check their pulse and they are still alive. You don't do

anything to help them. And we've got people that
testified to the grand jury, and other people have
talked to us, including your own son, who said [that
Wanda said], "You've got to kill them."

Wanda: No, I did not.

Moody: "You've got to kill them because they know
who you are and they know what you've done. . . ."

Wanda: No, I didn't.

Moody: ". . . And they are going to identify you." They
took you back down there because they reached the
point where they didn't know what to do.

Wanda: No, now hold it

Moody (matter-of-factly): And you went—no, you
wait a minute—you went back down there and you
fixed things up for them. And you continued to cover
up the whole time. You thought about yourself and
you thought about your son. That's all you thought
about during this whole investigation, and that's all
you've done is cover up for everybody else.

Graeber: And Phree was still alive. So therefore she
could testify against John, so John had to take her
out—because you told him to.

Wanda: No, I did not tell John to kill them. I did not
tell Dave to do anything to the girls.

Moody: And Phree could testify you were there. Because she told you—she asked you—she pleaded
with you—to go get her dad.

Wanda (whining): But I didn't know where to go. I
mean, I don't know where, right today, where Bennie
Morrow lives.

Moody: So what? Where was the nearest pay phone?

Wanda: Right across . . . down the street . . . but I still
didn't know where Bennie was.

Graeber: You know what you were seeing happen was
not right, but yet you chose not to do anything because your son was in the middle of it and your

husband was in the middle of it. You chose to let two little girls die.

Wanda: I am telling the truth. I did not tell them guys to kill the girls. I love kids.

Moody: You showed it.

Wanda: I love kids. I wish I would have called the police.

Moody (exasperated): You're not even listening to what I'm telling you. You showed how you loved kids.

Wanda: I know and I'm sorry.

Graeber: Well, you loved your kid.

Wanda: I will tell Bennie and them that I am sorry for not getting the help.

Moody: They don't want to hear it from you. That's not good enough.

Wanda: I know that. I wish I would have come the first night.

Graeber: You could have ended this stuff a long time ago, Wanda—a long time ago.

Wanda: When I went to bed, I was tired. I was, you know; I had the girls on my mind. And they told me to shut up and go to sleep. I mean, I didn't know what to do, where to go, who to go to, or nothing.

Graeber: What you should have done is, like any intelligent adult, is got on the phone and called 911. And you didn't say anything until we came to you— and we're talking about a long time later.

Wanda: Because they had told me to shut my mouth. You know, because John has . . . I have taken threats by John and everything else.

Graeber: When you "checked pulse," how many pulses did you feel?

Wanda: I felt at least three—three pulses. Martha was already dead. Because she wasn't moving—she wasn't moving at all. I did not have to touch Martha, but Phree I did. But when I took Phree's pulse—and

I knew how to do it because I had taken Eleanor's pulse every morning. . . . That was my job to take her pulse. And just like I have said, I wish to God that I had never learned how to do it. But they all told me that that was my job and I had to do it or I would get in trouble for not doing it.

Moody (disgusted): Evidently, no one had the job to go to the phone, huh?

13

*There was never any doubt in my mind that they were
there. The only thing that frustrated me was I knew
there was somebody else that we didn't have yet . . . that
they were protecting.*

—Sergeant Barry Eggers

On November 10, 1994, common pleas court judge Dou-
glas Geyer signed a search warrant allowing the investigators
to search a vacant apartment in a house on Linden Avenue.
Detective Eggers executed the warrant along with Detective
Graeber, Sergeant Moody, criminalist Tim Shepard, and Steve
Schumaker.

Handcuffed and dressed in his jail "uniform," David Marciszewski accompanied them to the large multiapartment
yellow brick house, located in a run-down section of the city
several blocks south of the Lion's Cage and Schuler's Bakery.
He walked the investigators through what he claimed had
occurred there on the night of August 22, 1992.

David alleged that the initial attack took place in this house
and that they had carried Phree and Martha out of there. He
said the girls were both "kind of out of it," so they were easy
to control.

The investigators sprayed luminol on the walls, the car-
peting, and the floors. They also stripped every layer of
paint off the walls with a heat gun, but found no forensic
evidence anywhere in the apartment.

During February and March of 1995, John Balser talked to

the detectives at least four more times and gave them at least two more names of the person who raped Phree and Martha.

On March 1, 1995, Wanda Marciszewski told Sergeant Moody that John had told her the night before, "Mom, you're going to die."

She also told him that about 9:00 or 9:30 the night before, someone tried to get in the front door of her house. She called the police about the prowler and Joe Jackson came over.

She claimed that John had told her, "Let the prowler come in and I'll fuck him up like I did the girls. I'll stick a pole up their ass like I did the girls."

Incredibly, on March 6, 1995, Wanda went public with the information she had about Phree and Martha's murders. She invited a reporter from WHIO-TV in Dayton, Ohio, to come to her home and interview her.

The next day, two reporters from the *Springfield News-Sun,* Delvin Harshaw and Miriam Smith, went to her house and talked to her at length. There were articles of clothing, shoes, and other odds and ends strewn everywhere in the less than clean, and very messy, living room. Wanda, clad in a hot-pink-and-white striped top and dark slacks, sat on a flowered sofa and drank coffee as she calmly told them about the events that she witnessed on August 22, 1992—the same story that she had told the detectives.

Until this time, the general public had been unaware of Wanda Marciszewski's existence, let alone her presence at the scene the night Phree and Martha were viciously murdered.

The girls' parents were outraged. The whole town was outraged.

John Balser called police headquarters repeatedly to talk to the detectives, mostly Al Graeber, to tell them who killed the girls. Sometimes he gave them a new name and other times he insisted that it was a person he had already told them about on an earlier occasion. He also called to talk about two of his favorite things: bicycles and lawn mowers.

Many times he just showed up at police headquarters for one reason or another. John, visibly upset, went in to talk to Detective Graeber in May 1995. His uncle Joe (Jackson) had told him that he and David would be the only people arrested for the murders. Al Graeber assured him that everyone involved in the murders would be arrested.

John said that he "wanted to get his prison time started so he could get out of prison sooner." He also borrowed $2 to get his lawn mower fixed.

John Balser called Detective Graeber on June 19 and told him that he was going to plead guilty to the murder of Phree Morrow, but he was not going to plead guilty to the murder of Martha Leach. John said all he wanted to do was go to prison so he can "get his time over." He also told him that "David will have served eighteen months of his sentence tomorrow and I have not even started mine."

John also wanted to know when the bike auction would be held.

The next day, Wanda Marciszewski testified in front of the grand jury in the case of the *State of Ohio v. John Balser*. She was the last of thirty-five witnesses to testify in a nine-hour session.

> Schumaker: How long did you stay with Eleanor that night?
> Wanda: I stayed until Joe came and got me and it was around nine. John called me and told me—this is his exact words: "Mom, I'm in trouble. Come and help me."
> Schumaker: You were at Eleanor's when you received that call?
> Wanda: Yes, I was and it scared me. I knew that John had always called me when he was in trouble and needed my help.
> (Wanda testified about meeting John on Main Street and being taken to "where the little girls was laying.

They told me if I moved at that time, that me and Willie would be dead just like the little girls was.")

Schumaker: Where was Willie?

Wanda: He was at home.

Schumaker: And where was Robby?

Wanda: I really don't know at that point. There was John and David and Boone and Turner and, just like I tried to tell the police at the time, there was somebody standing in the background, but I couldn't make out who it was. And I says, "Well, I'll just go home." And then after that they came back—after I got home—and John says, "You got to come and go with us. This is your job."

Schumaker: Now you are back on Light Street?

Wanda: Yes.

Schumaker: And they came back to get you again?

Wanda: Yes. And I says, "Where to now? I am tired and I want to go to bed." He says, "Come on."

Wanda (telling the jurors about taking "a pulse on Phree"): Well, I touched Phree and I says, "What in the name of God did you-uns do?" And John told me, "See, Mom, what little white trash gets." And that's when he came down with the rock on her head and killed her right then. She was alive when she looked at me and said, "Wanda, go get my daddy." Well, that's when John and them spoke up again and told me if I moved that, they would get me and Willie both, and I just stood frozen, more or less. I could not move. And when I got home then, I just went on to bed because I had to get up that next morning and go to work and try to do what I was supposed to with the old lady.

Schumaker: How smart is your son?

Wanda: They said at the school that—at Town and Country—that he has a mind of a four-year-old kid.

Schumaker: You live with him every day, how smart is he?

Wanda: To me, he is not that smart. The stuff that he does . . .

Schumaker: John had you come down the first time and he threatened you?

Wanda: Yes.

Schumaker: And then you left?

Wanda: Yes, I did.

Schumaker: And despite the fact that he threatened you, you went a second time instead of calling the police?

Wanda: That's because John told me both times that if I told anybody that night that me and Willie both would be dead and that the police would have four murders on their hands and they would not solve none of them.

Schumaker: Where did the girls' panties go?

Wanda: I don't know.

Schumaker: Where did the Schuler's bag go?

Wanda: I don't know, I never seen it. I never seen the Schuler's bags. They kept telling me that they gave the girls cookies. I never seen the cookies or the Schuler's bag or nothing.

Schumaker: And what about David Marciszewski, would he tell us the truth?

Wanda: I believe that, in my heart, that Dave did tell the truth. I really believe he did.

Schumaker: Are you still on good terms with him?

Wanda: Yes, I talk to Dave, maybe, three or four times every month or something.

Schumaker: Is he going to tell us the truth?

Wanda: I really believe Dave will tell the truth.

Schumaker: When Dave tells us that you made those statements—that you said to "kill the girls." Is that the truth?

Wanda: No.

Schumaker: You think your son is going to kill you?

Wanda: He has threatened me.

Schumaker: Is your son . . . Is he capable of killing his own mother?

Wanda: John has threatened me.

Schumaker: Why would he kill his own mother?

Wanda: He said if I said one word, I was dead.

Schumaker: Tell me about Jamie Turner jumping around in the pond.

Wanda: Well, he had blood on him and he was jumping up and down. When John came down with the rock, the blood squirted and Jamie was trying to get the blood off of him.

Schumaker: So Jamie was right there when the rock was dropped?

Wanda: Yes.

John Balser was reindicted that same day by the grand jury for his involvement in the murders of Phree Morrow and Martha Leach. He was charged with six counts of aggravated murder, two counts of rape, two counts of abuse of a corpse, two counts of kidnapping, and one count of tampering with evidence.

Finally, two years after the charges had been dismissed against him on the first indictment, Sergeant Moody and Detectives Eggers and Graeber arrested John at his home, where he still lived with his mother. Wanda, clad in shorts and a Mickey Mouse T-shirt, her long gray hair pulled back in a bun, stood on the porch of her home and sobbed as they took her son away in handcuffs.

This time around, John's right to a speedy trial required that the prosecutors bring him to trial within fourteen days of the new indictment. His trial was scheduled to start on Wednesday, June 28, 1995.

Retired judge Richard Cole was appointed by the Ohio Supreme Court to preside over the trial because the other common pleas court judges in Clark County were unable to clear their dockets in time to hear the case.

At Balser's arraignment the following Monday, he was represented by his court-appointed attorneys, Thomas Wilson and John Butz. When Butz voiced concern to the court about their client's competency, Judge Cole postponed the trial and ordered that John Balser be examined at the Dayton (Ohio) Forensic Center.

Butz argued that bond should be set because Balser had remained in the community for the previous two years, even though he knew that he would be reindicted, but Judge Cole ordered him to be held without bond due to the seriousness of the alleged crimes.

14

*That was a very, very eerie night. . . . It was really
[something] out of a crime-novel-type book . . . because
it was extremely dark and it was very foggy that night.*

—Steve Schumaker

The big, old house on South Fountain had been empty for
about five years when Robert and Molly Warner* moved
there in 1994. On Saturday, July 8, 1995, Molly decided to
participate in a "neighborhood cleanup" by cleaning out the
debris-filled double-car garage. While working in the south
bay of the dilapidated garage, she moved an old wooden door
and saw part of a tennis shoe stuck in the dirt floor. She
reached down to pick it up and realized, to her horror, there
was something inside it.

She quickly ran out of the garage to find her husband.
Frantic, she told him about the discovery, "There's something
inside that shoe, Robert! I think it's a body."

Disbelieving, he told her, "You're full of baloney."

But, at Molly's insistence, he finally entered the garage to
look at the tennis shoe—toes down, heel up. They called the
police.

When the officers and detectives arrived, they cordoned off
the area with crime scene tape and began the gruesome job of
uncovering the body. Only one officer, Sergeant Dave Anon,
entered the garage so as not to disturb the area any more than
necessary. Wearing a mask, he gently brushed the dirt away
with his gloved hands and was able to free the lower legs from

the ground. The tennis shoes had torn through the large trash bags that the body had been buried in.

As he worked, he talked to Sergeant Moody, who was standing at the entrance to the garage.

As he gently moved the dirt away from the upper part of the body: "The bag's a little chewed up. What was she wearing when she left? A purple blouse? I think I got a purple blouse. . . ."

Sergeant Moody: "I don't know. They're pulling the report up right now."

When the body was finally, very carefully, exhumed from the shallow grave and taken to the morgue, and the plastic bags removed, the investigators saw that there was a tattoo of a shooting star on one ankle and another one of a cross on the other ankle. Detective Eggers attended the autopsy, and even though they had to wait for the body, which now only weighed sixty pounds, to be identified through dental records, he knew.

Twenty-two months had passed before Belinda Anderson's badly beaten, decomposed body was found buried in the dirt floor of the garage behind the house on South Fountain Avenue, only a few blocks from where she had last been seen.

As fate would have it, Molly Warner knew Belinda. She had been a neighbor of the Anderson family when she lived on East Liberty Street a few years earlier.

Two weeks before her body was found, Richard, her oldest brother, and Karlene were blessed with the birth of a beautiful baby girl. They named her Jade Belinda. Karlene had told Richard, "When your sister comes back, she's going to be really honored to have one of her nieces named after her—just because we missed her so much."

On Monday, July 17, 1995—at long last—Belinda was given a proper burial. The memorial services were held in the chapel at Rose Hill Burial Park, with strains of her favorite song, "I Still Believe in You," playing softly in the background.

On Tuesday, July 18, 1995, the police exercised a search warrant at the house on Lagonda Avenue, where John Balser and Wanda Marciszewski had lived after they moved from Light Street. The police officers proceeded to dig up the backyard in search of evidence in the murders of Phree Morrow and Martha Leach. They found several articles of clothing unrelated to the case.

September 1995 was an eventful month for Steve Moody: He was promoted to lieutenant. And he also got married again—to an assistant prosecutor—and would, over the next several years, become the father of two more daughters.

Al Graeber was also promoted—to sergeant.

Two months later, Barry Eggers was promoted to sergeant and became the head of the Crimes Against Persons Unit.

In November 1995 retired judge Richard Cole found John Balser to be competent to stand trial. Two of the three psychologists who testified said they believed that, despite his mental retardation, he was able to assist his defense attorneys in preparation for his trial. The third psychologist said that although she didn't believe Balser was competent at that time, she did believe he could be restored to competency.

When John Butz, Balser's defense attorney, declined to enter a plea on behalf of his client, Judge Cole entered a plea of not guilty for him.

It was early in the evening of Sunday, February 25, 1996, that motorists traveling east on Interstate 70, south of Springfield, were startled to see the half-clothed, bleeding woman at the edge of the highway. She was barely able to tell those who stopped to help her that she had been abducted and driven away from the city.

A Care Flight helicopter landed on the interstate and flew thirty-two-year-old Ursula Thompson* to Miami Valley Hospital in nearby Dayton, Ohio. She had been stabbed in the face and beaten.

Detectives David Rapp and Debbie Burchett of the Clark County Sheriff's Office spent most of the night at the hospital with Ursula but were unable to learn the details of her attack because of her condition.

The following morning, Detective Rapp and Sergeant Roger Roberts returned to the hospital. Ursula was finally stabilized enough to be interviewed, but because of the knife wound to her face, it was very difficult for her to communicate. The knife had gone completely through her cheek, knocked out one of her teeth, and cut her tongue.

They spent most of the morning with her and were able to elicit the information that Ursula had been standing on the corner of High and Yellow Springs Streets when she accepted a ride from the man who later attacked her.

The slight blond woman haltingly—and painfully—told the investigators that she and the man then rode around looking for somewhere to buy some crack cocaine. He then drove to a dump site behind a building on South Limestone Street, near the city limits at the southernmost edge of town. The man claimed he had a cabin at the end of the rutted lane.

Ursula: I was in the front seat of his car when he stabbed me. He had two car seats in the backseat of the [station] wagon for kids.

Rapp: Did you know this guy?

Ursula: No.

Rapp: Can you describe the man for me?

Ursula: He was six feet tall, dark hair—shoulder-length brown hair. Dark glasses—black-rim glasses—frames were real thick. Had a mustache. Weighed two-ten to two-twenty. Blue jeans—long-sleeve flannel shirt.

Rapp: Did he have a gun?

Ursula: I didn't see it until he stopped. After he stabbed me, he stopped the car and got out. He stumbled and I took off running, and he hit me over the head with the gun.

(Finally she managed to escape and ran toward the highway.)

Rapp: What were you wearing?

Ursula: Blue button-up jeans and a red Coca-Cola T-shirt. Blue jean coat.

Rapp: Where is your purse?

Ursula: I don't carry a purse because I've been robbed before.

Rapp: We need to know if you got in the car . . . Was it your intention to have sex with him?

Ursula: No. I wanted a ride to go somewhere.

Rapp: You know this guy, don't you?

Ursula (protesting): I swear to God, I don't! Don't you think if I did, I would tell you?

Rapp: How was his hair combed?

Ursula: It was dirty. I guess it was straight back, but he had a ball cap on backward. He was in his thirties. I asked him for his name and he said his name was "John," but they always say that. He said he was going to give me thirty. I told him I had twenty.

Rapp: Was that for sex?

Ursula: No, it was for dope; I like to smoke crack.

Even though she didn't know the year or the make, she was also able to give a detailed description of the car he was driving: It was a dark blue station wagon—a little loud. He had a CB radio. It was a clean car. The car had two baby seats. He said he had twins—a boy and a girl. He had an empty pack of Marlboro cigarettes on the dashboard.

Detective Rapp and Sergeant Roberts observed that Ursula also had bruises around her neck.

Crime scene personnel from the sheriff's department found a tire track in the mud at the location where the attack had taken place and made a plaster cast. The investigators searched the scene and found a pair of jeans, a tooth, a pellet gun with a broken plastic handle, and several blood samples.

Later that day, Detectives Rapp and Burchett, along with Sergeant Al Graeber of the Springfield Police Department, canvassed the area where Ursula had accepted the ride and interviewed several prostitutes. The women told the detectives about a strange man with a mustache who wore thick dark glasses and drove an old station wagon with two car seats in the back.

The investigators were also able to locate an apartment near downtown Springfield where the prostitutes sometimes stayed, and they talked to two of the three men who lived there. George Pressley* told them that he "keeps an eye on the prostitutes" and also informed them that a man in a blue Chevrolet, possibly a Malibu, station wagon was harassing the prostitutes and could possibly be involved in some of the assaults on these women. He added that the car had a luggage rack on top.

When Detective Rapp returned to his office, he prepared an interoffice memo filled with the information they had gathered that day. Later that evening, Lieutenant Pat Sullivan called him at home and told him, "Hey, I'm coming over. I think we've got a good suspect."

After the lieutenant picked the detective up, he drove to an area just outside the city limits, close to the dump site where Ursula Thompson had been attacked. He explained that Sergeant James Howell had observed a man in the driveway of a house on Kinnane Street, in the Limecrest Addition, who matched the description of the perpetrator. The man was "doing something" to his car, which also matched the information in the memo.

The distance between where she was attacked and Kinnane Street is only about a quarter of a mile. Sergeant Howell was still there, watching the house, which sat farther back from the road than the houses on either side of it.

Sergeant Mike Roach had talked earlier to the middle-aged owners of the house, Mr. and Mrs. Carson*, and learned the names of the tenants—William and Karen Sapp.

Lieutenant Sullivan and Detective Rapp went to the sheriff's office and researched the criminal history of the man. They found that he had an extensive record in Jacksonville, Florida, several aliases—and that his previous address, in Springfield, was on Miller Street.

They went to interview the owners of the house who lived only two houses away from their rental property. Mrs. Carson said that whenever she saw Bill he was usually wearing a flannel shirt and a ball cap. She described him as having long, dirty hair, weighed 230 pounds, and wore thick dark black glasses. They both told the investigators that the man had a temper.

Mrs. Carson would later say that Bill and Karen were just ordinary people. Sometimes when Bill came to pay the rent—always on time—he would sit and chat for a while. Sometimes he brought sour gum balls for her grandchildren.

Bill helped Karen around the house, with the cooking and the cleaning, and did the yard work. He was a "good father" and helped care for the children.

Mrs. Carson would also say that Bill treated her—and her husband—"like gold" and would "do anything for them." "I don't have anything bad to say about them."

The law officers also wanted the license plate number on the car, so they obtained permission from Mr. and Mrs. Carson to go onto the property.

It was so foggy that night that they could barely see their hands in front of their faces. Sergeant Larry Fisher and Detective Terry Reed crawled through the yard, on their hands and knees, to get near the car. When they managed to get close enough to see the number, they also observed the suspect painting the car—with a paintbrush.

Lieutenant Sullivan called Steve Schumaker and provided him with the information they had, in order to obtain a search warrant. About 11:30 that night, Schumaker, Roach, and Rapp took the search warrant to Judge Gerald Lorig's home to have it signed.

About the same time the judge was signing the search warrant, Karen Sapp asked her neighbor Mary Lou Smith* to take her to the grocery store. On the way Mary Lou told Karen about a report she had seen on the local news about a woman being attacked the previous evening, not far from their neighborhood. She knew that Bill had not been home at the time of the assault; he had supposedly gone to the Laundromat to wash clothes. Karen had been worried because he was gone "for hours and hours." When he finally returned home, the clothes were still unwashed.

In the past, on more than one occasion, Mary Lou had seen Bill "fly into a rage." "He'd be all right one minute—and the next minute he'd be in a rage. If he didn't get his own way, he'd just go out in the yard and throw a fit."

She had witnessed him killing his son's pet rabbit. And he had shown her and her husband, Shawn*, his knife collection and his gun.

Referring to the news report, she now asked her friend, "Do you think Bill did that?"

Karen replied, "No." Then softly, "I don't know."

When they returned to the house, Mary Lou helped Karen carry the groceries in and then went next door to her own home, still pondering their earlier conversation.

As Lieutenant Sullivan, Sergeants Roberts and Fisher, and Detective Rapp approached the run-down house, to execute the warrant in the early-morning hours of Tuesday, February 27, 1996, the woman inside started yelling, "He saw you coming and ran out the back!"

But William K. Sapp was found hiding behind a furnace in a back room of his home. After a few tense moments they handcuffed him and read him his rights. Then they led him into the kitchen, removed the handcuffs, reread him his rights, and questioned him at the kitchen table.

With very little prompting, Sapp told them that he and Ursula Thompson had argued and she slapped him. He admitted that he stabbed her with a knife and hit her with a pellet gun.

After Sapp told them where to look, the law officers found the large Buck knife used in the attack hidden behind the paneling on a wall in one of the bedrooms.

Also present in the clean—but somewhat cluttered—house while he was being interrogated were his wife and their three young children. He did not have twins, as he had told Ursula, but in addition to a six-year-old son, he did have an eighteen-month-old girl and an eight-month-old boy.

It was odd that Karen had seen the sheriff's deputies coming. It was after midnight, but she had called out to them—and lied to them—before they even got to the door. Was she expecting them? Was Sapp expecting them? Had he told his wife what he had done? Was she protecting him? Or was she afraid of him?

The children had been awakened by the chaos and commotion. Karen tried to console them—and keep them out of the kitchen—as six-year-old Aaron* cried. He wanted his daddy.

After the 245-pound man was taken into custody, Lieutenant Sullivan and Detective Rapp returned to Miami Valley Hospital to see Ursula Thompson and to show her a photo array of mug shots. She was able to identify Sapp positively as the man who stabbed her.

Crying, Karen called Mary Lou about 1:30 in the morning and told her that Bill had been arrested and asked her to please come over.

Karen and Bill had lived next door to them for almost two years. For a brief period, Karen had even baby-sat for Mary Lou's six-year-old daughter, Alicia*, after school—until the night she and Karen were sitting at the kitchen table playing cards and she saw Bill bring Aaron's pet rabbit into the house. He went in the bathroom, started beating the small, defenseless animal, and then slit it open with a knife.

On another occasion Alicia caught Bill looking in her bedroom window. Shawn Smith, at 6'3" and 350 pounds, threatened to "kick his ass" if he ever saw him looking in their house again.

Karen was a quiet woman and seemed to take it all in stride. It was difficult to understand why she stayed with Bill. But Mary Lou remained friends with her even after these extremely disturbing incidents.

Even though Mary Lou had been suspicious of Bill, she was "utterly stunned" when she found out that he had actually been arrested. She dressed hurriedly and went next door to try to help her friend, and she was surprised to see that there were still sheriff's deputies present. Together the two women tried to calm the children and get them back to sleep as the deputies continued to search the house.

William K. Sapp, thirty-four, pleaded not guilty, in Clark County Municipal Court, to the charge of attempted murder and his bond was set at $100,000. He was indicted by the grand jury on Monday, March 4, 1996. The following Friday, he pleaded "innocent by reason of insanity" to the charges of attempted murder and kidnapping.

When Mrs. Carson was reminded that she—and her husband—had told the investigators that Bill Sapp "had a temper," she claimed that it was "nothing out of the ordinary." His arrest "was a shock."

Sergeant Graeber interviewed John Balser again, on April 30, 1996, after reading him his rights:

John: I was wanting to put on tape about Monty Walker*, one raped Phree and Martha. He raped Phree Morrow. I seen him and all. The whole truth and nothing but the truth. I think it was time to be truthful with you, Graeber, and I want you go after him. The whole truth . . . I think that would make it . . . I think that will make you happy when you get the right one.
Graeber: What's Monty do?
John: Monty works Main [Street]. He is a fag. And I

already know it. No one told me. And I did see
Monty having sex, Graeber.

Graeber: Okay, like I said before, John . . . now you've
given us a lot of names.

John: Yeah, I know.

Graeber: And we followed up on all these names you
gave us.

John: Yeah.

Graeber: And none of them was true.

John: I know. This name will be the whole truth, nothing but the truth. I want you to go after him for me.
To get him in jail. What he did wrong to my little
friend and all.

Graeber: Who told you to drop the rock on Phree's
head?

John: Wanda Marciszewski. And she give a direct de-
mand to do it. She said, "Kill her. If you don't, she
tell on you." And Phree look right at me. She said,
"John, I would never tell on you." And never hurt me
and all.

Graeber: And then you dropped a rock on her?

John: Yes.

On Wednesday, May 22, 1996, John Balser pleaded guilty
to two counts of aggravated murder. A three-judge panel
consisting of Judge Richard O'Neill, Judge Gerald Lorig,
and Judge Richard Cole (retired) accepted his plea and sentenced him to two life sentences in prison with no eligibility
of parole for at least forty years. Because of the negotiated
plea agreement, Balser, who had been found competent to
stand trial, did not have to face the possibility of the death
penalty.

The agreement required that Balser assist in any future
prosecutions.

The following day, officers obtained and executed a search

warrant for the blood of Monty Walker. They took the necessary samples and forwarded them to the FBI laboratory in Washington, DC.

On Monday, June 10, 1996, the Clark County grand jury reindicted Jamie Turner on thirteen charges: six counts of aggravated murder, two counts of rape, two counts of kidnapping, one count of tampering with evidence, and two counts of abuse of a corpse.

As part of John Balser's plea agreement, he testified in front of the grand jury that indicted Jamie Turner. Three years after the original charges were dismissed against Turner, he was again taken into custody after he turned himself in to the police.

The following Friday, Jamie Turner was arraigned in Judge Richard O'Neill's courtroom. After assistant public defender Noel Kaech told the judge that his client would not speak for himself, Judge O'Neill entered a plea of not guilty for Turner.

Kaech asked the court to release Jamie Turner on his own recognizance. He claimed that Jamie had made himself available to the authorities and had committed no other offenses since the original charges were dismissed in 1993. Assistant prosecutor David Smith said that Turner should be held without bond since it was a capital case.

Judge O'Neill ordered that Turner remain in jail without bond.

The results of the DNA testing on Monty Walker showed that, once again, John Balser had lied to the detectives about who had raped Phree Morrow and Martha Leach.

15

Sapp latched onto that because the detectives, by doing that, gave him an out . . . to rationalize what he was doing.

—Steve Schumaker

By the time William K. Sapp went to trial on September 9, 1996, for the attack on Ursula Thompson, the charges of felonious assault and attempted rape had been added to the charges of attempted murder and kidnapping. The trial took place in the Clark County Common Pleas Court with Judge Gerald Lorig presiding. The jury consisted of four men and eight women.

During the more than six months spent in the Clark County Jail awaiting his trial, William Sapp had lost more than seventy-five pounds. He was now clean shaven and his hair was cut very short. His boyish appearance was deceivingly benign in comparison to the night he was arrested.

On the first day of the trial, Sapp's plea of innocence by reason of insanity was dropped, and he entered a plea of not guilty.

Clark County prosecutor Stephen Schumaker, in his opening remarks, told the jurors that the case was simple: "Sapp deceived her and got her back in an isolated area so he could rape her and kill her."

During his opening statement William Merrell, Sapp's court-appointed defense attorney, told the jury that Sapp didn't do all that the prosecutors claim he did. "It's Ursula Thompson's word against the defendant's whether there was consensual sex and kidnapping."

Ursula Thompson, an admitted prostitute and drug user, testified that she voluntarily got into Sapp's car to go with him to buy crack cocaine. Sapp told her he needed to stop at his house for money, but instead he took her to the dump site on South Limestone Street and attacked her with a large knife and a pellet gun.

Ursula, the scar from the knife wound clearly visible on her face, told the jury: "I was scared and I was running. I was trying to get away from him.

"This man tried to kill me and he's going to prison."

Detective David Rapp had taped the interview with Sapp at his kitchen table on the night he was arrested. Sapp sat emotionless in the courtroom while the tape was played for the jury—until he heard the sounds of his children in the background. Crying, he turned away from the jurors and sobbed when he heard Aaron cry out, "Daddy!"

During the taped interview Sapp said that he thought he had killed Ursula Thompson, but that he didn't try to kill her.

On the second day of the trial, William Sapp took the witness stand and told the jury that Thompson kicked him in the groin and he grabbed a knife and swung out at her. "I really didn't mean for it to happen," he stated.

He claimed he wanted to help her, but Schumaker pointed out, during cross-examination, that he never even tried to help her. Sapp said, "I just freaked."

The prosecutor asked Sapp what he had meant when he told the deputies that he got violent.

"Sometimes I can't control my temper. Usually I punch a wall or a car," Sapp replied.

Later that day, after four hours of deliberation, the jury acquitted Sapp on the charge of attempted murder, but they found him guilty of felonious assault, kidnapping, and attempted rape.

Merrell asked the judge to be lenient and requested that Sapp's sentences run concurrently, but Judge Lorig imposed the maximum sentence of twenty-six to fifty-five years in prison. The soonest Sapp could possibly be eligible for parole would be in ten years, if he managed to get time off for good behavior.

Soon after William Sapp was arrested for the attack on Ursula Thompson, an unidentified Springfield woman called the Clark County Sheriff's Office and told Detective Rapp that Sapp's real name was William K. Lilly and that Sapp had lived in Jacksonville, Florida. She explained that while living in an apartment complex in Florida years earlier, she and her boyfriend had allowed Sapp to stay with them for a while.

They were all originally from Springfield and the woman had known Sapp since they were children.

She nervously related a bizarre story to the detective: She and Sapp had been in a grocery store in Jacksonville, and when a teenage boy with a patch over his eye entered the store, Sapp "just froze." She could barely hear him as he whispered, "I killed him."

The young woman was incredulous: "What?"

"I killed him the other night. He shouldn't be here. I killed him."

She reported this strange conversation to the Jacksonville Police Department and learned about an incident which had taken place a few days earlier behind a tavern, in which a juvenile had been stabbed in the eye with a screwdriver. Sapp was arrested, convicted, and spent some time in prison in Florida.

The distraught woman told Detective Rapp: "I have something that's been haunting me my whole life. Will you meet with me and talk with me?"

Of course he was more than happy to meet with the mysterious caller and find out everything he could about this violent man.

"This is what I need to confess to you. . . . We were poor then at the time—young—there in Florida. Trying to work to make ends meet . . ."

And then, lowering her voice, she timidly got to the point: "Bill always bragged about killing a lady in the alley—somewhere back behind our apartment. But I never noticed anything—didn't see any police or anything. I don't know how true it is."

Detective Rapp immediately relayed this information to the homicide division of the Jacksonville Police Department and they said they would get back with him. It would take some time to investigate, as this murder would have occurred approximately fifteen years earlier.

Two weeks after the trial was over, two homicide detectives from Florida flew to Ohio to investigate William Sapp, who was still being held in the Clark County Jail, awaiting his departure to Orient Correctional Institution.

Several days later, on September 26, 1996, Detectives Robert Hinson and T. C. Davis were ready to conduct an interview with Sapp. After he was brought from the jail to the sheriff's office and read his rights, he told them, "Sure . . . I'll tell you anything you guys want."

Deputy Danny Mitch and Detective Rapp, watching and listening from the other side of the two-way mirror, rapidly made the decision to set up a video camera and record the interrogation.

Sapp readily admitted to killing fifty-eight-year-old Shirley Ogden on April 14, 1981, on West Main Street in Jacksonville. Ironically, the inner city of Jacksonville is named Springfield and it was in this area that Sapp lived and the murder took place.

Then he started talking about the attack on Helen Preston.

Startled, the detectives called a time-out. The Clark County Sheriff's Office and the Springfield Police Department are both located in the Public Safety Building, at opposite ends. Since the attack on Helen Preston had taken place inside the city limits, Detective Rapp quickly walked down the wide corridor and retrieved Sergeant Al Graeber, Captain David Walters, and Lieutenant Terry Fisher of the Springfield Police Department.

Sergeant Graeber, barely able to contain his excitement, joined the Florida detectives in the interrogation room. When he asked Sapp if he knew anything about the assault on Helen Preston, he didn't deny it, but he claimed that "Bob," his alleged alter ego, was responsible.

Hinson (coaxing): Bill, tell Al about Helen. Tell him what you saw Bob do.

Davis (joining in): What names did she call him to make Bob mad?

(Sapp stared off into the distance, his eyes glazed over.)

Hinson: You can see it. Look at me! You can see it! Tell Al what you're seeing.

Graeber: What did he do, Bill?

Sapp (his voice raspy): He tried to rape the girl. He just hit her. I don't know what he hit her with—just kept hitting. . . .

Graeber: Did he hit her a lot?

(Sapp, slightly bent at the waist with his arms across his abdomen and his head resting against the wall next to him, nodded yes. "A train came by. He tried to rape her." Obviously distressed, he became reluctant to answer their questions. Tearfully, he cried: "But if Bob's involved in other stuff, that's more time!")

Sapp (continuing): He hit her with a piece of pipe. He was trying to rape her. (Sapp sniffles and wipes his nose with his palm.) He hit her about two times and then he hauled ass 'cause she turned around and started coming toward me.

Hinson: Let me ask you something. Look at me for a second. Can you stop Bob? Once Bob's out, can you stop him? Look at me. Can you stop him?

Sapp (rubbing his forehead nervously, cried): No!

Hinson: If you can't stop him, then tell me what he did.

You've got to stop him now. This is the only way you
   can stop him.
Sapp: He hit her with a piece of metal. He just hit her.
   He just kept hitting her. He hid the pipe—the rebar.
Hinson: Was she dead when he left?
Sapp (looking up at the detectives): God! I hope not!
Graeber: Did she get cut with anything?
Sapp: He's got a little brass pocketknife with three
   holes in it, in the handle. And it's sitting on top of a
   roof, at a church, on Miller [Street]. He tried to cut
   her throat! Ah, she's sick! She's all fucked up!
(He told them that her watch fell off and broke and he
   hid it under a loading dock.)
Sapp: She was sitting right in front of the dock. . . .
Davis: Come on; tell me what you're seeing. You're
   seeing it right now. You're rubbing your head—what
   do you see in your head?
Sapp: Her face is covered in blood. It's sick.
Hinson: This isn't the worst thing Bob's done, is it?
Davis: This is one of many things Bob has done.
Sapp (crying and turning his face to the wall again):
   He tried to kill my wife!

   The detectives questioned Sapp at great length about several unsolved crimes, but he denied involvement in any of
them except for two arsons: one in an old, abandoned log
cabin and one in an empty house.
   Sapp had told the detectives earlier about being neglected
and abused as a child, but Detective Davis didn't think Sapp
had told them the whole story and he was sure Sapp hadn't
told them everything about Bob's criminal activities.

Davis (with pen in hand): Everything didn't come out.
   Look at this a second. How many times do you think
   you were neglected? By your mother? By the people
   at home?

Sapp: I can't count them.

Davis: Once? Fifty? A hundred? Just an estimate.

Sapp: You're probably looking at four figures.

Davis: Four figures? One thousand? Two thousand? Is two thousand an accurate figure?

(Sapp nodded yes.)

Davis: How many times do you think your parents or anybody in charge of you physically abused you as a kid? Below ten? Twenty? Thirty?

Sapp: More than thirty.

Davis: You told us some things that happened to animals that you were around. . . . How many times did that happen? Once? Twice?

Sapp: Occasionally. I'd say fifteen—twenty.

Davis: How many times were you sexually abused?

(Sapp had misunderstood and thought "physical abuse" referred to sexual abuse, so "more than thirty" referred to how many times he had been sexually abused. He had included "physical abuse" in with the two thousand times he had been neglected.)

Davis: How many cigarette burns do you have on that arm? I counted eight there. And you got how many on this one? Okay. So ten's the number we can see. Do you have more than ten?

Sapp: Yeah.

Davis: What's a good number? Fifty? A hundred?

Sapp: Burns? A couple of hundred, maybe.

Davis: Two hundred times she did that to you—that's bad. And you watched your brother burned once, right? 'Cause we know you saw him suffer a lot of stuff.

(Detective Davis had been writing the numbers down as they talked and now he added them together.)

Davis: So we've got two thousand, fifteen, thirty, two hundred, and one. So at a minimum two thousand two hundred forty-six times—people's done horrible,

horrible things to you, right? Other than what you haven't told us about . . . You told us about the log cabin that you set on fire. The house on York [Street]. Down in Jacksonville—you told us you killed the lady in the alley. Up here in Springfield—you told us about the lady you hurt—that they arrested you for. And you told us about the lady at the railroad tracks. Are you telling me somebody did something to you two thousand two hundred forty-six times at a minimum and Bob only came out five times and did something back? Are you sure? And I'm not saying Bob did [more than two thousand] things, but wouldn't you think over a period of thirty-four years that Bob came out more than five times? All I'm saying is . . . Tell us now and get rid of it forever. Is there anything else? Anything? Do you agree with my math?

Sapp: Oh, I agree, but . . .

Davis: Bob probably came out more than the five times you told us about—or that you've already been arrested for. So you've only been mad five times in your life?

Sapp: Oh, God, no! I've been mad plenty of times!

Hinson: But every time you get mad, Bob doesn't come out?

(Sapp just looked at him and didn't seem to know how to respond.)

Hinson: Do you understand what we're doing?

(Sapp shook his head no.)

Hinson: This is kind of winding down. I don't want to walk away and wonder if there's something else that's bothering you that you haven't gotten off your chest. Is there anybody else? Here? Down in Florida?

Sapp (shaking his head): Anywhere.

Graeber: What's happened is . . . you've reached a point where a lot of weight's been taken off of you, okay?

I mean, I can even look at your face—your whole body. You can see that, okay? But just through experience—I've been doing this for a long time. Through experience—I'd have to guess that's there's still something in there. It may not be up front tonight. Because you got a big load—major, major things off—but you're still sitting on something . . . believe me.

(Actually, Al Graeber was as sure as he was sitting there that there was more. But this would do for now.)

Hinson: I need you to help me write a statement.

Sapp: What's this for?

Hinson: It's for the murder down in Jacksonville. You want me to help you?

Sapp (answering quietly): Yeah.

Robbie Hinson proceeded to talk Sapp through the statement, leaving a place for him to sign his name every time he wrote the word "I."

"I, William Kessler Lilly, having been advised of my rights do give this written statement of my own free will."

He stated that he was living in the Springfield area of Jacksonville, Florida, in the spring of 1981. And at that time he was renting a room from a man named Al Sapp and had fallen behind in his rent.

"I, William Kessler Lilly, had been forced to have sex with Mr. [Al] Sapp and his friend [in exchange] for the rent on several occasions. I, William Kessler Lilly, was told to get out and find some rent money any way I, William K. Lilly, could, by Mr. [Al] Sapp."

He then informed the detective that he had had "another person living inside of him" since early childhood. He further claimed that this "other person"—named Bob Lancaster—was the aggressive side of his personality.

"I, William K. Lilly, knew that this older white female 'bag lady' carried money on her person. I, William K. Lilly, waited in the alleyway about dusk and I, William Kessler Lilly, saw her coming down the alley. I, William Kessler Lilly, saw her stop and count her money and that is when I, William Kessler Lilly, attacked her. I, William Kessler Lilly, had a knife and was going to take her money. The attack 'went wrong' and I, William Kessler Lilly, stabbed her an unknown number of times to her back and abdomen area."

According to him, he then removed her underwear so he could have sex with her, but stopped "because it wasn't right." He took her money and ran away from the area.

He then told the detective that he had been in a "great deal of emotional pain" because of this and that he wanted the family to know that he was sorry and that he was taking responsibility for what he had done.

Sniffling, William Sapp (Lilly?) signed the confession.

(During the course of their investigation, Springfield detectives would learn that William Lilly claimed to have been adopted by Al Sapp and had taken "Sapp" as his legal name. For reasons known only to him, he chose to sign his birth name, Lilly, on his confession.)

The evidence also showed that the middle-aged woman was beaten and probably sexually assaulted. Her body was found in front of Sapp's apartment.

It was after the murder of Shirley Ogden that William Sapp moved in with the young couple that he knew from Springfield, Ohio, who lived in the same apartment complex.

The next day, Sergeant Jeffrey Flores from the Crimes Against Persons Unit and Tim Shepard, the forensic criminalist, paid a visit to Sapp (aka: Bob Sapp, Robert Lancaster, Billy Lilly, William Kessler Sapp, William K. Lilly, and Billy Bob Sapp) in the Clark County Jail. They read a "consent to search" form to him and he said he understood and signed it. They obtained samples of his blood, pubic hair, head hair, and saliva. These samples were sent to the FBI for DNA analysis.

Part 2

The Serial Killer

We serial killers are your sons, we are your husbands, we are everywhere. And there will be more of your children dead tomorrow.

—Ted Bundy

16

To me, that's what being, what we refer to as "a murder cop" is about. . . . You go into a room and you give some-one the moral "out" to tell you why they did something.

—Captain Steve Moody

The Springfield Police Department's Crimes Against Persons Unit continued their investigation of William Sapp until the following spring. When they received the results of the DNA tests from the FBI in March, the investigators were more than ready to interrogate him again.

On April 2, 1997, Sapp was brought from Orient Correctional Institution to be interviewed by Lieutenant Steve Moody and Sergeant Al Graeber. The interview was videotaped over a two-day period. There was eighteen and a half hours of tape—eighteen and a half hours in which Bob was never mentioned.

Sapp would tell them after the interview that he had "to make sure they had their shit together." What he didn't know was that this was Lieutenant Moody's favorite part of his job—that it was choreographed. Sapp may have thought he was leading the dance, but he couldn't have been more wrong.

At first, Sapp, who had been taking advantage of the prison's weight room and weighed a muscular 185 pounds, was very relaxed. During his trial for the attack on Ursula Thompson, his hair had been very short, a "burr," and he had been clean shaven. Now his hair was in a "businessman" style and he had grown a mustache.

But there was a feature of his appearance that he could not alter: the total emptiness in his hazel eyes.

Over coffee, in the small, bland interrogation room, bare except for a round table, three chairs, and a cabinet directly behind Sapp, he and the detectives talked at length about the different places that he had lived as a child in Springfield. His family had moved many times and he had lived in "three or four foster homes." (And, at some point in time, his parents were divorced and his farther remarried.) Sapp, clad in prison-issued pants and shirt a shade lighter than the brownish gold metal cabinet, referred to living in the penitentiary as "my own little secret hideout."

When the subject turned to J.R., Sapp's younger, mentally challenged brother, he got very serious: "God forbid I'd say this—especially right here—but if somebody hurt that boy, I'd kill them. I'd go to the electric chair. It wouldn't matter. He's been through too much. I couldn't stop it all. I could have stopped enough."

Sapp told the detectives that his stepmother had given him a bus ticket to go to Florida in 1977 or 1978, but Lieutenant Moody told him the year couldn't be correct because he (Sapp) was arrested in Springfield two days before his eighteenth birthday in 1980.

An acquaintance of Sapp's had beaten up J.R. Then Sapp "got high," went to the guy's house, took his rabbit out of its pen, slapped it up against a tree, left it on the guy's porch, and rang the doorbell. He was charged with cruelty to animals.

As the patient detectives tried to build a rapport with the violent but soft-spoken man, there was more small talk about the different jobs he had had. When Sapp and his wife, Karen, along with their two-year-old son, Aaron, came back to Springfield in 1991, they moved in with Kessler Lilly, Sapp's father.

Kessler Lilly lived on East Main Street, in the only house between the Japanese Connection and Dewine's Dairy Distributing. Susan Palmer lived one block east of Lilly.

Of course, the detectives now knew that Kessler "J.R."

Lilly was Sapp's brother. But when they had questioned J.R. after receiving several tips saying he looked just like the composite drawing, they were unaware that his older, look-alike brother had returned from Florida the previous year.

Because Sapp could not (or would not) find steady employment, he and his family ended up on welfare.

Sapp grinned and then laughed: "I wanted to be a brain surgeon when I was a kid, but about an hour or two into the books and I figured that wasn't for me. I can't even pronounce the words still today, let alone be able to know what's going on."

When Lieutenant Moody asked him why he and Karen decided to move to Miller Street, Sapp replied, "It was a lot of things." He and Karen and Aaron were sharing a room with J.R. at his dad's, and they needed their own room and so did Aaron.

Their upper duplex on Miller Street was only a few blocks from where Helen Preston had been attacked.

Sapp went on to say that he always seemed to be able to find work. Besides collecting scrap metal and selling it to junkyards, he also did odd jobs for their landlady, Janice McCormack* (who, ironically, was also Helen Preston's landlady). He proceeded to go into great detail about his many jobs.

"So what was going on [that] night . . . ? Tell me what happened with Helen. How'd that all start?" Moody inquired.

Sapp, almost casually replied: "I don't know. Tell you the truth, I really don't know. I was pretty fucked up. I was doing some drinking and shit. I got into doing some pills. God knows what it was. I done a little bit of everything. All I know is, I was walking across the parking lot there at South High School, and, uh, I happened to look over and I seen somebody crying over there on the corner."

Lieutenant Moody got up and went to the cabinet, took out a map, and laid it on the table in front of Sapp. The map depicted the area in question. Lieutenant Moody pointed out South High School and the YMCA and the surrounding area.

Sapp showed them where he was when he first saw Helen and also pointed out the corner that she was on.

Moody: You just walked across and said something to
   her?

Sapp (nodding yes): I just, you know, like I said, I
   heard her crying and then I went over and seen her
   crying, and I just asked her what was going on, and
   she started saying something about . . . What the hell
   was his name? Butch, I believe it was Butch. And
   then went into some long-ass detail about she walked
   into the bar and, apparently, she saw Butch drinking
   with another woman or a girlfriend or something.
   They had some words and a little push contest and
   she walked the hell out, from what I understand. I
   mean, I ain't gonna swear to it. We just walked. We
   talked about a lot of damn things. I mean, nothing in
   particular. I mean nothing—at first. I don't know
   how to say it. . . . I don't know, [she was] fascinated
   or just glad somebody was there, I guess, to listen
   to her. I can't remember who the hell it was, whether
   it was me or her, that had the beer. I think it was me.
   Anyway, I drank a little bit more, and off and on, I let
   her—if she wanted a drink—drink out of the can.

Sapp (showing them on the map which way they were
   walking, pointing out a spot where they stopped and
   watched for about five or ten minutes): Because there
   was two cruisers, one with flashing lights in the front,
   was in front of the YMCA. We didn't know what was
   going on. And we kept walking. And we went through
   here. I stopped to take a piss. Oh, sorry about that!

Moody: There's nothing that you're going to do or say
   that's going to offend us. You need to understand that.

(Sapp proceeded, in a slight Southern drawl acquired
   from living in Florida for ten years, to point out two
   places where he had "taken a leak" and one where
   Helen had done the same.)

Sapp: Then we seen a car go by and the lights kind of
   like flickered in and it startled the hell out of me. She

Crime scene at the pond where Phree Morrow and Martha Leach's bodies were found, hidden under the brush and skids.
(Courtesy of the Springfield Police Department)

Twelve-year-old murder
victim Phree Morrow.
(Courtesy of the Springfield
News-Sun*)*

Eleven-year-old murder
victim Martha Leach.
(Courtesy of the Springfield
News-Sun*)*

Belinda Anderson, 31, whose decomposed body
was found buried in the dirt floor of a garage.
(Courtesy of the Springfield News-Sun*)*

Phree Morrow's mother's house on
East Main Street. Martha Leach's
house is visible in the background.
(Author's photo)

Martha Leach's house on Lagonda
Avenue. *(Author's photo)*

Schuler's Bakery with Strahler's
Warehouse in the background.
(Author's photo)

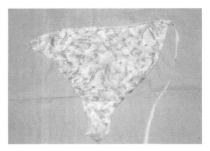

The multicolored underpants that were found floating in "Devil's Pond," just a few feet from Phree Morrow and Martha Leach's bodies.
(Courtesy of the Springfield Police Department)

The same pair of panties—cut right above the crotch—turned inside out.
(Courtesy of the Springfield Police Department)

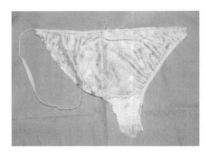

The flowered shorts that had been cut with a knife, found in the "Lion's Cage."
(Courtesy of the Springfield Police Department)

The same shorts turned inside out.
(Courtesy of the Springfield Police Department)

Top view of the bloodstained rock that was found on Phree Morrow's head. The slab was approximately 2 ½ feet long and 2 feet wide, and ranged from approximately 6 to 10 inches thick. *(Courtesy of the Springfield Police Department)*

The bicycle that the girls borrowed from a friend—to ride to the bakery—shown as it was found in the bottom of the "Lion's Cage." *(Courtesy of the Springfield Police Department)*

"Devil's Pond," the scene (several years later) where Phree and Martha's bodies were found. *(Author's photo)*

A portion of the "Lion's Cage," covered with graffiti.
(Author's photo)

Jamie Turner and Assistant Public Defender Noel Kaech,
at Turner's arraignment, June 1996.
(Courtesy of the Springfield News-Sun*)*

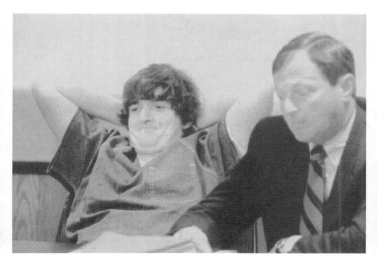

John Balser and John Butz, his attorney, at dismissal hearing,
June 1993. *(Courtesy of the* Springfield News-Sun*)*

David Marciszewski at his arraignment in the murders of Phree Morrow and Martha Leach, March 1993. *(Courtesy of the* Springfield News-Sun*)*

Wanda Marciszewski at her sentencing for her involvement in the murders of Phree Morrow and Martha Leach, November 1998. *(Courtesy of the* Springfield News-Sun*)*

Chief of Police Stephen
Moody, SPD. *(Courtesy of the
Springfield Police Department)*

Sergeant Al Graeber, SPD.
*(Courtesy of the Springfield
Police Department)*

Sergeant Michael Haytas,
SPD. *(Courtesy of the
Springfield Police Department)*

Sergeant Barry Eggers,
SPD. *(Courtesy of the
Springfield Police Department)*

Captain David Rapp of the Clark County Sheriff's Office. *(Courtesy of the Clark County Sheriff's Office)*

Clark County Prosecutor Stephen Schumaker and Steve Moody. *(Author's photo)*

William Sapp, soon
after his arrest,
February 1996.
(Courtesy of the Springfield
News-Sun*)*

William Sapp
(75 pounds lighter)
at his trial for the attack
on Ursula Thompson,
September 1996.
(Courtesy of the
Springfield News-Sun*)*

William Sapp arriving for his arraignment, April 1997.
(Courtesy of the Springfield News-Sun)

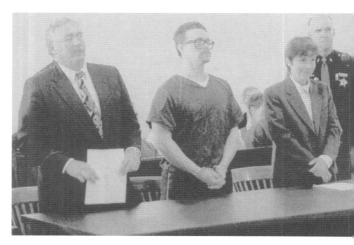

William Sapp, flanked by defense attorneys Dennis Lieberman
and Sharon Ovington, at his arraignment, April 1997.
(Courtesy of the Springfield News-Sun)

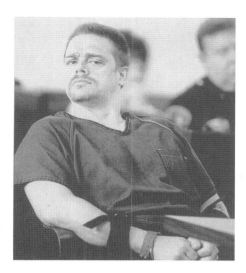

William Sapp at his
competency hearing,
April 1999.
*(Courtesy of the
Springfield News-Sun)*

William Sapp at his
competency hearing,
April 1999.
*(Courtesy of the
Springfield News-Sun)*

William Sapp during jury selection, September 1999.
(Courtesy of the Springfield News-Sun*)*

William Sapp during
his trial for the murders
of Phree Morrow,
Martha Leach, and
Belinda Anderson, and
the attempted murder
of Helen Preston,
October 1999.
(Courtesy of the
Springfield News-Sun*)*

William Sapp smiles for the *Springfield News-Sun* photographer Marshall Gorby after being found guilty on all twenty-five charges against him, October 1999.

William Sapp and attorney Dennis Lieberman at sentencing, October 1999. *(Courtesy of the Springfield News-Sun)*

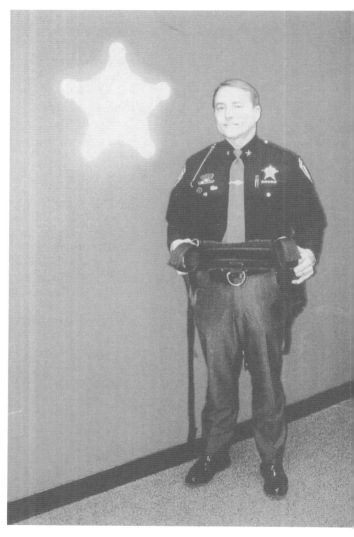

Clark County Sheriff Gene Kelly holding the stun belt that William Sapp wore during his competency hearing and trial.
(Courtesy of the Clark County Sheriff's Office)

was squatting—'cause she jumped up and then kind of stumbled. She was pretty inebriated herself. Kind of like the blind leading the blind, 'cause I was kind of like wasted.

(Sapp laughed hard at the memory of this.)

Sapp: I mean, I'm not joking because of what happened; I mean, it's just . . . I don't know. You'd of had to been there to see it. It was Three Stooges, kind of stupid stuff.

They continued walking and crossed the railroad tracks on South Limestone Street, until they were close to a loading dock at the back of one of the buildings. They were only about a block from downtown Springfield. "Out of the blue," Helen turned around and said, "You know, I like you. You're all right." They kissed and "messed around a little bit."

Sapp: And I'll tell you the truth, I really don't know. After that, I'm watching a train go by and . . . It wasn't nice—it really wasn't—it wasn't nice. All I know is that we were talking and I can't tell you exactly—I don't know—I don't know how to say it. Because all I remember is she, uh . . . An argument come out— and then all of a sudden it was just like, "You know, you're just like—why is it that all men, you know, got to have that stubble shit. You're just like Butch." And I got slapped! I don't know if I slapped back or . . . I couldn't help it. Of course, I don't expect anybody to understand or even believe it. (Sapp's voice gradually changed from casual to chilling.) It was just—it was like I was looking through the eyes of a different person. It was like my eyes were inside somebody else . . . and all I wanted to do was, uh . . . I couldn't, I couldn't stop. I watched all the hitting and the kicking. . . . This is what's probably going to hurt me—even saying it. At the time . . . the bitch needed to die. All bitches needed to die. It was time for that kind of shit to stop. It ain't going to happen no more.

Moody: What wasn't going to happen anymore?

Sapp: The slapping—the hitting—I think I even got raked with fingernails. I don't know. I can't be for sure. I can't say if that happened before or after.

Moody: So she fought you?

Sapp: Oh . . . yeah.

Sapp (after a long silence): All I know, it's like a large flash. Did you ever see where someone flashes you in the eyes with a flashlight? I mean, you're not expecting it. The effect afterwards . . . it's like clouds in your eyes—in front of your eyes. What the, you know, what the hell happened here?

(Sapp then showed them on the map, near the railroad tracks, where he hid the rebar, the weapon he used to beat Helen. Rebar is steel cable, used in construction, to reinforce concrete.)

Sapp: There's a culvert there. I can't remember if it's got a concrete cover over it or if it's metal. But up underneath it, there's gravel all around it; there's a little hole. That's where the rebar was put.

Moody: Well, where did you find the rebar?

Sapp: The rebar . . . Oh, God, I can tell you the truth, I really don't know. I don't know if they had some laying on a stack there somewhere or what. I don't know where it came from.

Moody: Do you remember where you hit her at with the rebar?

Sapp: No. I envision some kind of a monster looking up at me. But I'd imagine probably the head—the face. I don't know.

Moody: Did you use it as a club? Or did you poke at her with it?

Sapp: No, I was swinging.

Graeber: You say she was looking up at you. What'd she look like?

Sapp (whispering): Ain't no words to describe it. Don't know what to put it with—I really don't.

Moody: You just used the term "monster"—

Sapp: Yeah, to put it with something. No, like hamburger or meat or . . . I just can't.

Moody: Okay. So, she's on the ground. You've beaten her with the rebar. What happens next?

Sapp: I guess . . . I just . . . couldn't believe it. Hid the rebar. I thought she was dead.

Moody: Well, now, it's just like I told you, Bill. We've talked to Helen and she's told us some things about what occurred here and there. Now, there are some other things that you did. Where does the knife come into this?

Sapp (after another long silence, laughing nervously): I don't know. (He holds his thumb against the side of his throat.) I remember going . . . (pulling his thumb across his throat) . . . like that.

Moody: Now listen to me, Bill. Is she standing when you do this to her throat? Is this what starts it all off? When she insults you? And you, "This is it!" You know, you've "taken enough off these bitches" [and] "This is the last straw"?

Sapp: Ah, hell . . . I stabbed her in the stomach.

Moody: Was she standing when you cut her throat?

(The interrogation was now punctuated with many long silences. After yet another one, Sapp shook his head no.)

Sapp (voice low): She was sitting.

Moody: Well, take us through it.

(Sapp stared off into a place in time that the detectives could not see. Then he continued, his voice distant, and very soft.)

Sapp: She was just sitting . . . [and I] grabbed a hand under her chin and just . . .

(He demonstrated with his hands how he had held one hand under her chin and slashed her throat with the other. He said he was standing behind her at that point.)

Sapp: I just start trying to hide all that shit.

Moody: Well, before we get to that—I mean, you mentioned something. Once again, you've got it together. What about the stomach? How did that come about? Tell me about that—the positions and everything. What was going on there?

Sapp: I remember the stomach, possibly even how, but I don't know why. I don't know why I stabbed her in the stomach. I just remember doing it. I think I was in front of her. I don't even know if it ever went in.

Sapp (using his hands again to demonstrate how he used the knife): I think it was like this . . . [that] the knife was sideways. But I don't know if it ever went in.

Moody: Now let me ask you something here. I know you like knives. I like fishing lures; you like knives. You've always liked knives. And you know how to use a knife. So you know how you used it because you know what you're good at with it. And I know you can even tell me which knife it was you used.

Sapp (agreeing): Oh, I know what knife it was. It wasn't dull.

Moody: Well, you know how you used it then, because this is an instrument that you like.

(Sapp told them again that the knife was "sideways," but this time he also demonstrated with his hand the forward stabbing motion.)

Graeber: What else did you do with it?

Sapp (shaking his head): The knife? Nothing, I don't think.

Moody: You made a comment a while back—you

thought she was dead. But once she stops fighting and moving, what happens then?

Sapp: Well, I sure wouldn't come call you guys. I mean, it wasn't no joking matter, but . . . I didn't know what the hell to do. I tried to put her up under the dock. And then I went and hid the shit.

Moody: Tell me about how her clothes came off.

(Sapp seemed slightly startled, and turned first one way and then the other to look at each detective. Sergeant Graeber nodded yes, indicating they already knew. Sapp then stared straight ahead for a long time.)

Moody: Listen to me for a minute. This is just another instance where someone has wronged you, and because of the way you were brought up, this is how you react. And you're coming to grips with this.

Sapp: It doesn't matter. It's another human being.

Moody: It's Bill. It's about you. You talk about the clouds in front of your eyes and everything else. That's the alcohol and the drugs. But the rage is something you carry inside of you because of what occurred to you early on. And she just brought it back out and this is your way of dealing with it. You're walking along. You come to her aid. She's crying. You're walking along. You even share your beer with her. And once again, it's just another bitch that slaps you. You've got things pent up inside of you from way back when and this is what occurs. And you're clear on what occurred that night, so what we need to be clear about, because she's talked to us, because she survived: Now, how does she get undressed? What happened?

Sapp: I don't know how she got undressed.

Moody: Well, before you got rid of everything, there was some time there that was spent. And she's in and out of it, and she remembers some things and she's told us about it. You need to bring this back. And you've helped us out with a lot of things. You've taken us step-by-step through what happened. Now we're to the point where she's on the ground. What's going on next?

Sapp: We had sex long before that.

Moody: You had sex long before that? Long before what?

Sapp: The beating.

Moody: Now let me ask you something here. Look at me. So what you're trying to tell us here—and you need to think about this. You're saying you had consensual sex with her before you beat her?

(Sapp stared at Lieutenant Moody for a minute, then turned to Sergeant Graeber.)

Sapp: What's "consensual" mean?

Graeber: Consensual is when both of you agree to have sex.

Sapp (almost flippantly): She wasn't saying no.

Moody: How did her clothes get off?

(Sapp, once again, stared off into that place known only to him. He didn't answer.)

Graeber (after a while): Bill. How did her clothes come off for the sex?

Sapp: I guess I took them off.

Moody: Well, now wait a minute here. Look at me for a minute. You talked about picking up the rebar, using it on her. You're definite on that. You're definite about how you used the knife. Now, you and I both know, you know what happened.

Sapp: Just sitting there, playing around.

Moody: And you're saying that this is before you assaulted her?

Sapp: Yeah. Messing around . . . I don't know, being different. Being not married for the moment.

Graeber: When you had the sex, how much of her clothing came off?

Sapp: Just her pants, I think.

Graeber: Just her pants? How did they come off?

Sapp: I just pulled them off.

Graeber: Wasn't there a special way you handled that?

(Sapp seemed startled again and looked up at the detective.)

Moody: Who took them off, Bill?

Sapp: I guess I tore them off.

Lieutenant Moody walked over to the cabinet behind Sapp again and took out a package. He opened it and laid the contents on the table in front of Sapp. It was the pants Helen Preston had been wearing the night she was attacked. The whole inseam, including the crotch, and the outer seams on both legs, up to the hips, had been cut.

Lieutenant Moody gestured at the pants.

Moody: Now let's look at this here for a minute, okay? You've got the knife out. These pants aren't ripped. What's going on here?

(Sapp didn't seem to realize what he was looking at, so both detectives told him that it was Helen's pants. He leaned forward and stared at them.)

Moody (folding back some of the material): Bill, what's going on here while you're doing this? What are you thinking about?

(Sapp didn't answer.)

Moody: Well, let's go back to something you said, for a minute, okay? You're telling us that the pants came off before she insulted you. Before she slaps you. Look at all the blood on them. When you took these pants off her, what was she doing?

Sapp: I don't know. . . . I guess bleeding.

Moody: Bill. Bill?

(Sapp looked at the detective.)

Moody: You do know. You're clear on what you used. You're clear about the rebar. You're clear about how

she insulted you. You're clear about how you used
the knife. Now, is she talking to you? Is she awake
when you're doing this?

(Sapp stared at the pants, and was visibly shaken. Even
with the long silences, he had been fairly forthcoming up until then. But with the appearance of Helen's
bloodstained pants, he became increasingly reluctant
to respond.)

Moody (coaxing): What's going on here, man? What's
going on with this?

Sapp: I don't know.

Moody: Yeah, you do. Has this happened to you?

Graeber: Is there a reason why this is open like this? Is
there a reason why?

(Moody reached into a notebook and pulled out a picture of Helen. The picture had been taken after she
had been beaten and stabbed. He showed it to Sapp.)

Moody: Listen to me for a minute. This is your anger.
Part of it . . . all right?

Moody (laying the picture down and manipulating
the pants to show the cuts): But this is meticulous.
Do you understand what I'm saying? This took
some time. Here's the fly. . . . This pant leg goes up
here. . . . You come across and come down. What's
going on here with you—with this? I know you're
good with a knife. This wasn't ripped. This was cut.
Each seam's cut. Is it part of a fantasy or what?
What's going on here? You can help us here with
this. I mean, we're going from you getting angry
because she's insulted you and slapped you . . . to
this slow . . . taking your time-type thing. Why
would you put yourself in that situation of getting
caught? This took some time.

Graeber: How long did it take you to do that? Just take
a guess.

Sapp: Seven . . . seven to twelve minutes . . . who knows?

(Lieutenant Moody tried to keep Sapp's attention. Sapp's chin was touching his chest and it became increasingly hard to hear what he was saying. Moody tapped Sapp on the leg, as if trying to wake him.)

Moody: Hey, Bill! Hey! Help us to understand this.

Sapp: There's no understanding it.

Moody: I guess—help me understand this.

Sapp (voice low and raspy): Have you ever seen somebody set on fire? Have you ever seen them cut the shit away from them?

Moody: Their clothing?

Sapp: Skin . . . blood . . . it just peels away! All you have left is the shell.

Sapp (reaching over and holding one of the pant legs): Just a shell.

Moody: So whose clothes did you see cut off of them, Bill?

Sapp: Baby brother. I couldn't do a damn thing about it. (Crying, he removed his glasses and wiped his face.) What kind of brother am I?

Lieutenant Moody had investigated William Sapp's history for seven months prior to the interrogation and had learned "everything there was to know" about him, so he was aware of the incident that Sapp referred to. Sapp claimed that his mother had set his "baby brother," Paul, on fire. In turn, his mother had always blamed Bill for this horrific act.

After giving Sapp a moment to regain his composure, Lieutenant Moody directed Sapp's attention to the task at hand by touching Helen's pants. "What happened after you did this, Bill?"

Sapp: Tried to run and jump in between the damn cars of the damn train. I tripped—like usual.

Moody: But that's before you tried to shove her up under the dock to hide her, right?

(Sapp barely nodded yes.)

Moody: When you're doing this—cutting these pants off of Helen . . . is she fighting? What's she doing when you're doing this?

Sapp: Nothing.

Moody: Nothing at all? What are you thinking while you're doing this?

Graeber: What's going on with you, man?

Sapp (whispering): It wasn't Helen.

Moody: Who was it?

Sapp: It will always be there.

Graeber: Who was it?

Sapp: To do to her what she did to me all those years. . . . Hell, I'll always be locked behind bars. I've always lived this tortured-ass life.

(He reached across the bloody pants and picked up the picture of Helen and studied it.)

Moody: You go from all that anger to this meticulousness. Who's this about? You said that this wasn't Helen. Who is it?

(For several minutes Sapp didn't answer. The legs of Helen's pants were hanging over the edge of the table, in front of him. Deep in thought, he caressed the stiff denim material. The detectives sat quietly and studied his face.)

Sapp (finally): Why is it that the people you look up to the most is the ones that hurt you the most?

Moody: Man, if I had that answer, I'd be rich. Who we talking about?

(Sapp reached over and touched the pants again, but did not answer for a very long time.)

Sapp (tearfully): Now that I'm in prison, I was her most favorite son. How do you tell? How do you lay it on that motherfucking man? . . . Made to see and do things . . . maybe the right place for me is the chair. Then I wouldn't have to live this shit no more.

Moody: You're not living it because you're not doing this to anybody anymore—for one. You're not doing it. Listen to me. You're not having anybody. Your mom hurt you. And you're not having anybody—there's no woman that's insulting you or slapping you again.

Sapp: No. But it's kind of rough having her end up looking like that—all because of me.

Moody: Now listen to me. She's alive. And the emotional scars that you have are going to heal. (Lieutenant Moody nodded toward the picture of Helen.) And so are these scars. So when you're doing this, she's unconscious, is that what you're saying?

Sapp: I don't know. I never paid attention.

Moody: Were you afraid of getting caught? Or were you even thinking about that?

Sapp: I didn't care. Like I told you—I knew you'd be back.

Moody: Do you understand, by coming back and talking with us, how much help you've been to us? Do you understand that?

Sapp: Yeah.

Moody: After you got the pants off her, did you have sex with her?

Sapp (whispering): Yeah.

(He said that Helen was on her back. ". . . Can't really say we were having sex." Sapp said he didn't come "because I didn't want to." He also said he didn't think she was moving while they were "having sex.")

Moody: When you had sex with her, were these pants still under her, or where were these?

Sapp: I can't tell you. I don't know. . . . I would imagine probably still under her.

Moody: We had our forensic people look at that (the pants). That's why we knew these were cut. This isn't a rip—this is a cut. So this is very important, to understand why you did this.

Sapp: I think it's time for me to be in the penitentiary. I don't need to be outside no more.

Moody: There you go, man. There you go. I think that's the most important realization that's been said. That's the most important thing that's been said in this room today. Why do you think that is, Bill? Why do you think you need to be in the penitentiary?

Sapp (voice laced with self-pity): Sick. I'm fucking society's maggot. That's my home. They say, once somebody don't give a damn about you, you know it's true. So we're all tied—I already know that.

Moody: Do you understand that's the best place for you? That's where you can get some help? The proper medication? The proper therapy?

Sapp: Ain't no help for me.

Moody: Well, there is. Because until you can learn how to deal with the anger and the proper response when someone insults you or slaps you in the face or talks to you like you're dirt, you need to be locked up for a while.

Sapp: I know . . . I ain't safe to be around. But it's so weird—I never hurt my wife or any of my kids. Or then, again, maybe I did. God, I hope my kids don't grow up to be like me!

(After another long silence Sapp reached across Helen's pants, picked the picture up again, and studied it. He didn't seem to notice that one of his arms was resting on the blood-soaked material.)

Sapp: You know what they need in this country? An eye for an eye.

(He laid the picture down and sat back in his chair.)

Sapp: There's somebody out there walking around right now, with my heart signature on them. . . .

Moody: You left a signature. I'll give you that.

17

That whole technique . . . Bill's very "visual." That's
why we used the maps. . . . That's why we had the cab-
inet. . . . Every time I'd go to that cabinet . . . he liked
that. . . . You had to show him that you knew what you
were talking about.

—Captain Steve Moody

Sapp told them he ran most of the way home and then cut
down an alley and threw his green fleece jacket in a Dumpster. Then he walked "down to the corner," where he threw
"my knife, which is the brass one with two or three holes in
the handle, on top of the roof."

Sapp: Go across the street. Go upstairs. That's it. I'm
    sure y'all got the knife by now.
Moody: Why'd you get rid of the jacket?
Sapp: Had blood on it, I guess.
Moody: You know, one thing you said that really was
    interesting—I mean you talk about "signature of the
    heart." You're wounded that way, right?
(Sapp raised his eyebrows and shrugged.)
Moody: Have you ever done this before?
Sapp: Done what?
Moody: Well, just like we were talking about—how
    meticulous these pants are cut.
Sapp: Oh! No.

Sapp (barely shaking his head and then whispering):
No. I wish to God I'd never done that. I wish it was
something I could put in a bag and keep . . . myself.

Moody: Now, why would you want to do that?

Sapp: It would show . . . It'd be a reminder.

[Author's note: And, no doubt, a very effective way to
relive the whole experience.]

Graeber (pointing to the pants): What gave you this
idea, then? How'd you get this idea?

After a long pause Sapp haltingly told them about a "real
surgical steel scalpel" that he had in his knife collection. He
had gotten it from his mother and claimed that it was the
"same one she cut my pants off with." He described how she
had cut "each stitch" in front of the zipper on his pants and
told the detectives that he had thought he "was gonna get
stabbed or sliced."

"Did she ever stab you or slice you?" Graeber inquired.

Sapp softly replied, "Yeah, I got my scars."

He claimed that he had "some sear marks, where she took
it one time on each side of my nuts" and that she had also
poured candle wax on him.

Moody: Did you use that scalpel on these pants?

Sapp (shaking his head): No.

(There was a very long silence while Sapp just stared
at the pants.)

Graeber: Did you ever do this to anyone else?

Sapp (voice husky): No, and I'm never going to again
either.

(Lieutenant Moody picked up the pants and laid them
on top of the cabinet behind Sapp. Sapp turned
around and watched as Moody opened the cabinet
door and pulled out another map.)

Sapp (amazed): What y'all got a big rock in there for?
(Laughing) Man!

On September 26, 1991, shortly after Sapp came back from Florida, he set fire to a log cabin in a wooded area not far from his father's house. The log cabin and the scene of the attack on Helen in 1993 were only a few blocks apart, alongside the same set of railroad tracks.

Sapp did not deny the arson, and Lieutenant Moody marked the cabin's location on the second map.

"I've always been fascinated by fire. It just hit me. . . . Torch it! I don't know why," Sapp revealed.

"Did somebody make you angry that day about something? Did somebody screw with you?" Moody suggested.

Sapp finally answered that he might have gotten into a fight with "the ol' lady," then added: "Just a lot of arguments."

"So things aren't real good between you and Karen?" Moody asked.

Sapp answered, "No. She's just the only woman in the world who ever loved me. I threw that away."

The "maps" that the seasoned detectives used were actually aerial photographs of the neighborhoods in question. They pointed out some places on the map that they knew Sapp was familiar with and asked him about some others. They, of course, had a destination in mind. A place in time that they knew Sapp could take them, as much as it was possible through someone else's words and eyes. It proved to be a much more difficult task than visiting the crime scene where Helen was attacked or the site of the log cabin fire.

There was more casual conversation and Sapp even reminisced about some of the places in the neighborhood. Sapp's father's house was in the picture and the site of the log cabin. Also, in the picture: Penn Street Hill, Schuler's Bakery, and Strahler's Warehouse.

Moody: Well, let me ask you something here. We got this fire here in the log cabin, okay? Things aren't going real good at home. What else is going on down here? You doing anything else down here that we need to know about?

Sapp (shaking his head): No, just a bunch of "scrapping" that's about it. (Scrapping is a slang term for collecting scrap metal and selling it to junkyards.)

Moody (pointing to places on the map): You've got all these woods. You've got some water back here. . . .

Sapp: Water back where?

Moody: Right back here. This is Schuler's Bakery—this L-shaped building here. This is Strahler's Foods—you know where that is.

Sapp (having trouble placing it): Strahler's Foods . . . Strahler's Foods . . .

Moody: Right here is a pond. And you know what's significant about that pond back there?

Sapp (shaking his head and looking at Moody): Uh-uh, what?

Moody: In August of 1992—in this pond area—we found two young women that were dead.

Sapp: You're talking about . . . Oh, what was his name? He was in the west wing [of the jail] with us.

Graeber: What was he in there for?

Sapp: Killing them little girls. I just can't think of his name. John . . . John something . . . Is that what you're talking about?

Moody: Talking about the two young women that we found back behind this place. Yes. You don't remember when that happened?

Sapp: I don't remember when it happened. I remember my dad telling us about it. Telling us [the police] had come over and messed around with J.R. and come out with some kind of composite and stuff like that, but I don't know where it ever went from there, other than when I got arrested up here.

Moody: What do you know about these two young women?

Sapp: I don't know nothing about them two young women.

Moody: You didn't have any involvement with them at all? Did you know them?

Sapp: No. I don't mess with little girls.

(That was exactly why the detectives referred to Phree Morrow and Martha Leach as "young women." They knew he would balk at the insinuation that he had hurt children.)

Moody: Well, these were young women. I mean, they were made-up that day. They had makeup on. They didn't look like little girls.

Sapp: I ain't never seen them before—never even heard of them.

Moody: Do you know what their names were or anything like that?

Sapp: Not until we were in jail.

Moody: Who's "we"? Who are you talking about?

(Sapp told them about being in jail with John Balser. They were right across the hall from each other and, according to Sapp, stayed up all night talking. Sapp claimed that this was how he knew John.)

Moody: You never knew him from scrapping or anything like that?

Sapp (shaking his head): I never seen John before, but he was all right. I kind of felt for him 'cause he's kind of like my brother—he's mentally handicapped.

Moody: What'd you think about what he told you?

Sapp: Some of it I don't know whether to believe or not. Because my dad had said that he would think that John didn't do it—at least by his self. He said that he just didn't think he could do it, 'cause he said he knew John or knew of John. I guess my brother went to school with him.

Moody: Where'd he go to school at?

Sapp: Town and Country, I think it was. . . . I think

that's where my brother went. John went to Town and Country and I think he said he graduated from there, as a matter of fact.

Moody: Do you remember when Paul was going out to Town and Country?

Sapp (sadly): No, I don't remember too much about Paul.

Moody (asking Sapp again about being in jail with John Balser): What'd he tell you about this? This case here?

Sapp (trying to remember a name): I swore I'd never forget that name—'cause he was up there after John left. 'Cause John—that's all he ever talked about— was bringing this Jamie character in. I remember [John's] mom on TV, saying that she was there when it happened.

Moody: So did you know any of these people? Did you know his mom? Did you know John before?

(Sapp shook his head.)

Moody: You didn't? Did you know Jamie Turner?

Sapp: That's the name. . . . That's the name. No, I never even knew Jamie Turner.

Moody: And you don't know anything about these two young women? You didn't have dealings with them . . . ever?

Sapp: No.

Moody: And you don't know anything about how they were found or anything like that?

Sapp: Well, I've heard stuff about the way they was found, but one of the deputies up there at the police station said that wasn't true.

Moody: What did you hear that happened?

Sapp: "They" was going around saying that sticks had been shoved up their . . . uh . . . female parts . . . and into their butts, and all that other stuff.

Moody: So what do you think happened to them—
based on what you know?

Sapp: I don't know. I couldn't even begin to guess. I
wouldn't even want to—not at all.

Moody: You don't know anything about these young
women?

Sapp: No. I don't even know them. I ain't never met
them. I couldn't tell you what they look like—or
anything. I mean, I'm already in prison. I know I'm
there for a long time. I mean, you know, hell, I already confessed to a murder in Florida. I mean, you
can't get worse than that. I do a lot of things. I may
have a lot of problems, but the one thing I'm not
gonna do is run around and hurt little kids. I'll be
damned.

Moody: Well, the thing about it is—like I said—these
two looked like young women. They had makeup on
and everything else. They were healthy, young
women and the older of the two was a little bit
"quick" with her mouth. You know, they grew up
close by, so . . .

William Sapp did not budge from his story that he had
never known and had never seen Phree Morrow and Martha
Leach.

18

You've got to be patient. . . . You've got to be really patient. . . .

—Captain Steve Moody

Lieutenant Moody got up from his chair and went to the cabinet again and Sapp turned to watch. This time he took out a stack of papers and brought them over to the table. Sapp leaned forward in his chair to see what he had.

Moody: I don't know whether you remember this. This is a property receipt, okay? This is when they took your blood, back on September 27, 1996. They took saliva from your mouth. Do you remember sticking that piece of paper in your mouth? Got it all wet? They took some pubic hair. The guy that came in— Mr. Shepard.

(Throughout all this, Sapp nodded and agreed and was unperturbed.)

Moody: So then he sends the blood to the Federal Bureau of Investigation in Washington, DC. They have a laboratory there and this is the letter talking about sending your blood—William K. Sapp. This is the letter that goes with the samples of your blood and your—I'll say "spit," 'cause that's what it is—and the hair samples. That gets sent to the FBI lab and they do DNA testing on blood. And your blood is what we would call a "known sample" because it comes from you. We know it comes from you—they drew the blood. Here's the receipt. There's the report from Mr. Quill in Washington, DC, who is the DNA laboratory technician—the specialist who analyzes the blood. We compare samples of semen that were taken from these two young women because they were assaulted. They both had semen in them. So we have that and that was sent to the FBI a long time ago—they had that. So they can take that semen and they can do what they call a DNA profile, which is unique to anybody, okay? Semen that comes out of me or blood that comes out of me is unique to me. Al's is the same. Yours is the same. We're all unique in that way. So what happens is, he sends a report to the FBI and they go through a process of extracting the DNA from the known sample of blood; in this case, your known sample, okay? And they compare it to the semen that they knew came out of those girls. Now, what do you think that told them?

Sapp: Nothing.

Moody: Your specimen number was K-75—"dried blood sample from Sapp." This is the report that Mr. Quill sent back to us. It says, "Based on the results of the genetic and the DNA profile from specimens Q-1 and Q-2"—now, that's the semen from both those young women. Q-1 is from one of the young women. Q-2 is from the other young woman. And they're from the same man. Those specimens of semen taken from those girls match K-75—Sapp.

Sapp (seemingly shocked): Huh? Huh-uh!! Oh, hell no! I think not.

(Sapp leaned back in his chair and was no longer calm and relaxed.)

Moody: Bill, this is a report from the FBI.

Graeber: It's from the FBI lab, Bill.

Sapp (firmly): Well, I'm sorry, but it ain't me. I'm gonna tell you that right now!

Moody: Let me show you something here.

(Sapp leaned forward and followed along closely as Lieutenant Moody explained the report.)

Moody: Do you understand how this is? They take your blood, they analyze it, and it comes out with your chemical makeup. Your DNA—which you get part from your mom and part from your dad—that makes us all unique. The blood and the semen that they recovered from this crime scene match the "known" person.

Sapp (interrupting): How the hell can they match me when I ain't never been there?

Moody: Well, there were seventy-five people checked and out of those seventy-five people, the blood from your arm matches the semen found in those young women.

Sapp: Huh-uh.

Moody: Bill, how do you get by your semen being in these girls?

Sapp (increasingly agitated): I don't know! Man, there ain't no fucking way; I done nothing to no kids! Oh, hell no!

Graeber (emphasizing each word): They didn't look like kids. Believe me, they did not look like kids.

Moody: Bill, the blood that came out of your arm and went to the FBI lab matches the semen in those two young women.

(Sapp got up out of his chair, walked over to the corner of the tiny room, and ran his hands through his hair.)

Sapp: Aw, man . . . you gotta be kidding me!

Moody: Come on over here and sit down.

Graeber: Sit down!

Moody: Now you need to straighten this out with us right now.

Sapp (extremely agitated): There ain't nothing to
    straighten out. How can I straighten something out I
    don't know nothing about? I'm telling you—I don't
    know nothing about that! Man!

Moody: You need to talk to us about this.

Sapp: I—don't—know.

Moody: You had sex with them.

Sapp: How in the hell could I have sex with them when
    I wasn't even with them?

Moody: Your semen is in them. You were with them.

Sapp: I did not kill no kids!

Moody: I'm talking about having sex with two young
    women. You're semen is in those two. We need to
    discuss how it happened.

Sapp (spreading his arms wide and shrugging): I don't
    know 'cause I wasn't there.

Moody: You were there long enough to have sex with
    them.

Sapp (incredulous): You think if I would have done
    this, that I would have been so willing to give all that
    stuff? You gotta be crazy!

Moody: Bill, it happened. We have the scientific evi-
    dence to prove it.

Sapp: Man, do you think I'm gonna stand around and
    watch somebody kill little kids? I don't think so.

Moody: I'm talking about having sex with two young
    women—

Sapp (interrupting): Sex with two young women.
    Yeah—too young. That's the key—too young!

Moody (picking up the report): And here's the evi-
    dence that shows that you did it.

Sapp: Which means now I'm tied in to a fucking mas-
    sive murder case and I didn't . . . Whew, no, I didn't,
    no! I ain't killed nobody like that. No, no, no, no!

Moody: But what I'm telling you is—we're talking
    about sex. We're talking about you having sex with

them. And you need to straighten it out with us. Just like you straightened it out about Helen.

Sapp: How can I straighten something out when I tell you I was never there?

Moody: You're not telling the truth. Your semen was located in those two young women—it's yours—only unique to Bill Sapp. You. Now we have to talk about this and get it straight.

Sapp: There ain't nothing to get straight. You might as well just go on ahead and give me the electric chair.

Moody: No. There's no one talking about that except you.

Sapp (leaning forward, beseeching): Don't you think I want to get everything off my mind?

Moody: I would hope you would.

Sapp: I did not witness nobody or participate in anybody being beaten—especially children.

Moody: Okay. Tell me about the sex.

Sapp (whispering): I don't know nothing about the sex.

Moody: Well, yes, you do. Because you left your signature there—your signature was your semen.

(Sapp removed his glasses and wiped his hand over his face.)

Moody: That is completely . . . I mean, there's no getting around it.

(Sapp finished wiping tears from his face and put his glasses back on. There was a long silence as Sapp sat with his arms across his chest and stared off into that unknown place.)

Moody: Talk to us about this. What happened?

With occasional prompting from the very attentive detectives, Sapp told his first version of what happened that day:

"They come out of Schuler's Bakery, laughing and giggling. And I don't look like I am right now. I was stout, I guess, hair a little longer, different glasses. I just whistled at them and they whistled back.

"We talked. We joked. We laughed. We started bullshittin' around and I told them a few things—how pretty they was . . . and I don't know—you'd have to ask some other little girls, I guess. I don't know how to say this—excited, I guess, that somebody older was paying attention to them.

"We started talking and bullshittin' around and I offered one of them some money. I don't know, maybe they was bullshittin' or something."

He claimed the three of them walked to a secluded area, hidden by pallets and trees, several blocks from the bakery behind Cramer's Mill on York Street.

"We was just messing around. I gave them the money. I know I shouldn't have."

He said that when they left that area, they walked up York Street to Harrison Street. According to Sapp, they were at the corner of Harrison Street and Linden Avenue when he and the girls went in opposite directions.

Moody: How much did you give them?
Sapp (hanging his head): I gave them ten apiece.
Moody: Tell me how it went. How'd the sex go?
Sapp (whispering): But then they say they found them dead.
Moody: Just take me step-by-step through it, Bill.
Sapp: This ain't easy.

With much prodding from Lieutenant Moody, Sapp went into graphic detail about what he had done with Martha: "The only thing she said was that it hurt a little bit. And then after that, that Phree was a virgin. And that's when stuff got a little edgy."

According to Sapp, there was a disagreement between the two girls about whether or not Phree was a virgin. He said that Phree was a little nervous and embarrassed, but finally they "just did it." (The autopsy reports showed that, despite Sapp's rhetoric, both Phree and Martha were virgins prior to August 22, 1992.)

> Sapp: I told them if they ever needed something to just let me know.
>
> (Sapp repeated his story that they had walked to the corner of Linden and Harrison and then parted company. He added that he thought the girls had said something about a "party." He claimed he didn't know where they went from there.)
>
> Moody: And the whole time you were with them, you never went to the bakery? With one of them?
>
> Sapp: No.
>
> Moody: I want you to be sure about what all occurred and be straight with us. Not about having sex with the girls. Let's get it all out—about everything that occurred that day.
>
> (Sapp sat with his elbows resting on his knees and stared at the floor for a long time.)
>
> Sapp: What's there to . . . ? I mean . . . I said what I had to say.
>
> Moody: What happens to these two young women? Where do they end up?
>
> Sapp: I don't know.
>
> Moody: Yes. You do know.
>
> Sapp (laughing): Okay, well, okay, maybe I do. But I'm telling you seriously—I don't know.
>
> Graeber: This piece of evidence is your signature, Bill. Okay?
>
> Sapp: Okay . . . what is it now?
>
> Graeber: How many signatures have you given us today?
>
> Sapp: I don't know. I don't even know who the hell I am anymore.
>
> Moody: We do.

Graeber: We do. We know who you are.

Moody: We're sitting right here with you.

Graeber: We know who you are.

Moody: We know what you're about. We found out everything there is to know about you. And we've shown you that. Hell, I've shown you things today that you don't even remember happened to you! Right? I mean, you said it, Bill! We got our shit together. We know what it's about. What happened to those two young women after you guys "parted company"?

Sapp: You all are making it look like I'm the killer! I'm not gonna go around killing little kids!

Moody: The only time anyone has mentioned "killer" today—in reference to these two young women—has been you.

Graeber: What did happen, buddy?

Sapp (whispering): It was just a party.

Moody: I know it was—so tell us about it.

Sapp (voice low): What's to tell?

Moody: No. We need to know. What are you talking about?

Sapp: The party at the house. The brick house up on the hill.

19

*I think it started over on Linden Avenue. . . . The girls
might have been picked up down by the bakery. . . .
That's where they were taken to. . . . We believe now
that's where the initial attack started.*

—Captain Steve Moody

The house that Sapp referred to on the map was a house he
had told them earlier that he had never been in. The house he
said he saw Phree and Martha walking toward after they "went
their separate ways." It was the house on Linden Avenue

Moody: Let me ask you something here, all right? This
    story here (the "Cramer Mill story") didn't happen?
(Sapp barely shook his head no.)
Moody: So let's go back. . . . How did you hook up
    with the girls?
(Sapp told them that he was out scrapping, and when he
    got to the corner of Linden and Harrison, he heard
    music and people "bullshittin' around." He looked to-
    ward the sounds and someone asked him if he wanted
    a beer.)
Moody: So you go in there—and who do you recognize?
Sapp: There was a black guy. Well, half, I guess—half
    mixed. I know John. I know Dave.
Moody: Where are Phree and Martha when you go in?
Sapp: One was tied up on a chair. And the other one

was tied up on a coffee table. People were having fun—and I guess I just had fun too.

Moody: Which one was tied to the chair?

Sapp: I'm gonna say Martha.

Moody: What's she saying?

Sapp: Wasn't much she could say—she was gagged. But she wasn't crying. All I know is they was fucking around and playing around, and we—we all done it. I didn't wear one of the protective things. Never did like them. So . . . I guess I left myself inside of them. I mean, I thought, you know, they'd eventually go to the bathroom and use it and, you know, whatever they do.

Moody: They didn't get a chance to go to the bathroom, though, did they?

Graeber: What time did you leave that party?

Sapp: As soon as I seen what the hell happened.

Moody: No, Bill. They didn't have a chance to go to the bathroom, did they?

Sapp: No.

Moody: What happened?

(Sapp had tears in his voice as he said something about putting "a blanket over their heads.")

Sapp: They had this big stick. And they had this fucking rock—huge rock.

Graeber: Where did all this take place?

(Sapp took his glasses off and ran his hand over his face and then put his glasses back on and stared straight ahead.)

Sapp (whispering): At the house.

Moody: Which one did you have sex with first?

Sapp: Martha.

Moody: How did you do that?

Sapp: From behind.

Moody: You told me she was tied in the chair. Help me figure this out. Tell me how it went.

Graeber: Bill, how does that work? How's that work?

(Sapp leaned forward, rested his elbows on his knees,
   once again removed his glasses, and started crying.)
Sapp: It didn't work.
Graeber: It didn't work? What happened then?

Neither of these versions was true, even though they contained some truth. It was obvious that William Sapp was not
mentally challenged. No doubt, on some level, he was enjoying the whole experience of finally telling "his" story, and he
seemed to want to make it last as long as possible.

After the "Cramer Mill story," in which he only "admitted"
that he paid Phree and Martha for sex, and the "party at the
house story," in which he basically admitted raping the girls,
but put the blame for the attack on everyone else, he continued to give the detectives bits and pieces of the truth, in more
than one version of the "pond story":

"I left my dad's. I was drinking. I was gonna go hunt bottles there on Penn Street Hill. I used to hunt bottles there all
the time when I was a kid. That's where they was having their
little party at."

They offered him a beer and he accepted. "We all sat there
getting drunk—getting fucked up. But the little girls wasn't
drinking, 'cause I know they didn't have any pot or anything
in their system. It was actually Martha that said that she was
the virgin and Phree wasn't. . . .

"No. They never got a chance to use the bathroom. The
motherfucker picked up this rock . . . huge rock! Like it was
a piece of pie! Tripped out—didn't know what the hell to do!"

Moody: Who picked up the rock?
Sapp: David Marciszewski.
Moody: Well, let's back up here a minute.
Sapp: It never happened in the house.
Moody: Where did you have sex with them?
Sapp: Right there.

Moody (referring to the map): Right here?

Sapp: Yeah.

Moody: What's there?

Sapp: "Devil's Pond." That's what it is now.

Graeber: How many people were there?

Sapp: About five or six—not including myself.

Graeber: Was all of them males?

Sapp: No, there was a couple of females.

Moody: Well, Bill, when you came up there—tell us how it went. They offer you a beer—how does it go from there? Take us through it!

Sapp (sounding tortured): Is there any more after this?

Moody: Sit back up in the chair and take us through it!

Sapp: We was all just sitting around, fucking around, drinking, bullshittin' around. And then the conversation went to, you know, pussy. The women grabbed the girls—well, not actually grabbed them—took hold of them. They wasn't yelling or fighting or— that's not to say they probably wasn't scared the fuck to death. One by one—everybody had a nice little time. Me—I never brought no rubber. They was holding the girls down—made them put their face in the dirt. I thought they was just bullshittin'—until they let the first rock fall. Then the game was over. Then they done the other one. And they kept doing it. There's not a fucking thing you could do.

(He claimed that the girls weren't yelling, but that one of them said, "Are you gonna kill us or just fuck us and let us go?")

Sapp: I told them, "Ain't nobody gonna kill you. Where'd you get that from?"

Moody: Well, who were the two women that were there?

Sapp: I don't know who the hell they were. I'd know them if I seen them.

(Sapp told the detectives that he knew three other people

had sex with the girls besides him and that he was the last one to have sex with them.)

Sapp: I know Dave . . . John. . . . I'm gonna tell you the God's honest truth—I don't know if Jamie was there. I don't remember seeing the boy there. I mean, he might have been, but I didn't see him.

Moody: So you had sex with Martha first?

Sapp: Yes. Phree was on her knees with her ass in the air and her head on the ground. The rock—they slammed it into her head. You don't understand. Oh, God! To have somebody die like that! It's something you can't forget. It's something that'll haunt you for the rest of your life. Then they started covering everything the hell up with twigs, branches. They said they's gonna bury them—right by the goldfish.

Moody: When people are having sex with them, are they struggling? While you're having sex with them, are they struggling?

Sapp: No.

Moody: How did their clothes come off of them?

Sapp: They were tore off. I ain't never in my life seen anybody tear people's clothes off like that— especially jean material. They just grabbed them and it was like it was a piece of paper. They just come right the hell off.

Moody: Did they say anything? Were they conscious? What did you think their condition was then?

Sapp: I knew what it was. I knew what it was when the rock hit their heads.

The detectives left Sapp alone in the interrogation room while they went to get him something to eat. The picture of the pond area was still on the table. The skids, with Phree and Martha's bodies underneath, were visible in the picture. Sapp (not knowing he was being videotaped) leaned forward and started talking out loud to the photograph: "I told you two, didn't I? We're all gonna go to hell together. They never should have done that to y'all. I'm sorry."

He removed his glasses and laid them on the picture and wiped his eyes. He replaced his glasses and stared at the picture for a long time. Then he picked it up and said: "I won't let you all get away." He held it against his chest for a moment and then stared at it again before placing it back on the table. After a while he moved the picture and looked at the map. He whispered: "I knew they'd catch me sooner or later. I was hoping they would."

Perhaps he had guessed that he was being videotaped.

Sapp, once again, studied the picture with his face only a few inches from it: "I'm sorry, Dad. I was hoping to see home again. It's just as well. I never had a home in the first place. I wish there was something else I'd done. Maybe I could stay here—forever."

Sapp (softly): What's gonna happen to me?

Moody: We've got a lot to talk about, you know? But you said it earlier—the best thing right now for you is to be where you are.

Sapp: So how much more time do you think I'm gonna get?

Moody: I don't know, man.

Sapp: Death row . . . I guess I need to get ahold of the old lady—and my kids—and tell them I ain't never coming home. Oh, I knew the time was coming.

Moody: It's about getting at the truth.

Sapp: I've been waiting for you to come back.

Graeber: I told you I was coming!

Sapp: I know. You said you was gonna come and talk to me about this. You two talked to John and them too, didn't you? That's all John ever talked about—

was either Graeber or Moody. That's my dude. I miss him.

Moody: Let me ask you something straight up. Did you know any of these guys before this shit jumped off? Did you know them at all? Had you known them before?

Sapp: No.

Moody: When you guys were upstairs, across from each other in the isolation cells, did John ever bring this up to you?

Sapp: Yeah.

Moody: What did he say? Did he know what you were in for at that time?

Sapp: Yeah.

Moody (referring to the map again): What did he say about you and this?

Sapp (smiling): "I'm gonna go over there and tell Graeber that William Sapp was with me!" I said, "Go ahead." I like John.

Graeber: He never did! He never did.

Sapp: I wonder why ol' Jim didn't say anything.

Graeber: Who's Jim?

Sapp: That's what I call John—"Jimmy Boy." He's a good kid.

Graeber: Was John's mother down there that night?

(Sapp nodded yes.)

Graeber: Who was the other woman?

Sapp: I don't know.

Graeber: So do we know any more secrets about you?

Sapp: No. That's it. That was the one you was looking for.

Graeber: I still got some secrets.

Sapp (shrugging and then laughing): I ain't worried about them. I don't know. I guess maybe I'm a sick person. I should be nervous, mad, and blaming the world. I can't kill myself—not even with all this garbage coming down. I got a seven-year-old little boy that made me promise not to. I wonder how he's gonna come out. . . . He's got mental problems now. I turned out to be a hell of a father.

(Moody offered him another soda or a cup of coffee, and Sapp said he could use a cup of coffee.)

Sapp: I could smoke a pack of cigarettes!

Moody: When was the last time you had a cigarette?

Sapp: About an hour before you all come to pick me up.

Moody: Oh, yeah? You're allowed to smoke over there?

Sapp: Oh, yeah.

Moody: I didn't even know that, man. 'Cause you haven't said anything about it! I didn't even know you smoked.

Sapp (shrugging): I didn't and then I started back up again.

Moody: Did you? Once you got in?

Sapp: Yeah.

(Graeber set a cup of black coffee in front of Sapp.)

Moody (casually): You understand what this is about, don't you?

Sapp: Yeah.

Moody: This is about justice. This is about finding the truth. This is about being honest with not only yourself, but also us being honest with you.

Graeber: We've definitely been straight up with you.

Sapp: Oh, I know that.

Graeber (rolling up his shirtsleeves): It's been enjoyable talking to you tonight, you know.

Sapp (speaking with audacity): I always thought I'd make somebody's career. I just never thought it'd be like this.

Graeber (countering): Gee, let me tell you something: we made our careers a long time ago. What happened is—during our tenure of duty—we happened to run into you. Which is part of our job in this situation. And both of us are just the type that we're going to follow it through all the way to the end. Steve and I didn't know you five years ago, but we weren't going to let you go.

Moody: We knew you were out there.

Graeber: But you're not a number to us, you know? And like I told you a minute ago, you're not a career to us. But you are part of our job.

20

Part of the job . . . to me . . . is getting people to tell on themselves.

—Captain Steve Moody

More truth . . . more lies. Each time the long-suffering detectives took Sapp through his story, more of the truth emerged.

Moody: Okay. Well, let me ask you this: who did you hear Phree say to them, "You're ugly! Get away from me"?
(During the break Sergeant Graeber had brought some mug shots into the interrogation room for Sapp to look at.)
Sapp: That guy that was in the picture.
Graeber (laying the sheets of mug shots in front of Sapp): Which guy?
Sapp (pointing to one of the pictures): Right there.
Graeber: Jamie.
Moody: We talked a little bit earlier before and you said that none of them said anything out of the way. But she looked right at him, didn't she? And told him, "You're ugly! Leave me alone!" We know that. Who else did she say stuff to? She had a quick mouth, man.
Graeber: What'd she say to you?
Sapp: She didn't say nothing to me. I don't know if it was

John or Dave—one of them—she called a fucking retard.

Moody: How'd that make you feel when she made the comment about "retards"? I mean, you got Paul that you care a great deal about and you got J.R. that you care a great deal about. You know what I'm saying? And I'm sure they've been called names too.

Graeber: What were you feeling then—when that came out of her mouth? What are you feeling, Bill? Did you feel dislike for her?

Sapp: Dislike? No.

Graeber: What were you feeling, Bill?

Sapp: Hate.

Graeber: Hate for who?

Sapp: For them.

Moody: What'd you feel for her?

Sapp: Don't know.

Graeber: Yeah, you do, Bill. You're a real precise person. You know what you felt for her.

Moody: You knew what you felt when Helen slapped you in the face and talked that trash to you. You know what you felt when Ursula Thompson stole your crack from you and kicked you in the balls. Don't you? You knew how that felt. This is one more incidence of a woman wronging. . . . You guys are sitting up there. You're enjoying yourselves. You're having a few beers. There's no one getting hurt. Everyone's laughing and carrying on and she's got to turn her mouth loose on Jamie—tell him he's ugly and then turn it on John and call him a "fucking retard." Now she may as well have spit in their faces or slapped them! You probably would have respected that more.

Graeber: What were you feeling then, Bill? Come on, buddy.

Sapp: I don't know. There wasn't no feeling.

Graeber: You were pissed at her, weren't you? Bill? Weren't you?

Sapp: I guess.

Graeber: No. Were you or weren't you?

Sapp: Well, I wasn't happy.

Moody: What'd she say to you? Bill, she wasn't just going to save comments for these two guys. We know. She was a smart-mouthed young woman.

Sapp: She was foul-mouthed. She wasn't just smart-mouthed. She wasn't that little innocent thing people thought she was.

Moody: And she had a good teacher, didn't she? Right from her mom! So what's she say to you, man? When she's passing around all the foul-mouthed comments, what's she say to you?

Sapp: Called us all a bunch of little limp-dick mama's boys and then hit John. He got hit with a rock!

Moody: So then . . . the shit's on, isn't it?

Sapp: He got hit by the rock and I said, "I'll show you. . . ." And they just all gathered around them. While they was falling, all they said was "Are you gonna kill us?" "Ain't nobody gonna kill y'all!" They said, "What are you gonna do? Just gonna fuck us and let us go?"

Graeber: What else happened? You're in a rage, Bill. What else happened? She just insulted your buddies. She just insulted your brothers. And you're pissed. What happened, buddy? Huh?

(Sapp just stared straight ahead.)

Graeber: Hey, Bill! What happened?

Sapp: They were just taking their clothes off of them. Talking about showing them who the hell's the limp dicks around here.

Moody: Did any of the other guys have sexual intercourse with those two—with Phree and Martha? We know you did.

Sapp: Yeah.

Moody: Okay. Now you said—you told us something earlier about Martha being on top of Phree. What's the deal there? Is that true or what?

Sapp: Yeah. The way they set it up was put them on top of that—that way they didn't have to—I don't know, something about getting dirt on you or something. I didn't much pay attention to all the jibber jabber.

Moody: What'd you have on your mind?

Sapp (taking a long time to answer): Showing them who the hell was a limp dick. I finally did manage to do something. I went over and got on top of the other one. She had her ass in the air. . . . Then they . . .

Graeber: Then they what?

Sapp: This monster fucking rock, or boulder, or whatever the hell it was . . .

Moody: Did you pick it up?

Sapp (looking at Moody): I couldn't pick that damn thing up. I'm not a weakling, but I couldn't pick that up. Hell, I'm half inebriated as it is. Kind of hard to be able to pick up a rock when you're up inside someone.

Moody (incredulous): You're having sex with one of them when the rock hits her in the head?

Sapp: Yeah.

Moody: Is that what you're telling us?

(Sapp nodded yes.)

Moody: Who dropped the rock on the head when you're having sex?

Sapp: Dave. I mean, I thought he was just bullshittin'. I guess not.

Moody: So, you're having sex with—and this is the one that called you guys names and threw the rock at John?

Sapp (staring at the picture): Yeah.

Moody: So what happened then?

Sapp: Body tightened up.

Moody: Whose body?

Sapp: Hers.

Graeber: What'd the other girl say when this happened?

Sapp: I don't think she was even alive.

Moody: What were you thinking? Weren't you worried about being caught? I mean, you took a chance here. What's going on here? What are you thinking? When this is going on? I mean, is anybody helping you carry those pallets across?

Sapp: No.

Graeber: We know someone did.

Sapp: He's a good kid. He don't need to . . . I did it.

Moody: No. You need to tell us who helped you.

Sapp: Jimmy Boy.

Moody: Who?

Sapp: John.

Moody: Your ol' buddy John? John Balser?

Sapp: Yeah.

Graeber: Who had the knife, Bill?

(Sapp didn't answer. Graeber looked at Moody and gestured toward the cabinet behind Sapp.)

Graeber: We got some scientific evidence over there?

Moody: Uh-huh.

Graeber: Show him that.

(Moody went over to the cabinet and took out a large paper bag.)

Sapp: John . . . John had a knife and so did . . .

(Moody removed an article of clothing from the paper bag and laid it on the table in front of Sapp.)

Moody: You've seen these before, haven't you?

(Sapp looked stunned and nodded yes.)

Graeber: Would that be your name there? Bill? Is that your signature there, buddy?

Moody: That's what you called it earlier.

Lieutenant Moody went over and got Helen's pants off the top of the cabinet and held them alongside the clothing on the table—the flowered shorts that had been cut almost identically.

He put Helen's pants back on the cabinet, and when he returned to the table, he put his hand on the shorts: "That was cut off, Bill," he said.

Sapp just stared at the shorts.

Graeber: What is this? Did you sign this, Bill? Bill? Talk to me, buddy.

Sapp: I guess.

Moody and Graeber (simultaneously): No. Don't guess it!

Moody: Listen to me here. Let's talk about this.

(Sapp leaned forward and touched the shorts.)

Moody: When this is going on . . . what's she doing?

Sapp: Nothing.

Moody: Why?

Sapp: Terrified, I guess.

Moody: Terrified?

(Sapp shrugged.)

Moody: Or is she not able to do anything?

Sapp: No.

Moody: Were her eyes open? How was she laying?

Sapp: Yeah, her eyes was open.

Moody: Well, I'm going to tell you something. She was either unconscious or something—because there's not a mark on her. You didn't even scratch her. When you made this cut here and on down the leg— no scratches—nothing; you did a good job. You're good with that knife, man.

(Sapp laughed.)

Moody: So what's the deal here? What's her state?

Sapp (looking down): Terrified.

Moody: Is she still alive? What are you saying to her when you're doing this?

Sapp (whispering): I didn't really say nothing.

Moody: Why? What did the talking for you?

Sapp (staring at the shorts): The knife.

Moody (leaning closer to Sapp and lowering his voice):
You told me before when we were looking at Helen's
pants, you never did this before. You did this—before
you met up with Helen. This happened with Martha
and Phree before Helen. This was in August of '92.
Helen was in December of '93—a year and four
months later. What's going on, man? What are you
thinking? What's this doing for you?

(Sapp continued to stare at the flowered material.)

Graeber: Who you getting even with, Bill? Hey, Bill!
Who you getting even with, buddy?

Sapp (whispering): Nobody.

Moody: This is your thing, isn't it? This is part of what
gets you off.

(Sapp looked up at Moody.)

Moody: This is part of the excitement, isn't it? Right
here.

Sapp: No, not really. . . .

Moody: Well, let me ask you something: How'd you
feel when you were making these cuts and she's
lying there and, in your words, she was terrified?
How'd that make you feel?

Graeber: What'd it do to you, Bill? She's laying there . . .

Moody: Terrified! You know, you've been called a
limp-dick motherfucker.

Sapp: I guess we all were.

Moody: Yep. You're thrown right in there with them.
And you showed them that you weren't a limp-dick
motherfucker. And that's what you said. What's
going on here, man?

Sapp (whispering): Revenge.

Graeber: Revenge? Revenge on who?

Sapp (tormented): The bitch who took my soul—took

my life. I never got to be a kid. Hey, they were right—
I'd never amount to anything.

Moody: These are Martha's shorts, man. Or was Phree
wearing them? Or do you know? Who was wearing
these—the virgin or the nonvirgin?

Sapp: Non. (Sapp meant Phree.)

Moody: Yeah . . . this is where you got your juice. This
is what it's about! She's lying there terrified and you
made these cuts careful enough that you didn't hurt
her. After you cut this away, what'd you do?

(Sapp didn't answer.)

Moody: Bill! Bill! After you got done with this—after
you did your thing here . . . what happened then?

Sapp: I don't understand what you're trying to . . .

Moody: Well, after you got done with all this—what
happened then? Pants come off of her?

Sapp: Yeah.

Moody: What else came off of her?

Sapp: Panties.

Moody: You ain't kidding! Where'd you cut them?

Sapp: I cut them?

Moody (pointing to a place on the shorts): You cut
right through here to cut them. So after you got her
underwear off of her, what'd you do?

Sapp: I guess we had—I guess she was raped.

Graeber: Did you rape her at this time?

Sapp: All of us did.

Moody: Did you look in her eyes?

Sapp: Yeah.

Moody: What'd that do for you?

Sapp: I don't know. It wasn't terror—it was a lost feeling. It's the only way you could describe what was in
the eyes. Just lost.

Moody: What's going on with you when you're doing
this? You're right back into this meticulous—just
taking your time—getting the juice, man.

Sapp: There is no juice.

Moody: Aw, man, we're talking about the vicious assault that you described—just like with Helen—remember that? That anger? You know that anger jumps out there, man. And then it goes from that extreme to . . . (touching the shorts) this extreme—to the slow cutting—cutting down the threads. You know, these shorts are up—cutting across—cutting on down—until it's wide open. From that explosive anger to this meticulous—controlled—taking care of business. What's going on?

(Sapp stared at the shorts with the loose flaps lying open.)

Moody: You've got to help me with this, man. What's going on with you when you're doing this? Change chairs with me. Do something! Put me there! What's going on in your head? What's this doing for you? Is it a fantasy?

Sapp (laughing): Yeah, right.

Moody: Well, what is it? Help me understand.

Sapp: There is no understanding.

Moody: There is an understanding and I'll tell you why: Because there's been two times I've seen this and you're responsible for both of them! There is understanding, Bill! What's it about this time? This is the first time you did it! That I know of—I know of at least twice. You told me before you didn't do it but the one time.

Graeber (tapping his fingers on the shorts): What is this, Bill? What is it? What do you get out of this? Spit it out, man. What'd you get out of this? Bill?

(Sapp did not answer.)

Moody: Let it go, Bill.

Sapp (finally speaks, agonized): I lost so much. My hopes—my dreams—security—childhood—my children—all that's sacred—over and over. How'd I lose it? Nobody gave a shit. Something to look forward to when you come home from school . . . How do you tell the man you love (his father) that the woman he married . . . ? It's not important.

Graeber: It's important to us.

(Once again Sapp removed his glasses and wiped his face.)

Moody: Where else have you done this?

(Sapp shook his head no.)

Moody: Have you done this in Florida? Am I going to have to call Rob down there and them guys down in Jacksonville and say, "Hey!" Am I going to have to look down there?

(Sapp sat back and put his hands behind his head and shrugged.)

Sapp: Probably.

Moody: Where else? Where else here am I going to have to look for things? Maybe not only this (pointing to the shorts), but other things that we've got to clean up.

Sapp: There ain't nothing else to clean up.

Moody: See, that's what you told me earlier.

Sapp: Well, I knew this was coming around.

Moody: How'd you know it?

Sapp: I can see it in the eyes.

Moody: Well . . . you also know in your heart you can look right in my eyes and know that we've still got some unfinished business.

It was almost midnight on April 2, 1997. They had been talking for over nine hours.

21

*He sat there with Phree's shorts . . . with Helen's pants
. . . (rubbing the material) between his index finger and
thumb. . . . He was living it again. . . .*

—Captain Steve Moody

About 9:30 the next morning, Lieutenant Moody brought
Sapp a cup of coffee. He was still in the same room where he
had been questioned the day before. A bed had been brought in
for him to sleep on instead of taking him over to the jail. All of
the evidence and pictures had been put away the night before.

Lieutenant Moody said, "I'll be right with you"; then he
left the room.

Alone in the room, Sapp laughed hard: "I'm not going
anywhere!"

A few minutes later, Lieutenant Moody and Sergeant Graeber came in and Moody read him his rights again because
"there was a break in the action." Sapp acknowledged that he
understood his rights and signed the paper.

Moody: I guess what's hard for me to understand is . . .
    you know that we've talked with them. You know that
    we've talked with John. We've talked with David.
    We've talked with Jamie. We talked with Alex—the
    biracial guy. You're trying to tell us that—and you
    need to think about this—the first time you ever had
    any dealings with Jimmy Boy, as you call him, or
    David, or Jamie, was at that pond that day.

Sapp (nodding): Yep.

Moody: I mean, put yourself back in our position, okay? You're the guy with the tie on today. Think about how strange that is—how strange that sounds. I mean, here you are and you've got to think about the truth now because you told us three different stories. So you've got to think like the detective—like the cop. Which one's the true story?

Sapp: I told you which one's the true story.

Moody: You're the first person that's told us about two women being there. You're the first that's told us about two women being there at the time you put them there.

(Sapp just stared at Moody.)

Moody: What time did you start drinking that day?

Sapp: It's hard to say. I guess you could call it daybreak.

Moody: So what's going on this day, man? You and Karen have it out—again?

Sapp (staring straight ahead for a long time and then finally answering): Yeah.

Moody: So because you love her—and I mean you do care for her—you get the hell out. But you are mad—you're pissed! So tell me where do you go from there? What's going on?

Sapp: I went up to Kinsler's (Bar)—I guess that's the name of it—got some more beer and set off walking. Just walked, over there by Penn Street.

Moody: So do you walk up there to them? This wasn't the first time that you saw some of these guys, was it?

Sapp: No.

Moody: When you walked up there, who was familiar to you right off the bat?

Sapp: John.

Moody: How'd you get to know John? Think about that because John's talked to us about it.

Sapp: I know. John knows my brother.

Moody: Did you go scrapping with John sometimes?

Sapp: Yeah. He knew a lot of them places. Actually, for who he is, he knows a lot. He's not as dumb as people think he is.

Moody: We know that. We know that. So, you walk up there. . . . You know John. Who else do you know there?

Sapp: Well, I knew Dave, but I didn't know Dave was actually his dad. I seen him around with John a time or two.

Moody: How many times did you go over to John's house on—where he lived?

Sapp: Lagonda Avenue. Went to the white house. The house we went to on Lagonda was on the other side of the overpass.

(John and Wanda moved to the house on Lagonda Avenue, upstairs, after Phree and Martha were murdered, so it would seem that Sapp still had contact with John after that night.)

Moody: Who else did you recognize and know? From before that day?

Sapp: Jamie. But I didn't really know him—too much.

Moody: So we've got John, David, and Jamie that you know. We talked last night about the biracial guy, right? Curly hair?

Sapp: Yeah.

Moody: Did you know him before that day?

Sapp: I'd seen him before. He's got a smart-ass mouth and nobody liked him—'cause he's a punk.

(Moody reached over and picked up one of the mug shots and held it up.)

Moody: Picked him out last night. Remember?

(Sapp stared hard at the picture and barely nodded yes.)

Moody: So, they tell you they got there in a car. Did you come in the car with them? Were you out riding with them?

Sapp: Guess it'd be stupid to say no, huh?

Moody: No. It would be stupid not to tell the truth. We're dealing in facts. This is about your movements before everyone ended up down here. So, that day, how and when did you hook up with them? What was going on?

Graeber: Come on, Bill.

Moody: We know . . . Listen to me. Look at me for a minute. We know Jamie Turner told two different sets of people that he had a date that day with two girls and you were hooked up in it too. Now you need to straighten this out—now. And you know from dealing with us, we ask a question, we know the answer. "A date with two girls." And then he told somebody else he had a date with two whores. So let's go with it—the facts, man. The truth. You need to tell your side of this. The truth.

Sapp: Down by the pond. That's where the girls was at.

Moody: All right. How'd you come to get there? Where were you before that?

Sapp (whispering): Riding around.

Moody: Who was riding around?

Sapp: Everybody.

Moody: Who was driving?

Sapp: Me.

Moody: What were you in, man?

(No answer.)

Moody: Now I'm going to tell you something else right now. At a certain time that day, we've got Marciszewski standing on—right here—right here out on the sidewalk next to Schuler's. We've got John walking across the street to a vehicle. And we've got somebody sitting in that vehicle—parked right there behind the wheel. And we know what time that is from some people that don't have anything in the game. They're not even involved. They're witnesses.

More evidence. "A date with two whores." We've got Dave and John right here and we've got somebody else in that vehicle behind the wheel. It's about facts. It's about the truth.

Graeber: Let it go, Bill.

Sapp: John told you.

Graeber: You tell us.

Moody: I'm telling you. You guys had "a date with two whores." It was planned from the start. Other people have told us where people were at certain times. How'd you hook up? Where were you? What were you driving? Take us through it. Tell us what you did! It's your turn now to get right.

Sapp (indifferently): I guess it don't even matter, does it?

Graeber: Where'd you hook up?

Sapp: Just a little ways down from the house (on Linden Avenue).

Graeber: What kind of vehicle?

Sapp: Mercury Marquis.

(Sapp's wife, Karen, owned a Mercury Marquis.)

Moody (leaning close to Sapp): Jamie's going around telling everybody he's got a date with two whores. How'd that get set up?

(Sapp shook his head no.)

Graeber: Bill, you already know. . . . You've talked to us long enough. And you're shaking your head no? You know better than that, right? Huh? Don't you? Who set the meeting up?

Sapp: Jamie.

Moody: Okay. How did he know them?

Sapp: That I really don't know. I don't know how he come to know them. But apparently he said he'd met them. . . . Well, he met the one, I guess, 'cause her mother used to pimp her out at the bar all the damn time. It made John mad. 'Cause I think John liked . . .

Phree? But he really liked her a lot. Well, they's talking about if they had a car, they could have a—go out riding around and have a party. A Mercury Marquis is a big car—extremely big.

Moody: So, who all meets you down here to get in the car?

Sapp: The whole gang.

Moody: So, you're driving. Right?

Sapp: Yeah.

Moody: John, Dave, Jamie—the biracial guy?

Sapp: Yeah.

Moody: Okay. That's who you called the "Neanderthal"?

Sapp (laughing softly): Yeah.

Moody (referring to the pond): Kind of a pleasant place to be?

Sapp: Yeah! If that right there had never happened, you could—almost like a sacred little place.

Moody: So when did Martha and Phree get there that day?

Sapp: They were already there. They was sitting down right there—bullshittin'. By this time we was all over the area. I'm not quite sure the name the boys and Jamie had called them little girls. But you should of seen John. He started shaking. He started stuttering. When he gets real upset, he stutters. He can't really do much—started crying. Didn't think too much about it at the time—until Jamie slapped the one.

Graeber: What did you do?

Sapp: Nothing until they started messing with John. Took all the names and all the scorn—held them down while I cut the clothes off.

Graeber: Who'd you hit?

Sapp (whispering): I don't know.

Moody: You do know. It was just like J.R.—you were there for John. You've always been there for John too. And here Phree is—the one that John had a crush on—and she tells Jamie that he's ugly and calls John a "fucking retard." And this is the one that John had known since he'd been a little guy and since Phree had been a little girl—that he had a crush on. And she calls him a "fucking retard." Someone picking on somebody that you care about that is their own special person—through no fault of their own.

Sapp: You have to know John.

Moody: We do know John.

Sapp: So much hurt.

Graeber: How'd you hit her?

Sapp: With my fist.

Graeber: How many times?

(Sapp shook his head.)

Graeber: You don't remember?

(Sapp shook his head no.)

Moody: Where'd you hit her at, man?

Sapp: Side of the head.

Moody: You're damn right! Right in the mouth—right in the head. How many times?

Sapp: I don't know.

(Sapp lifted his right hand and looked at it,)

Sapp: That can tell you.

Moody: Yeah. Let me ask you something, Bill. Hey!

Moody (tapping Sapp on the leg): Did you do it till she quit? Did she call him a "fucking retard" anymore? Did you drop her like a rock?

(Sapp stared at his hand, then sniffled and shook his head.)

Sapp: I don't know. You should've seen the hurt in his eyes. His will disappeared. Just shut her fucking mouth! There was no need for them to take the rocks and stuff. . . .

Moody: It was just another bitch—just like Helen and all the rest of them—and she wronged somebody you cared about.

Sapp: Yeah, that's a lot of justice.

Moody: But it's the truth and it's something we deal
with. Now how many times did you hit her? In the
head?

(Sapp looked at Moody and shook his head.)

Sapp: I don't know. I opened my whole hand up! (Sapp
held up his right hand.)

Moody: Where at?

Sapp (pointing to a place on his hand): That's why
that's like that.

Moody: From hitting her?

Sapp: So, you'd think I'd never forget that.

(Moody grasped Sapp's hand and examined it closely.)

Sapp: Every time I eat—every time I write . . . that's
why I don't like shaking hands! (His voice broke.)
You don't want to shake hands with a dead girl!

Moody: How many times did you hit her?

Sapp (whispering): I have no idea. That I don't know.

Moody: Did you hit her till she dropped?

Sapp: Oh, I imagine if you checked the tree, it's probably got me on it too! 'Cause I hit it a time or two!

Moody: Your blood? So after you hit her, what happened to her?

Sapp: Everybody took turns.

Moody: How many times do you think you hit her?

Sapp (looking at him): If I say "one"—I can say a
"thousand."

Moody: Okay. Did she fall to the ground when you
kept hitting her? Did she say anything?

Sapp: No, 'cause I thought she was dead. I honestly
thought she was dead.

Moody: Where was Martha when this jumped off?

Sapp: Right there. Yeah, just right beside us.

Moody: Did anybody scream?

Sapp: There was no scream. There was nothing. They
didn't scream.

Moody: So, this story about these two women grabbing these girls—that's not true, is it?

(Sapp shook his head no.)

Moody: Were there two women there at that point in time?

Sapp: Not at that point in time.

Moody: No. That's right. There wasn't. Okay, Phree's on the ground. What's going on with Martha?

Sapp: She was already naked. I don't know about where her clothes are or how they got—or anything like that. Phree's the one that had on . . .

(Moody went over to the cabinet again.)

Sapp: . . . the shorts with the flowers on them.

(Moody came back to the table with the paper bag in his hands and reached inside the bag. He pulled the shorts out of the bag and laid them on the table.)

Moody: 'Cause these two liked to switch clothes. Mom's told us that. So you punch her out—she goes down—because of what she does to John. She takes that light right out of his eyes. She hurts him deeper than he's been hurt in a long time. Doesn't she? And you reacted just the way you—you take care of business. So she's on the ground. Dave's got Martha's pants off. Is that what you said?

(Sapp barely nodded.)

Moody: What's he doing?

Sapp: Telling her to "flip the hell over." Then she gets on—I guess, I don't know, his knees are hitting in the dirt or something. So they tell Martha to get on top of Phree.

Moody: But before that happens, what are you doing with Phree?

Sapp (staring at the shorts): I guess I'm leaving my name.

Moody (touching the shorts): Right here. Leaving your

name. And this isn't the first time that you've left your name, is it?

Sapp: There was Helen.

Moody: Helen was after this, Bill.

Sapp: I can't tell you anything that happened before—I'm going to tell you that—'cause I was far beyond what I am now.

Moody: Okay. Well, let's deal with this . . . (He touched the shorts again.) . . . right here first. You're leaving your name right here. When you're doing this, what's Phree doing?

Sapp: Nothing.

Moody: You thought she was dead?

Sapp: Yeah.

Moody: Let me ask you something. When you're doing this—now we've already talked about it—you're zoned in to this. You're on this. You're locked in to this. How do you concentrate on doing this with all the other chaos that's got to be going on around you?

Sapp (voice hushed and full of wonder, trying to explain): There is no other chaos around me. I don't hear nothing. I don't see nothing. Feel nothing. And I don't give a shit about nothing. Everything around me is black. The only thing I see is what's in front of me. I don't pay attention to nothing. It's like being in outer space or being out there in the wide open with just a set of eyes. Nothing else exists! I've left—I am the environment!

Moody: Look at the precision here, man.

Sapp: I don't see precision, though.

Moody: You told us yesterday you wanted to be a brain surgeon.

Sapp: Well, what you want and what you get is two different things.

Moody: You told us yesterday about the scalpel.

Sapp (suddenly agitated): Oh, that's just lovely! I'm a walking modern-day damn Jack the Ripper!

Moody (pointing to the shorts): What are you doing this with, here?

Sapp: Big Buck knife. About eleven inches—extremely sharp—like a razor. It's mine.

Moody (nodding): You've got it with you all the time, 'cause you've always got your knife with you. It's your thing, man.

Sapp: Once you get past being scared of them, they become your friends. If they're held to your throat—while people do what they want with you—you respect them! (Sapp laughed.)

Moody: You said something yesterday that got me thinking last night. Listen to me. "How do you tell the man you love that the woman he's married to . . . ?" And then you stopped. You need to finish that right now. Let it out, man. Finish it. Free yourself of it, Bill. Right here and right now.

Sapp: I ain't never gonna be free.

Moody: Yes, you are. We're going to do it right now. What'd your mom (biological mother) do to you, Bill? This is troubling me. I need to know why. We need to know why. She dropped candle wax on you. She seared your testicles.

Sapp (dumbfounded, looked at Moody): How the hell did you know that?

Moody: You told us.

(Sapp shook his head no.)

Moody: Yes, you did, last night.

Sapp: You're not going to tell my dad this, are you? That would kill him. He would kill her.

Moody: Bill. She had sex with you.

Sapp: No. It wasn't sex. It was torture.

Moody: What else did she do to you?

Sapp: Fucked me. She had sex with me.

Moody: How? What would she do to you?

Sapp (laughing and then whispering): Everything. I could go on for a long time. Cigarettes . . . lighters . . . needles . . . knives . . . What do you do when you're a little kid? There ain't one person in the whole world to look up to. The only two people you think you can trust—and one of them . . . I used to think, "It's just a dream."

Graeber: What kind of sex did your mom have with you?

Sapp: She would make me screw her. She would give me "jobs." She would even sit down in my face. And then you got your people telling you: "You should've never been born." So you see, prison's nowhere. I'm nowhere. That's where I need to be. (Continuing sarcastically) Hey, Springfield had her! She set the baby on fire, but she has psychological problems, so she gets to leave. Probation. One of my brothers . . . [she] watched him drown in a lake. Again—psychological problems. I know what she did. She told me. Bitch! (Looking at Graeber and then Moody) You can't tell your dad. How do you . . . ? That bitch took everything he done all his life for his boys. Done without.

Moody (leaning toward Sapp and speaking softly, coaxing): Listen to me. We need to go back here. You've given up the biggest ghost in your life. Everything else is insignificant. You need to tell it right now—how Phree and Martha died.

Sapp (after a silence): They were turned over on their stomachs, facedown in the dirt. They took rocks. Everybody took a rock. One time each. That rock's on Penn Street Hill. Yeah, it is. Only they just decided to go up there and push the damn dirt over on top of it. That's what they did with the rock. Down to their uncle's junkyard. Unless y'all got it.

Moody (getting up and telling Sapp to turn around for

a second. Going to the cabinet and opening the doors. On one of the shelves lay a huge rock): It's right there, Bill.

(Sapp shook his head no.)

Moody (voice low): Yes, it is. Bill, I'm going to tell you something. I'm going to tell you something and I'll show you if I have to. That was left right on Phree's head. That one right there. It's got her blood on it. You want to see it?

22

He's evil . . . but then again . . . to me . . . and to the other men and women who investigate homicides and try to learn all we can about people who do this . . . he's an interesting evil. . . .

—Captain Steve Moody

Sapp stared at the huge rock lying on the top shelf of the cabinet.

"That ain't quite the one," he remarked.

Lieutenant Moody shut the cabinet doors and Sapp turned back around.

"That's not the one. There's another rock. I'm telling you, I know what that rock looked like," Sapp insisted.

Moody sat back down. "Why? Because you had it in your hand?"

Sapp: We all had it in our hands.
Moody: You used it on their heads, didn't you?
Sapp: Yeah.
Moody: Was that before or after you had sex with them?
Sapp: Before.
Graeber (leaning closer to Sapp): Bill, because of what your mother did, is that why "the bitches had to die"?
Sapp: Tell you the God's honest truth—I never know when it's gonna happen!
Moody: Yeah, you do—because this always follows

something by some woman that's wronged you. Your mom wronged you.

Sapp: Yeah, but I mean I just don't go out there and deliberately . . .

Moody: Listen to me. Your mom wronged you. Ursula Thompson wronged you. She stole from you. She kicked you in the nuts.

Sapp: Ursula Thompson is a fucking . . . lying . . .

Moody: She had a foul mouth too, didn't she?

Sapp: She's a liar.

Moody: Phree Morrow had a foul mouth.

Sapp (mockingly): Oh, no. Phree Morrow was the innocent type.

Moody: We both know the truth to that, don't we?

Sapp (whispering): John really loved that girl.

Moody: What'd you do to Phree with that rock?

Sapp: After they all just had a turn—there was this gurgling—just the damnedest thing! "You'll be sorry!" "Like hell we will!" So I picked it up, held it over my head, and throwed it down. Trying to send the son of a bitch on the other side of the world!

Moody: Then what'd you do to Martha?

Sapp: I had to slam the rock on her. I think the rock hit her in the back of the head, by the neck. I wasn't picking that rock up again. They wasn't getting rid of that rock.

The huge rock in the cabinet was, of course, the one that had been left on Phree's head. The other rock that Sapp referred to was, no doubt, the missing lava rock.

And he was obviously incorrect or confused about the order in which things happened because the enormous rock was not moved from Phree's head. He claimed he "wasn't picking that rock up again" when it was on Martha's head.

From what the detectives already knew, Martha was

undoubtedly killed—or, at the very least, rendered unconscious—first, with very little struggle, and was probably
already dead when the large rock was dropped on her head.
But Phree had fought them, as much as a twelve-year-old
child can fight five grown men.

Moody: Phree was defiant right up to the end, wasn't
   she? She was going to show you guys.

Sapp: She was strong.

(Sapp told the detectives that he and John took a shirt
   and wiped the sides of the pallets, to eliminate any
   fingerprints that may have been left on them.)

Moody: Whose idea was that?

Sapp: That was mine. I just killed somebody. I'm not
   stupid.

Moody: No, you're not. Just to make sure we're clear
   on something: you have sex with them—each one of
   them—before or after you drop the rock on their
   heads?

Sapp: One was before. One was after.

Moody: Who was "before"?

Sapp: Martha.

Moody: Before you started covering them up, what
   else gets done here?

(Sapp didn't answer. Moody went to the cabinet and
   brought back a picture of the girls' bodies and laid
   it in front of Sapp and pointed to something in the
   picture.)

Moody: What's laying there?

Sapp: Tennis shoes.

Moody: Who puts those there?

Sapp (finally): I guess I did.

Moody: There's no guessing about it—the truth. Who's
   in control? Who's got to straighten things out?

Sapp: How do you straighten things out like this?

Moody: You did the best you can. That's what you

been doing all your life. You did the best you can under the circumstances.

Moody (pointing to the picture): Who does this?

Sapp: Me.

Moody: All right. You have the shoes there. You have Phree and Martha there. Start putting the brush on them, right?

(Sapp sounded tortured as he told the detectives that he carried one of the pallets from the dock over to where the girls were and laid it on top of Martha. He helped John with the second pallet and they laid it on top of Phree, slightly overlapping the first one.)

Moody: Okay. At this point in time, they're covered. Who all's still at the pond?

Sapp: Me, John, and Dave. Everybody else is running back to the car.

Moody: Who would that be? That ran back to the car?

Sapp: That would be the Neanderthal. . . .

(Sapp turned his head and stared at the floor, then looked up and motioned toward the picture of the girls' bodies.)

Sapp: I don't have to look at that anymore, do I?

Moody (ignoring him): Who else ran back to the car?

Sapp (looking down): The Neanderthal and Jamie.

Moody (laying the picture closer to Sapp): So you and Dave and John were here, right?

Sapp: Yeah. We're here.

Moody: So what happens then?

Sapp: We started gathering shit up and Dave's got the bike and he says he's going to meet me over here by the church on the hill. And I had to haul ass around there.

(Moody moved the pictures so they could see the map.)

Moody: Where are we talking about?

Sapp: The church on the hill.

Sapp: And Dave said he had a place to get rid of it. We all went over there.

Moody: What'd you have with you?

Sapp: The shirt and the shorts.

Moody (pulling the shorts from underneath the map): You left your name on them, didn't you? You're not going to let this go too far from you, are you?

Sapp: I don't know if I had them with me or not. Man, I guess.

Moody (tapping Sapp on the shoulder): Okay. So come on up here. Let's look at the map. You turned down this road right here (beside the railroad tracks). Here's the bridge. Then what'd you guys do?

Sapp: We parked the car under the bridge (leaning forward and pointing to a place on the map). Yeah, this little area right here, I guess. . . . It's all grown with scrubs, so it's kind of hidden. We just went along this little roadway here—'cause this is a little path that goes all the way around here.

Moody: What's back there? What's that called?

Sapp: I don't know what they call it.

Moody: What do you call it?

Sapp: Lion's Cage.

(Moody went over to the cabinet and got some more pictures. He laid one of them in front of Sapp.)

Moody: How'd you get down in there?

Sapp: Climbed down the ladder and I handed the bike down to John.

Moody: You went down there too?

Sapp: Yeah.

Moody: What else went down there?

Sapp: The clothes . . . I thought the shorts, the shirt, and the underwear went down there. They used to keep that place clean. It was fun watching the water go down in it.

Moody (laying another picture in front of Sapp): Like that?

Sapp: Yeah, but a lot worse.

Moody: What's down there? What do you see down there?

Sapp: I see a wheel, a frame, a seat of a bike.

Moody: Who tossed it down there?

Sapp: I tossed that down there.

Moody: What else did you throw down there?

Sapp: All the stuff.

Moody (taking the picture away and laying the shorts on the table): You know what you threw down there? You threw your name down there. What'd you throw down with it? So your name wouldn't be found?

(Sapp leaned back and looked at Moody and then at the shorts.)

Moody: Do you remember throwing these down there?

Sapp: I thought I threw down a shirt and panties down there.

Moody: Well, you can see that you didn't throw their shirts down there. Because they still got their shirts on.

Graeber: Who do you think the shirt belonged to?

Sapp: My shirt? I threw my shirt down there?

Moody: Ah, we're asking you, man. Whose shirt did you throw down there?

Sapp: Maybe it was my shirt, but I thought I was wearing a T-shirt, though.

Moody: Do you want me to go to the cabinet?

Sapp: Yeah! (He laughed.) Seriously!

Moody: When you threw that shirt down there—why did you throw it down there? What'd it have on it? That you knew you had to get rid of it?

Sapp: Probably blood.

Moody: When you hit them in the head with the rock— what happened to their heads?

(Sapp hung his head and didn't answer.)

Moody: When you took that rock and tried to "send it to the other end of the world"—you tell me what happened.

Sapp (barely whispering): I guess blood was everywhere. Shit just sprayed out all over the place.

Moody: What were you wearing that night?

Sapp: Tennis shoes, a pair of jeans, white muscle shirt. I want to say a flannel shirt, but—or a blue shirt. Blue keeps coming to my mind.

Moody: Did you get blood on you?

(Sapp barely nodded yes.)

Sapp: My face.

Graeber: When you got blood on you, what did you do?

Sapp: I ran to the water.

Graeber: When John got blood on him, what'd he do?

Sapp: He wiped it off. Some of it.

Graeber: When Jamie got blood on him, what did he do?

Sapp (shaking his head): I helped John wipe off.

Graeber: What did the biracial guy do?

Sapp: As far as I know, they just kept wearing their clothes.

Moody: What'd Jamie do? When he got blood on him?

Sapp: Started just hopping around a little bit. He wanted to get the blood off of him. (Sapp laughed softly a couple of times, then smiled.) He jumped—he jumped in the pond!

Graeber: Would you believe we already knew that?

(Sapp laughed harder.)

Moody: You can still see it, can't you?

Sapp: That's my dude.

Moody: Who? Jamie?

Sapp (serious again, whispering): Yeah.

Graeber: Where's Phree's underwear? Panties?

Sapp (after a very long silence): I don't know.

Moody: Where'd Martha's go?

Sapp: Somebody's went down the "hole."
Graeber: So where'd Martha's panties go?
Sapp: That I don't know.
Graeber: You don't know where either pair of panties
    went?
Sapp: I believe it went down in the "hole," but that I'm
    not for sure.

Once again they questioned Sapp about who was at the
pond "at the end." The detectives knew he had left someone
out.

"Did anyone leave and come back with anyone, Bill?"
Graeber asked.

Sapp didn't answer. But then after a long silence, Sapp, answered, "It's kind of hard to get John calmed down. Y'all
know that, don't you?"

Moody: Yes, we do.
Sapp: Seems like his old woman can do that pretty
    successful. I don't know who left. I mean, you know,
    you got to run around trying to get shit covered up
    and took care of. So you don't pay too much atten-
    tion then. Your head's rushing too fast. The woman
    that—it was an older-type woman.
Moody: You knew who it was. There's only one person
    that can calm John down. Who came back up there
    and calmed him down?
Sapp: He said it was his mom.
Moody: Tell us what happened when she got back
    there, Bill.
(Sapp didn't respond.)
Graeber: Hey, Bill!
(Sapp looked up at him.)
Graeber: What'd she say?
Sapp (hanging his head again): Just a lot of stuff.
    Cussing Dave out for bringing John back and getting

him involved, and this other dumb shit. And, uh . . .
she was trying to find out what was going on.

Moody: What is going on? I mean, at this point in
time, are Martha and Phree covered up yet? When
she gets there?

Sapp: No.

Moody: 'Cause you got your hands full with John,
don't you? They're already dead, aren't they?

Sapp: Yeah. No sense in it.

(Moody held the picture of the girls' bodies in front of
Sapp's face.)

Moody: They're already right here, aren't they?

(Sapp looked away.)

Moody: Bill? Are they or aren't they?

Sapp: Yeah.

Moody: What'd she do? Did she walk around?

Sapp: Yeah, she was up around them.

Moody: What did she do?

Sapp: She was calling them—like she knew them—by
personal names. Like, I don't know, maybe it was all
over because of John being there. I don't know . . .
"Little tramps" and that she "needed to die."

Moody: That's what she's saying?

(Sapp nodded yes.)

Sapp: "Wasn't gonna do nothing but grow up and be
a little whore anyways" . . . "Dragging John down—
corrupting him. . . ."

Moody: What'd she say to you?

Sapp: "I can't believe that you would do this to John.
That I expect out of his dad."

Moody: Did you see her touch the girls? Did she help
cover them up?

Sapp: I know she stooped down and took the necklace off of . . . one of them.

(Moody held the picture in front of Sapp again.)

Moody: Which one?

Sapp (looking closely at the picture and nodding his head): Martha.

Moody: Did you take anything from them?

Sapp: No. (Then Sapp pointed to the shorts.) Well, I guess I took them.

Moody: There's no guessing about it!

Graeber: What happened to Phree's underwear?

(Sapp cracked his knuckles and stretched his arms in front of his chest, then sighed.)

Sapp: They was in Dave's pocket. I don't know what he done with them. They should've went down into the "hole" with the rest of it. That's why I said that stuff went down there.

Moody: Well, when you cut these pants off—what happened to the underwear? How'd they come off?

Sapp: They were ripped off.

Moody: Who ripped them off, Bill?

Sapp (whispering after a while): Me.

Moody: And where'd they go from there?

Sapp: In the air.

After establishing Wanda's presence at the crime scene, the detectives resumed their questions pertaining to the events at the Lion's Cage.

"Did you take the shorts down with you?" Moody asked.

Sapp thought for a while, then shook his head no, but he said: "Yeah, maybe I did. Maybe they were on me."

Moody was incredulous. "Huh? They're on you?"

Sapp barely nodded yes.

Moody: What'd you do with them?

(Sapp leaned back and stretched his arms.)

Sapp: That'd be after we threw the bike down. We climbed up the stairs—I wiped all the bars down that we might have even touched. Everything. I even wiped the bike down before it went down.

Moody: Did you throw the shorts down?

(Sapp nodded yes.)

Moody: What'd you do with the shorts, though, to try and make sure that we wouldn't find them? When you threw them down?

Sapp: Threw them in the water, I guess.

Moody: Yeah, but you did something, man. You're thinking. You've got it . . .

Sapp: Ohhh! Wrapped them in a rock!

Moody: Yeah! There you go! You wiped all that down, and you're right! We got that bike out of there and there wasn't a print on it! You did a good job! And you wrapped these up in a brick and we've got the brick. You were thinking!

Sapp (shrugging): Well . . .

Moody: You were in control, weren't you? Somebody had to be in control.

Graeber: You know, when you guys went over there and dropped this stuff, where was John's mother?

Sapp: I don't know! She damn sure didn't go with us!

Moody: Okay. So you got everything down and you wiped everything down. Once again you've taken control of the situation, man. You got rid of things. What happens then?

Sapp: Well, we pretty much . . . well, uh, started to get together what the hell we're gonna do and say. I mean, that's gonna be important. I mean, we have to say something if we got talked to, but we all had to sound the same without being the same story, so— words had to be kind of different.

(Sapp looked up, shrugged, and laughed self-consciously.)

Moody: So who decided . . . ? I mean, where'd you guys do that? Where'd you go when you got back in the car? Did everybody get back in the car?

(Sapp hung his head and nodded yes.)

Sapp: Went to a house down on Lagonda—in back.
See, we got a shade tree, so you can sit right there
and . . . It was kind of secluded, you know, nobody
could really walk up on you. John—he likes fooling
around in the grass anyways.

(This is the same house where John and Wanda later
moved upstairs. At the time of the murders, Wanda
was working downstairs, caring for Eleanor.)

Moody: What was the conversation?

Sapp: What to do—definitely, don't go the hell back
up there!

Moody: Who's making sure everybody understands
that?

Sapp (laughing): Well, I mean, you know . . .

Moody: Who's taken control since the shit went bad?
Who wiped everything down? Who told everybody
not to go back up there?

Sapp: It didn't work.

Moody: Why didn't it work?

Sapp: 'Cause I believe John went the hell back up
there.

Moody: When?

Sapp: The day they were found. As a matter of fact, I
think he was probably one of the first up there.
Which made me a little mad because he had told me,
when he come back, that somebody had made a
comment about "I survived the Penn Street Hill
killings!"

Moody: You went back, didn't you? You couldn't help
but go back.

Sapp (looking down): It was the next day.

Moody: Before they were found?

(Sapp shook his head no.)

Moody: After? Where were you standing?

Sapp: Behind the doctor's office—the hill.

Moody: Looking down on us? Looking down on me?

(Sapp didn't respond.)

Moody: Who were you there with?

(Sapp looked up at Moody and then back down.)

Sapp: Me and John. I think Dave was down there by Schuler's. The other characters kind of like spread out. It bothers me why John didn't say nothing about me.

Moody: Why do you think he didn't say anything about you?

Sapp: I don't know.

Moody: Well, you've got to have a feeling about it. Was he scared of you?

Sapp: No. I would doubt that very seriously.

Moody: Do you think it was out of a sense of loyalty? To you?

Sapp: I just treated him like he was normal. He is—to me. He's my "brother."

Moody (pointing to the shorts): You wrapped these up in a . . .

(Sapp reached across the table, picked up the shorts, and laid them on his lap.)

Moody: . . . in a brick.

Sapp stared at the shorts for a minute and then folded them. He held the shorts in his hands and stared at them for a long time, no doubt reliving the experience of cutting them off Phree. He finally looked up at Lieutenant Moody and put them back on the table.

"What were you thinking?" Moody inquired.

Sapp stared at the shorts. "I didn't believe this shit could happen. I blocked it out! I don't know how many times I went back to there—hoping it wasn't true," Sapp remarked.

Moody: Back to the pond?

Sapp (shaking his head): There at the cage. Stood on the cage—sometimes for hours. Just stood there waiting, thinking maybe somebody would come. I figured y'all would be watching the areas for a while.

Moody: You went back to where Helen was, didn't you? You could stand on the cage and look [at] where Helen was.

(Sapp didn't answer.)

Moody: I'm going to tell you something.

(Moody moved the shorts and the pictures out of the way so they could see the map.)

Moody: Here's what we know: Here's where you live—right here. Look at all the things that are happening around where you live. You come back from Florida. You burn the log cabin. The carriage house gets burned. The house on Harrison Street gets caught on fire. Phree and Martha. Helen's right down here. What else we got, man? What else is down here?

Sapp (shaking his head): Nothing.

Moody: After the girls—this happens in August—you move up to Miller Street. Did that help you get away from that? You're still drawn back down to this area, aren't you? You're standing on the cage. You're going back to the pond. Did you go back over and make sure if we missed anything at Helen's?

(Sapp barely shook his head no.)

Moody: Between the time that Phree and Martha met you guys at the pond—then you did Helen by yourself—what else happened right down here? October 22, 1993.

Sapp (shrugging): I don't know. What?

Moody: Here's the pond.

(Sapp leaned forward to look at the map.)

Moody: Here's Penn Street Hill. Right here. You're walking down the street here and there's a—one of the whores down there. You guys walk right up through—up the hill here—'cause she says she'll trick with you. And then something happens.

(Sapp shook his head.)

Moody: You're just another piece of shit again. Here's another woman calling you a piece of shit.

(Sapp shook his head again.)

Moody: And later that morning, we find Caitlin Levalley right here.

Sapp: No.

Moody: Now I'm going to tell you: She's alive—just like Helen. She survived. She survives. She's got the same—it's the same deal as Helen, man.

Sapp (exclaiming): You got two motherfuckers out there doing the same thing then, 'cause that wasn't me!

Moody: We're sitting here and you know as well as I do, the worst things we've talked about, we've talked about today.

Sapp: Yeah. But I don't know nothing about that area right there.

Moody: It's right across—if you stood there, you could look right across to the pond. Right across Penn Street, right to the pond.

Sapp (shaking his head): I don't know nothing about that area, though.

Graeber: Well, it's the same area.

Moody: It's the same area.

Moody (looking Sapp in the eye): There's more things we've got to talk about, Bill. Isn't there?

Sapp (nonchalantly): No. Not really. But he (Graeber) said we was probably going to talk about something, so . . .

(Sapp laughed and looked at Moody.)

Moody (matter-of-factly): There're more things we have to talk about. Are you hungry?

23

To get across to people that no matter what life they may have lived . . . what race they are . . . what station they're at in life . . . we take homicide very personal. . . . It's a personal thing.

—Captain Steve Moody

"Who else's family can we help deal with what happened to them? That their daughter might have wronged you—insulted you," Lieutenant Moody pressed.

Sapp shrugged and shook his head.

"Let's get things squared away. What else have you done that we need to know about?" Moody challenged.

Sapp looked at Moody. "Nothing," he answered.

Moody: Now we both know—I'm looking right at you—and we know that's not true.

Sapp: I ain't got nothing here.

Moody: Yeah, you have! And I guess I thought we were beyond this—not being straight with each other. The worst part of this is over with. Put yourself in our seat. We've got to straighten out what else you've done.

Sapp: Goddamned tennis shoes, isn't it? It wasn't the pants—this time. It was the goddamned tennis shoes!

Moody: Tell us how it went, man.

Sapp (answering softly, finally): I'd never seen her before, but sure was pretty. I don't know how to explain her. Blond. Kind of long hair. Pretty body. Pretty face. She had a real pretty face. Kind of round. Full cheeks. She wasn't the dope head they said she was. At least she didn't look like she was strung out.

Moody: How often had you seen her around?

Sapp: That was the first time.

(Sapp told them that when he first noticed her, she was walking by Deborah's Attic, a vintage-clothing store around the corner from his house. Lieutenant Moody patted Sapp on the leg as he got up to go to the cabinet again. He brought another map back to the table and spread it out in front of Sapp.)

Moody: Here we go! All right? Let's get it done. The girls (Phree and Martha) were August of '92 and you moved in here (Miller Street) September 7, 1992.

(It was one year to the day after Sapp moved to Miller Street that Belinda Anderson disappeared.)

Moody: September 7, 1993. And it was a mild fall. So, it was almost springlike. So tell me what . . . How'd you first meet her?

(Sapp told them that he was out in his backyard with his dog, Fangs.)

Sapp: Then I seen her. She come around the corner. She looked not too happy at first. Fangs ran over toward [her]. . . . I asked her where she lived at and she said she didn't live around here. I'm not quite sure—I think Bellefontaine. I took the dog upstairs. I don't know where Karen was at, at the time. And then I come back down and she was still around. We just kept talking. We must have talked for—God, I don't know—thirty, thirty-five minutes. Just shooting the shit. I don't know. Something . . . somehow I got the impression that maybe she might be a [prostitute] . . . and I asked her if she dated. I asked her how much she usually charged. She said, "How about forty bucks?" Whew!

Moody: Did she say for what?

Sapp: Yeah, for everything. You know, that was steep, but I don't know—somehow I just knew she was clean. Different. Jeans and white tennis shoes— maybe pink tennis shoes. Jacket—pink jacket—I believe it was a pink jacket.

Sapp related their conversation to the detectives:

I asked her, "Well, you got a place to go to?"

She said, "Well, don't you?"

I said, "Yeah, but I don't know when Karen's coming home."

Sapp: I mean, you know.

Moody: That could be touchy, huh?

Sapp: Well, it wouldn't be too good. So we started up the alley.

Again, Sapp related their conversation:

She said, "Why don't we go in a garage?"

I said, "I'm not walking in somebody's yard and going up in their garage."

She said, "Don't have to. You can crawl through the hole."

Sapp: Climbed through the back—through the hole. It's pretty dark, but it's not, you know, real dark.

Graeber (pointing to the garage on the map): What happened in there, Bill?

Sapp: She started giving me a blow job after I paid the money. Seems like that's all she wanted to do. That she wasn't doing the rest now.

Moody: She's got your forty dollars in her pocket?

Sapp: Yeah.

Moody: And she's not going to do what she said she was going to do. Does she?

Sapp: "I'm gonna go get John" or somebody like that.
Or "Bear," or some strange name like that. To beat
my ass! She was a strong girl. She can hit!

Moody: She wasn't a lightweight, was she?

Sapp: No.

Moody: Did it surprise you?

Sapp: There's no need in it. Started fighting . . . Don't
know what the hell it was she picked up, but I remember she picked it up to keep whacking the fuck
out of me with it—on my elbow.

Moody: Did it bleed?

Sapp: Yeah, it bled. Hell yeah, it bled! Took it to what
was laying on top of one of the cabinets. Pushed it
into her where she never would work. It's a piece of
pipe. I swung the motherfucker at her. I thought
she'd step the fuck back! Somewhere in the head—
side of the head. She dropped. Figured I was going
to get what I paid for. Or I was getting my fucking
money. But, you know . . . I never did get it.

Moody: Get what?

(Both detectives had leaned forward in their chairs because Sapp was talking so softly they could barely
hear him.)

Sapp: I never did take her—take it.

Moody: Are you telling us you never had sex with her?
Other than the blow job? Did she finish you on the
blow job?

Sapp: No. She got up. Well, she was gonna start to get
up. She said, "I'm gonna go up here and call the police. I won't get you now. While you're in jail, I'll
come back and get your wife and your kids." All of
a sudden I just felt hot—real hot. Hot like I was on
fire inside. I, uh, this old piece of metal—steel—or
something—hit her about twice. That's all it took—
that time. (Sapp looked up at Lieutenant Moody.) I
didn't know what to do. I crawled out the back. I was

in a daze for a day or so. I think it was the next day
or after that, I went back.

(Sapp explained to the detectives where he had found
the large plastic bags. He said he was "coming from
work" and passed a factory.)

Sapp: They got a chute out in back. It's got big bags to
catch all the paper. That's probably the fibers you
picked up—was that paper. I went back, put her in the
bag—vomited all over the fucking place. It was . . .
The smell was awful. You wouldn't believe the smell.
Well . . .

Moody: Yeah, we would.

Graeber: Yeah.

Moody: We've smelled it.

Graeber: We've been there, buddy.

Sapp: So I put her in the bag. One over the head all the
way down and one over the feet all the way up. Well,
actually, I think I done the feet first. Rolled her over.
Took a shovel and dug a little grave—just enough for
the body to barely fit in. Threw the dirt back over—
some scrap and debris—I think I left a door there.
Maybe not.

Sapp (looking at Moody): That fucking tennis shoe!
One on—one off.

Moody: Yep.

(Sapp then stared straight ahead.)

Moody: How many times did you hit her in the head?

Sapp (chillingly): You know, when you hit somebody
in the head, you'd think they'd die. Real fast. Don't
happen like that. They keep making sounds. I can't
even explain how it is. It's like trying to talk and the
only thing you can do is gurgle. I mean, Jesus Christ,
how many times you gotta hit a person before they
stop fucking trying to get up? (Sapp looked at
Sergeant Graeber.) I had to stop. Wouldn't stop—she
wouldn't stop. God, I don't even know where exactly

all I hit her at. I know I hit her in the head. I might've hit her in the back . . . shoulder . . . neck . . . I don't know.

Moody: You did.

Graeber: You did.

Moody: You hit her in the neck. You hit her in the head. You hit her in the face. You did. Just like you hit Helen. Just like you beat Helen.

Sapp (shaking his head and whispering): No. No.

Moody: How was that different, then? Tell me how that was different.

(Sapp used both his index fingers and both his thumbs to make a circle with about a three-inch diameter.)

Sapp: This pipe was like this.

Moody: How long was it?

(Sapp thought about it for a few minutes, then stood up and put his hands out as though he were holding an imaginary pipe beside him.)

Sapp: About that tall.

Moody: So about five foot high. How much blood was on it?

Sapp: I don't know.

Moody: Tell me about how you got her pants off.

Sapp: I didn't even ask her. Taking them off. I figured I done bought them. So I took them off for her. I think I started in the back. Pulled the waistline up. Cut some and ripped the rest.

Moody: Which knife were you using?

Sapp: The Smith and Wesson—very unique knife. It's all stainless steel. Double-edged—got a groove down the middle. It's a "bleeder." It's an assault knife—a hunting knife.

Moody: So where do you start cutting on the pants at?

Sapp (standing up and turning around to demonstrate): You grab them right here by the waist. When you got them pulled up, there's a space in between—in here.

Stick it in there and go straight up. And then I ripped the rest of the pants off. (Sapp sat back down.)

Moody: You didn't cut them?

Sapp: I suppose you know. You ain't got the pants?

Moody: I know. You're going to tell me where the pants went. But I want to know about you putting your name on this one too.

Sapp (shaking his head and whispering): No.

Moody: Well, you started to. What stopped you?

Sapp (shaking his head): I really don't know. Maybe it's a fact—being too close to home. Christ, it might as well be in the backyard! It was!

Moody: Is she moving? Or is she done?

Sapp: No, she's not done yet.

Moody: Okay. So you've got some time here.

Sapp: Yeah.

Moody: You can't tell me things aren't blowing up— things coming back. . . . This is just another example of another bitch getting it over on you. Promising you something and then pulling it back away. She might as well have smacked you in the face. Or spit on you! You held up your end of the bargain and all she was going to do was take.

Sapp: I should of let her go get her stupid half brother! Or uncle. Or whoever the hell he's supposed to be!

Moody: Yeah, but didn't she threaten to have Karen and the kids taken away?

Sapp: But she didn't. But they still got me anyways.

Moody: What'd you do with the pants?

Sapp: Took them over to a Dumpster. Had to get rid of my shirt. I loved that shirt!

Moody: What kind of a shirt was it?

Sapp: Long-sleeve, button-up . . . it was a pretty shirt. Blue.

Moody: Was it? You like blue, don't you?

Sapp: I used to. Blue was a happy color.

Moody: So did you cut the pants the rest of the way off of her?

Sapp: Yeah.

Moody: How'd you do it?

Sapp (softly): Like opening up a Christmas present. Some kids tear it open. Me, when I was a kid, I used to make sure to take the tape off. Unfold it—pull by pull—it was open!

Moody: So how'd you open this Christmas present?

Sapp: Stuck it (the knife) in where I said I did—go up the back—and just followed it all the way around. Get to the zipper—open up the legs. Threw them away.

Lieutenant Moody got up and went to the cabinet again. Sapp looked at Sergeant Graeber and then turned toward the cabinet. Moody took a loose-leaf notebook out of the cabinet and looked at Sapp. "You never know what I'm going to pull out of there, do you?"

Moody sat back down and looked through the notebook until he found what he was searching for. He removed a page with several pictures of Belinda on it and laid it in front of Sapp.

Moody: She was pretty, wasn't she?

Sapp: Yeah.

Moody: Do you remember what kind of shirt she had on?

(Sapp thought for a few minutes, then whispered, "No.")

Moody: She had pretty blue eyes too, didn't she?

Sapp: Yeah.

Graeber: How many times did you go back there, Bill?

Sapp: Twice.

Graeber: What did you dig the little hole with?

Sapp: My knife and my hands. I rolled her over in it. Facedown, I think. In a bag, you really don't know.

Moody: You're right. You're right.

Sapp: Yeah, I believe so. 'Cause the foot was sticking

up out of the . . . Apparently, I didn't dig it long enough or something. That foot was sticking up over the little shallow—whatever you want to call that.

Moody: When this hit the media, what did you do? How did you hear about it? When they found her?

(Sapp thought about it for a minute.)

Sapp: I think Karen told me. Or it might have been the television. Somebody heard about it on the news. So I drove past.

Moody: While we were there?

Sapp (nodding his head): Yep.

Moody: When you drove by, what did you see?

Sapp: The empty—the blackness of the garage. The tape. People running around with jackets that said "Police" on it—I think it said "Police" on it. They were blue and yellow—or something like that—I don't know.

(By the time Belinda's body was found, Sapp and his family had moved to the house on Kinnane Street in Limecrest.)

Graeber (motioning toward the pictures): And you never saw her before? When you lived up there?

Sapp: No. If I had . . . As a matter of fact, when I met her, she said she was up here visiting. She had just got here—"today" or "yesterday."

Graeber: Did she tell you her name?

Sapp (pulling the pictures closer to him): Yeah. If I heard it or if I seen it, I'd know it.

Moody: Just so I'm clear, okay, about what went down in the garage—you crawl through the hole, right? You agreed to a blow job and what? Sex? For forty dollars?

Sapp: Yeah. She said she changed her damn mind. She wasn't doing the other and she wasn't doing that. (Sapp, sitting with his arms folded across his chest, stared at the pictures.) It should've never happened. I told her she was fucking crazy. "Give me my money back!" Or I was going to do something. I reached down to grab her. Apparently, she had her hands on something—I don't know what the hell it was. All I know is, she whacked the hell out of it. That wasn't nothing, though. She made it hurt. Strong. I grabbed her by the throat. I remember that now. I just wanted to squeeze her head off her fucking shoulders. She scratched me.

Moody: Where'd she scratch you?

Sapp: In my face and on my arms.

Moody: Did it bleed? Were the scratches bloody?

Sapp: Oh, yeah! I would say. (Sapp almost whispered.) She kept fighting. Figured I was gonna get what I paid for anyway, or else I was gonna get my money back. That's when she managed to slap my glasses off my face. And I threw her against the fucking wall! And when she went down, I found her. I guess I just knocked her senseless for a few seconds. (Sapp stared at the pictures again for a long time.) But you can't right a wrong. It wasn't about . . . She wouldn't shut up! (Sapp slumped in his chair and seemed dazed.) It was like talking like a gargle. It wasn't really talking, it was . . . (Sapp shrugged.)

Moody: Was she down when she was doing that?

Sapp: Yeah.

Moody: See, that's something you talked about with Phree too. So when did you realize that she was dead?

Sapp: I didn't . . . I stayed there for a little bit. When I come back—my wife says sometimes I get up in the middle of the night and I don't remember it. I'd disappear—three or four hours at a time. I was thinking maybe I could take pictures of her. Take the body and sneak it into a Dumpster. Put it in the back of the car and go dump it somewhere. Thought about burning the building down at one time.

Moody: When she was still buried there?

Sapp: Yeah.

Moody: Why didn't you?

Sapp: I don't know!

(Sapp was totally absorbed in looking at the pictures of Belinda.)

Graeber: What are you thinking about there, Bill? Hmmm?

(No response.)

Moody: Bill?

Graeber: What are you thinking about?

Sapp: Trying to think of her name.

24

*He could step out his side door . . . on the alley side. . . .
He could stand on his porch and look right to where
Belinda was . . . in the garage. . . .*

—Captain Steve Moody

Sapp wiped his face on his shirtsleeve and then sat back
with his hands behind his head.

"When you lived on Miller Street—I was talking to Janice McCormack—she says you're all over the place here,"
Lieutenant Moody observed.

"There's no doubt," Sapp replied.

Moody: "Trolling the neighborhood" is how she put it.
By your own admission last night, you referred to
yourself as a "creeper." What else was going on
down there in that area? What do you have going on
right next door to you? You guys are trying to live
there. You're trying to raise your family. What's your
family subjected to?

Sapp (shaking his head): I mean, her son—or her grandson, I think it is . . . Yeah, I'd say probably dealing.

Moody: You told Al back in September, when you
talked to him, what was going on at that house. And
the drug dealers in this area—the ones we talked
to—didn't like you. You were a threat to them.

Sapp (incredulous): How in the hell could I be a threat
to them?

Graeber: They considered you a threat for whatever reason.

Moody: But, during this time also, we know that you've got a drinking problem. You've got a problem with "rock" (crack cocaine) too. Now I want to know what these people here did to you during that time?

Sapp: Hah! They ain't never done nothing to us! As a matter of fact, the old woman—I guess the grandmother—she'd be coming over all the time and talk with Karen. Sometimes the kids would go out there and play together. I never had any problems with them. No cross remarks.

Moody: What about who was dealing dope out of there from time to time? Did you ever buy any crack over there?

Sapp: No.

Moody: Maybe not out of the house—maybe in the backyard?

Sapp (vigorously shaking his head): No, I wouldn't even bring it around the house. I wouldn't even allow it around the house.

(Sapp apparently knew that the detectives' questions were leading to the tragic fire on Miller Street—next door to where he had lived—that had taken four-year-old Avery Bailum's life in August 1994.)

Sapp (casually): You gonna ask whether I set the fire or not? No. As a matter of fact, I was inside that house. I liked that house. I would have liked to have had it, but for five hundred dollars a month . . . (laughing) That's too much.

Moody: How did these people pay for that?

Sapp (shaking his head): I don't know. I tried not to get into too many people's business. I just took it upon myself that he was doing basically a lot of dealing.

Moody: You might've liked the old woman that lived there—but you didn't care for what was being brought around your house, did you? 'Cause you didn't bring the crack around your house, did you?

Sapp: Well, they didn't bring it around either.

Moody: They dealt out of there! We know they dealt out of there.

Sapp: Well, he dealt out of there, but he never done it in a open kind of way.

Moody: People stopping for a minute at a time, running in, running out—that's not open? We both worked Drugs a lot of years, man. We know how it runs. We know how it affects neighborhoods. And we know how it angers people.

Sapp: Well, it never angered me—like that. We weren't even living there at the time.

Moody: Now wait a minute, okay? We still haven't found her (Belinda) yet! So you're still going by this area because you're checking on this.

(Sapp shook his head no.)

Moody: You still drive by. Bill! You went back to the Lion's Cage and stood on it. You went back to the pond. You went back down around Helen's spot. You go back to these places.

Sapp (tapping the map with each word): But—I—didn't—go—back—to—here!

Moody: Well, what I'm telling you is, you set the fire, but you didn't mean for anything to happen that day.

Sapp (emphatically): No. I didn't set the fire. If I set the fire, I'd tell you, "I set the fire." I mean, I'm already in prison for the rest of my life. It's not gonna bother me or hurt me any more than what's already happened. But I didn't set that fire and I didn't get that girl on Penn Street Hill either. The rest I'll be in court for—'cause I done them.

Moody: What kind of fire do you think this is? Do you understand what I'm getting at here? Use what you know—why you set fires and tell me—'cause you came back by that day when the fire marshal was still there, and everything. You told Al about that.

Sapp: Yeah. Well, we were kind of curious. I mean, God, right there. We seen it from the car, but never got out and looked at it or anything.

Moody: You never got out and stood across the street in the parking lot with the people and looked?

Sapp: No.

Moody: Where do you think the fire started?

Sapp (laughing): I don't know.

Moody: Well, you looked for a while.

Sapp: Yeah, but it looked pretty wasted from what we seen. Maybe one of them kids was playing with fire.

Moody: Well now, this is an arson fire. Nobody in that house caused that fire.

Sapp (exclaiming): I don't know!

Moody: Where you go—where you're at—where you're living—where you're working—we can draw a circle around things that happen. Can't we? Something else happens and you move out to Limecrest. When you're at Limecrest, Ursula happens.

Sapp: Yeah, I moved to the state penitentiary. I wonder what's gonna happen now.

Sapp found that thought to be quite amusing and laughed very hard at his own remark.

Sergeant Graeber asked Sapp if he needed to use the rest room and he replied that he did.

Moody then remarked, "One more thing to talk about. One more thing to straighten out."

As they all stood up to leave the room, Sapp said, "I'm serious, though."

Lieutenant Moody patted Sapp on the shoulder, "I know. I know."

"That one down there is not me," Sapp stated.

Sapp (laughing): Well, I know what this next one's about.

Graeber: We have to get that other map.

Sapp (laughing again): Another map? Man!

Moody: I guess what's interesting about you . . . I mean, just before we took this break, what we noticed is every time something happens—in a short period of time—you move. Okay? I mean we saw that with Martha and Phree. You come back into town, the log cabin burns. Martha and Phree—that's in August, and in September you move over on Miller Street. Belinda disappears—that's the name of [the] girl in the garage—Belinda. And we also know, just like you did with Ursula, that you guys—when you have your problems with the rock and you need something like that—you hook up with one of these chicks. You go do that. They get what they wanted. You get what you wanted. You guys get high. Boom! Part company. Okay?

Sapp: Ursula's the only one I ever done that with—the only one I ever trusted like that.

Moody: Why? What other women did you run into that beat you out of stuff?

Sapp (shaking his head): Never been one to beat me.

Moody: No, I can honestly say, just by looking at you . . . you never allowed any of these women to get over on you. That stopped after the hurt of being young. That's why we're talking about taking control. You took control. You took control when Helen insulted you. You took control with Martha and Phree. You took control with Belinda. You took control with Ursula.

Sapp: The problem is, I should've done what I got accused of doing. Then it wouldn't have been so bad.

Moody: Done what? What should you have done that you were accused of doing?

Sapp: She said I raped her!

Moody: Who? Ursula?

Sapp (protesting): She said I kidnapped her! I didn't do none of that shit!

Moody (feigning astonishment): Hey! Bill! Does it surprise you that a woman would get on the stand and lie about you? After all the shit you've been through? After the way these bitches have treated you?

Sapp: Yeah.

Moody: It surprises you that she'd get up in a court of law and raise her right hand and lie about you?

Sapp: About something I didn't do. Yeah!

Moody: Why should that surprise you? Look at it! Look at what she did to you! She stole your dope! Then she kicked you in the nuts!

Sapp (shaking his head): Yeah, but still . . . She said she never knew me—never seen me before.

Moody: So let's get this last one done. All right?

Sapp: Where am I supposed to be at now?

(Moody unfolded the map.)

Sapp: Where in the hell is this at, man?

Moody: On East Pleasant. You go on down—on down this road. That's where it comes out onto Kenton Street. You know where we're at now?

Sapp: Umm, yeah. I think I do.

Moody: You've got railroad tracks here. Mill Run runs down through here.

Sapp: Yeah, I used to steal the blasting caps out of the cabooses.

Moody: Back down here at the DT and I railroad yard?

(Sapp nodded yes.)

Moody: Then you know this area pretty well.

Sapp: Umm, back then.

Moody: Well, it hasn't changed much. What we need to talk about happened down here in this area.

(Sapp shrugged.)

Moody: Back in February of 1994. You were living on Miller Street. Something happened in February of '94 and just like clockwork—just like always—in March of '94, you move off Miller Street out to Kinnane. Every time something happens, you make a move.

Sapp: Mmm, no. That ain't necessarily true. I moved off Miller 'cause Karen was pregnant and I didn't want her going up and down the damn stairs in the winter. That's why we moved off Miller. She already fell once and hit her—messed up her back and her backbone. I wasn't having it

Moody: And that may be part of the reason because you do care so much about Karen. But you've got to think about what else is going on during this time. Are you working then? Is it anything steady?

Sapp: Whew! I don't know.

Moody: You've got that crack problem. You're drinking. You say she's pregnant?

Sapp: Ah, we spent most of the time, I think, in and out of welfare.

Moody: Vanessa*'s born in August—three days after the fire on Miller Street. So, Karen's pregnant in February, isn't she?

(Sapp nodded.)

Moody: She's three months along. What else is going on during that time?

Sapp (shaking his head and sighing): Nothing much.

Graeber: Were you happy about the baby coming?

(Author's note: Sapp's answer, to put it mildly, was disturbing.)

Sapp: Hell, yeah! Especially when I found out it was a girl.

Moody: How did Karen feel about it?

Sapp: What? A baby? Ah, she loved it. We were going to make this our last one.

Moody: But you didn't stop, though, did you?

Sapp: Nope—Brad*.

Moody: June 14, 1995.

Sapp: That's when I gave her a present. I went and had myself fixed.

Moody: After Brad?

Sapp (nodding): Yeah.

(Then laughed.) Oh, well!

Moody: What else is going on during that time, man? How are you feeling about things?

Sapp: Shoot, pretty good. Especially when we found a place for Karen—I mean, it needed a little work, but it was worth it. I don't know . . . It was a whole house. It had a front yard. The kids could go out. The dog. Loved it on Kinnane! It was ideal. Beautiful. Peaceful.

Graeber (tapping a spot on the map): You tell us about here. This wooded area right here.

Sapp: I can't tell you nothing about no wooded area. I told you everything I know. I can't tell you something I don't know nothing about.

Moody: In February of 1994—in the middle of February—we found a woman here. She was reported missing on February 2, 1994. She was found February 19, 1994. We know where this young woman was—the last place anybody saw her. We know what she was about. She had a crack problem too.

Sapp: Well, not everybody that uses crack . . . we all don't hang together.

Moody: I'm not saying that. She was a prostitute. That doesn't make her a bad person either.

Sapp: No. She's just gotta take care of herself and her habit.

Moody: That's right. But what's interesting about this is—she fits right in with some of the things that you've done. This woman wasn't alive, but she still told us things. You've got to fill in the blanks for us.

Sapp: I ain't filling in the blanks, 'cause she didn't tell them about me.

Graeber: Why wouldn't she tell them about you?

Sapp (laughing): It wasn't me. I mean, I'm not trying to be a smart-ass. I mean, bear with me. I mean seriously. That's not me. That's—not—me! I told you what I done.

Moody: Okay. But you understand where I'm coming from here?

Sapp: Oh, yeah! I understand! I mean, you've got to do your job. You've got to ask questions. But I'm telling you, that's not me there!

Graeber: Helen . . . you hit her with a piece of rebar. Right?

(Sapp nodded.)

Graeber: See, this lady here—she got hit with rebar also. Left marks on certain parts of her body.

Sapp: That wasn't me. I'm telling you, that wasn't me.

Moody: It's not like you've got anything to lose here.

Sapp: Right! I don't. But I'm not gonna cop out to something I didn't do!

Moody: I don't want you to, Bill. I don't want you to.

Sapp (firmly): I'll tell you—that one—Penn Street (Caitlin Levalley)—and that fire—that's not me. Wasn't there. Didn't do it.

Graeber: You want to know something? I believe you. I know it doesn't mean anything to you, but I believe you.

Sapp: Well, you know, coming from a convict . . . Maybe I'm the world's greatest liar, but I don't think I can lie that damn good.

Moody: No. You can't.

(Sapp laughed.)

Graeber: You actually can't lie worth a shit.

25

My wife has told friends about how Graeber and I sat there and ate with him . . . laughed with him. . . . I mean, he is what he is. . . . We are what we are. . . . Our job is to make sure he doesn't do it again.

—Captain Steve Moody

The detectives had a few more steps before they could call the dance complete.

"Let me ask you something, Bill," Lieutenant Moody stated. "We talked about here and we've talked about Florida. Is there any [other] place in Ohio?"

"No," Sapp replied.

"Is there anything else in any other state or city or town that we need to know about? That we can make straight for you?"

Sapp (shaking his head): No. Nothing. I've only been to Florida and Ohio.

Moody: What about the states in between?

Sapp: Well, you know, that's in a car, traveling with the wife and kids—which she did the driving—nonstop. It's just not a nice thing to think about.

Moody: Let me ask you about something, since we're talking about Karen. How much of this stuff did Karen know about? Which ones did Karen know about?

Sapp: Nothing. She suspected, I think, but she didn't know nothing.

Moody: She suspected on Helen. She knew about Helen.

(Sapp stared at Moody.)

Moody: Because she tried to help you out. She tried to throw us off the track.

Sapp: No. 'Cause I was totally somewhere else—I told her I was totally somewhere else when . . .

Moody: Well, but why—the next day after Helen . . . what about the police report you made about being assaulted at Fountain and Miller? What was that about? That was to cover the injuries you got from Helen, wasn't it?

Sapp (angrily, but irrationally): No. That's 'cause that little fat-ass, tub-of-lard, hookin' ass, little bitch staying in that corner house went to running her fucking mouth—yelling "nigger." And they come over there and three of them little bastards said they was gonna hit my wife and hit my kids. And that ain't gonna jump off with me!

Moody (unconvinced): So, you're telling me that Karen didn't give that police artist that sketch just to throw us off?

Sapp (calm again): No. What she seen . . . You know that could've been somebody just totally innocent looking for Helen. I don't know.

Moody: Well, evidently, it was—someone totally innocent—because we know who assaulted Helen.

Sapp: But she never knew. I think she kind of felt—only after what happened with Ursula.

Moody: What about the scratches and the marks you got left on you from Belinda in the garage?

Sapp: You know, that's not real hard to take care of.

Graeber: What about the scratches from Helen? How'd you explain them to Karen?

Sapp (shrugging): Fight . . . Of course there was the missing shirt and everything, but, you know, if you're gonna be a liar, you gotta do it right. You gotta at least be muddy and dirty. You gotta at least have swollen-up body parts. If there ain't nobody there to do it for you—and you don't want nobody to do it for you—you do it yourself.

(Self-inflicted injuries so that he could tell Karen that he had been in a fight or had been assaulted.)

Moody: There's nothing else you think we need to know about?

Sapp: No.

Moody: You haven't hurt anybody else that we need to know about?

Sapp (shaking his head): No.

Moody: How do you feel?

Sapp: I feel good . . . light. (He touched the back of his head.) I also feel like—fire back here. And I'm scared the hell to death. 'Cause I know what's coming. I know exactly what's gonna happen. I got a feeling it's gonna be max on everything.

All the maps and evidence were locked up in the cabinet and they took a break. When Sapp came back into the room, he stared at the bare table and then turned and looked at the cabinet and sighed. He spoke while alone in the room: "Sorry. I hope they catch the . . . He needs to be caught—just like me. I thought I was the only sick, deranged son of a bitch out there. I guess not."

He turned toward the cabinet again and whispered: "Well, Jimmy Boy, don't worry. We're gonna be together for a long time. If I can get over to Madison."

Then Lieutenant Moody came back into the room. "Do you need anything?" he asked.

Sapp replied no.

Moody: You know there's one thing that . . . You were talking earlier about the knives and stuff—and you talked about a Klan knife. How'd you come about getting that? It was a collector's thing, wasn't it? What was it? Ku Klux Klan—what?

Sapp: It's a "for members only" knife.

Moody: How'd you come upon that?

(Sapp laughed softly.)

Moody: How'd you get that?

Sapp: I'm a member.

Moody: What attracted you to that group?

Sapp: Wasn't really attracted much to the group itself. It was just—it's not so much that they're against niggers—they're against anything that's not them.

Moody: How did you feel about that? Were you like that?

Sapp: Values ain't all that bad.

Moody: How do you feel about the mixing of the races.

Sapp (after a long silence): I don't believe it should be done.

Moody: How do you feel about blacks?

Sapp: You got blacks—and you got whites—and you got niggers.

Moody: But how do you feel about black people?

Sapp (finally answering): About the same as I feel about white people.

Moody: Have you gone with any light-skinned black girls?

Sapp: Light-skinned? (He leaned forward and put his elbows on the table.) No, there wasn't no light-skinned.

Moody: Did you ever know a light-skinned black woman that was on the street down there by the name of Gloria? She had a crack problem too.

Sapp: No. I'd remember light skin.

Moody: Let me ask you something. Has any black

woman you've dated screwed you over—ripped you off?

Sapp (shaking his head): No, that's one thing I can say. I've yet to have found a black one that would do that.

Moody: The woman that we talked about—the last portion that we talked about—in the woods? The last map we got out?

Sapp: Yeah. What about it?

Moody: She was a black girl named Gloria who was a prostitute with a crack problem. Are you sure there's nothing you can tell me about?

Sapp: No. I'm positive.

Moody: I mean, I was just thinking . . . You were talking about the Klan knife and all that stuff, you know. Are you going to have a problem with—everybody else involved in what you've done has been white—are you going to have a problem admitting that this was a black woman?

Sapp: No. As a matter of fact, it never even dawned on me—everybody being white.

Moody: All right. Okay, man, I just, I guess . . .

Sapp: Well, you know, you're wishing. You've got to . . .

Moody: No, I'm not wishing. Just making sure to check all—you know, cover all the bases.

Sapp: But I won't cave in even an inch on something that I didn't do.

Moody: And I don't want you to! I don't want you to!

Sapp: I mean, I know I may have used rebar, and God forbid if another one is. If there's somebody out there, then he's got a real problem.

Moody (agreeing): Yeah, he sure does. (Moody got up from the table and left the room.) Let me see what's going on.

(A minute later the detectives came back into the room.)

Graeber: Hey, Bill! (Graeber laid a picture on the table in front of Sapp.) Do you know this woman?

298 Carol J. Rothgeb

(Sapp leaned over the picture and looked at it and shook
    his head.)
Sapp: Never saw her. I ain't never seen her before.
Moody (heading out of the room again): That's who I
    was just talking to you about.
(Sapp studied the picture.)
Graeber: Pretty, isn't she?
(Sapp shrugged.)

Alone in the room again, Sapp put his head down on the
table, then laughed and sat back in the chair. Then he leaned
forward and started singing softly. Resting his head on his
arms, he tapped his fingers.

A few moments later, he sat back again: "I bet I could
catch that other fucker. Guarantee it.

"Well, it's over. All over. Finally. Now I can quit worrying."

He stood up, spread his arms, and sighed. Then he walked
over to the cabinet and leaned on it.

"Even though I'm gonna be in the pen for the rest of my
life, I'm the freest fucking man in the world!

"I been waiting on y'all for a long time."

26

[Sergeant Al Graeber] was a good man. . . . He was a good police officer. . . . He was like a little bulldog. . . . He was all cop. . . . Al's job was his life.

—Captain Steve Moody

John Balser, of course, had told the detectives many names, but Sapp was certainly not one of them.

The next day, on the long ride to take William Sapp back to Orient Correctional Institution, Lieutenant Moody asked him, "How are we going to get Balser to come up off of this?"

Sapp replied, "You go there. You tell him Bill said, 'It's okay to tell, Jimmy Boy.'"

Steve Moody and Steve Schumaker left Orient and drove to Southern Ohio Correctional Facility in Lucasville, where John Balser was incarcerated, to pay him a visit.

They had brought a photo array of mug shots with them and now laid them in front of Balser.

Lieutenant Moody asked John, "Is there anyone here who looks familiar?"

Moody watched John's eyes and saw that he was looking directly at the picture of William Sapp, but he pointed to a picture of another man with whom he had been in the Clark County Jail.

"This guy looks familiar," John said.

"Well, John, I bet he does," Moody answered. "You were up on the floor with him. We know who did it now, John. We know. We've got the DNA."

Incredibly, Balser looked at Lieutenant Moody, pointed to Sapp's picture, and said, "Mooo-nee, I'll bet you if you test—I'll bet you five hundred dollars if you test this guy's DNA—that'll be the guy."

Moody was disgusted. "John, I wouldn't bet you anything. You know, Jimmy Boy, that that's the guy. Why, out of all these years, didn't you tell us?"

John's answer was quite simple: " 'Cause he treated me like a brother."

Several days later the Crime Scene Unit was dispatched to the home of Wanda Marciszewski, on East Euclid Street, to do a "consent to search" for possible evidence from the Phree Morrow and Martha Leach homicides. The focus of the search was jewelry that the young girls might have been wearing on August 22, 1992.

Among the many miscellaneous items of jewelry that were confiscated, the investigators found the necklace that Martha had been wearing the night she was brutally murdered. The piece of jewelry that Sapp referred to when he said, "I know she (Wanda) stooped down and took the necklace off of one of them."

Sergeant Michael Haytas also followed up on Sapp's claim that he had hidden the rebar that he beat Helen Preston with in a "culvert" in Clark State Community College's parking lot. Even though it had been over four years since the attack, he found it exactly where Sapp said it would be.

It was approximately sixteen inches long and two inches in diameter. When viewed as the construction material that it was, it was little more than interesting, but the investigators had seen the chilling results of what it could do when used as a weapon.

On Monday, April 7, 1997, William K. Sapp was indicted by the grand jury on nine counts of aggravated murder, four counts of rape, four counts of kidnapping, three counts of tampering with evidence, three counts of abuse of a corpse, two counts of attempted aggravated murder, and two counts of arson.

At this point in time, the public had no idea how the investigators had tied Sapp to the murders. They couldn't figure out why it had taken almost five years. They didn't know that not one of the other participants had ever mentioned Sapp's name. They didn't know that Sapp had told detectives, six months earlier, about the attack on Helen Preston. They didn't know that Sapp had left his "signature." Or that his blood had been drawn and his DNA matched the semen found in Phree and Martha. And they didn't know that, only days earlier, he had confessed.

There was much controversy and criticism surrounding the fact that Clark County prosecutor Stephen Schumaker would not discuss the events leading to Sapp's arrest in the murders of Phree Morrow, Martha Leach, and Belinda Anderson. He was indeed aware that the public wanted, and maybe even needed, the answers to many questions. The murders of the two girls had haunted the city for many years.

The citizens of Springfield had not known that they had a serial killer in their midst. They didn't know until Sapp was indicted by the grand jury that there was a horrifying connection between the children's murders and the murder of Belinda Anderson and the attack on Helen Preston.

And Schumaker was not about to try the case in the media.

Since the first newspaper headline proclaiming that two girls' bodies had been found, I, Carol J. Rothgeb, had been saving the articles, thinking about writing a book. With the arrest of William K. Sapp, I knew that I would write a book—something I had talked about and dreamed about off and on for twenty-five years.

All eight of the defense attorneys in Clark County with certification to try death penalty cases had already represented other defendants charged with the murders and rapes of Phree Morrow and Martha Leach. Therefore, since the indictment against Sapp included death penalty specifications, they were not eligible to represent Sapp.

Late Friday afternoon, April 11, Judge Richard O'Neill filed documents with the clerk of courts stating that two Dayton attorneys, Dennis Lieberman and Sharon Ovington, would be representing William Sapp.

On April 18, 1997, William Sapp was arraigned in Judge O'Neill's courtroom. Several sheriff's deputies checked the courtroom thoroughly to make sure no one had managed to hide a weapon under the seats, or anywhere else in the courtroom, before the public was allowed to enter to watch the proceedings. The small gallery only accommodated about fifty people and it filled up quickly, mostly with members of the victims' families.

Debi Segrest from the Clark County Prosecutor's Office asked Belinda's brother, Richard Anderson, if he was "going to be good." He replied, "You know what I want to do." She said, "Yes, I know. But are you going to be good?"

Sapp's court-appointed attorney Dennis Lieberman informed the court that his client would remain mute on the plea.

Judge O'Neill entered a plea of not guilty for Sapp.

There, for the first time, I saw the man who was accused of these horrendous crimes. The fear finally had a face. The brutal, and frightening, reality was that he looked like a laborer or a factory worker—not a monster.

Sergeant Barry Eggers recalled the day that he and Steve Moody had been in William Sapp's apartment on Miller Street—the day Karen agreed to help with a composite drawing. He had gone back later—by himself—looking for Karen, to follow up on the information she had given them. Karen wasn't home, so Eggers was in the house alone with Sapp.

"I think about that—and not being ready—not knowing that there was this kind of person there and not being prepared for a confrontation. He could've probably had me very easily. If he'd have thought at that time that we were looking at him as a suspect—that whole meeting may have been different. But he obviously felt safe that we didn't have a clue," Eggers stated.

In November 1997 Dennis Lieberman and Sharon Ovington filed a motion to suppress the videotaped statements of William Sapp. They said they believed his statements to detectives were a result of coercion and they claimed that, at times, Sapp was "incoherent, mentally unstable, and incapable of recalling statements he had made moments before."

The attorneys also claimed that Sapp was "borderline mentally retarded" and not competent to waive his rights: "In the course of interrogation, the police made false promises to the defendant that he would receive the psychiatric care he desperately needs, in order to elicit statements from him."

According to the court documents, the defense attorneys also said that the detectives administered "mind-altering" drugs, such as Prozac, to Sapp during the interrogation.

Other court documents revealed that doctors prescribed the Prozac for Sapp. He was already on the medication before he was brought back to Springfield to be questioned.

The suppression hearing was scheduled for January 12, 1998, and the trial was to begin on January 26.

In December 1997 the defense attorneys sent a memo to the court saying that they could be prepared to try the case the following month, but a more thorough psychological exam of Sapp was necessary. The psychologist couldn't meet with Sapp again until January 16. The defense lawyers alleged that they could not represent Sapp fully without a proper psychological examination.

Judge O'Neill postponed the suppression hearing and the trial. They were rescheduled to start in April 1998.

In March of that year, the trial was once again postponed when Lieberman told the court that they were having difficulties scheduling the specialists necessary for tests and preparation for trial.

Judge O'Neill moved the trial date to July 13, but the suppression hearing would still be in April.

On March 2, 1998, Sergeant Al Graeber officially retired from the police department at 4:00 in the afternoon. Five hours later, at 9:00 that evening, he died. He had been on extended sick leave, suffering from lung cancer.

The previous month, the city commission had named February 10, 1998, "Al Graeber Day," in recognition of his many accomplishments during his twenty-eight-year career. That same day he was awarded the Distinguished Service Award from the Springfield Police Department.

It was the last of many awards he had received over the years.

His longtime friend and partner, Steve Moody, would later say, "I believe Al knew he was sick long before he was diagnosed. I believe that once we interviewed Bill Sapp and that came to fruition . . . I truly believe that that's what kept him going. It was aggressive lung cancer, but I think he fought it for a lot of years. He was always the first one here in the morning and, a lot of nights, the last one to leave."

Al Graeber left behind his wife, Sharon, and his four daughters.

The suppression hearing started on schedule on Tuesday, April 14, 1998.

Lieutenant Pat Sullivan of the Clark County Sheriff's Office testified about the execution of the search warrant of the house on Kinnane Street, on February 27, 1996, at 12:01 A.M. He said that Karen, William Sapp's wife, told them that he wasn't home.

But they found him hiding behind the furnace, handcuffed him, and read him his rights. Sapp did not invoke his right to counsel. Lieutenant Sullivan said that Sapp appeared normal that night. After they handcuffed him, they took him to the main part of the house and removed the cuffs. They sat him at a table, reread him his rights, and questioned him.

Jacksonville, Florida, detectives Hinson and Davis gave testimony pertaining to Sapp's admission of guilt in the homicide of the Florida "bag lady" and the attack on Helen Preston.

Robert Hinson testified that Sapp wanted to talk to the detectives and that Sapp understood everything when he waived his rights.

Lieberman asked each of the detectives if they were aware of Sapp's previous illegal drug use, including crack cocaine and LSD, and whether or not they were aware that Sapp had been prescribed Prozac and lithium for a mental illness, which could have had an effect on him.

Both detectives replied that they were unaware of his drug use.

Dr. James Gibfried, a psychiatrist, told the court that he examined Sapp and prescribed refills of lithium and Prozac, enough to last for his stay in Springfield (April 2 through April 4, 1997). He stated that the drugs would not have an effect on Sapp's understanding of his rights.

Over the next several days, sixteen hours of Sapp's chilling videotaped statement was played for the court. Periodically, throughout the playing of the tapes, Sapp wrote notes on a tablet and gave them to his attorney Sharon Ovington.

On the last day of the suppression hearing, Lieutenant Moody took the witness stand and testified that William K. Sapp had voluntarily waived his rights on at least three separate occasions, including when he was picked up from the prison and transported back to Springfield for questioning. Sapp never invoked his right to remain silent nor did he ask to have an attorney present.

Lieutenant Moody also told the court that Sapp did not appear to be intellectually impaired and that he believed Sapp understood his rights.

Judge Richard O'Neill denied the motion to suppress Sapp's videotaped confession.

During the playing of the videotapes, the people in the gallery—the victims' family members and myself—were allowed to sit in the jury box so that we could have a better view of the large screen.

The sound of his voice on the videotapes, with the light Southern accent acquired from living in Florida for ten years, is worth noting. Much of the time he spoke in soft, hushed, whispering tones. It is not at all difficult to imagine how threatening and menacing he must have sounded to his terrified victims as he raped, maimed, and killed.

During his statement to the detectives, there were times when he showed—or attempted to show—something akin to remorse. But in the courtroom—if he did, indeed, feel any guilt or remorse—there wasn't a hint of it exposed.

Remarkably, after hearing Sapp tell the detectives about the atrocious things his mother had done to him, some members of Belinda Anderson's close-knit family expressed a certain degree of compassion and understanding—for the child that he had been. However, this was not for the adult, who, we all agreed, had to take responsibility for his own actions.

27

I think that was part of the strategy. . . . I think he [Mr. Lieberman] very much wanted a female co-counsel. . . . That didn't work because of what Mr. Sapp did . . . and was. . . .

—Steve Schumaker

As Sapp's trial date grew near, more problems arose. In June 1998 Dennis Lieberman informed the court that he had received a report from a psychologist who concluded that William Sapp was incompetent to stand trial at that time.

Judge O'Neill ordered psychological evaluations for Sapp, and both sides were asked to submit names of psychologists or psychiatrists to the court.

When Sharon Ovington came into the courtroom before the proceedings began, she took a seat at the end of the defense table, as far away from William Sapp as possible. Sapp remained shackled throughout the proceeding.

Lieberman informed the judge that Sharon Ovington wished to withdraw from the case "due to matters best kept confidential."

When Schumaker suggested that Ovington address the court, she told Judge O'Neill that after "some communication" with Sapp, she could no longer zealously represent him. She did not reveal the nature of the communication.

It was very probable that Dennis Lieberman's strategy had been to have a female co-counsel sitting next to William Sapp and talking to William Sapp in order to send a message to the jury that, despite the horrific accusations against their client, he was not out to destroy all women. As it turned out, the jurors would never see a female within arm's reach of Sapp.

Although I was never able to learn exactly what they said, the "some communication" with Sapp that Ovington referred to was, not surprisingly, threatening letters.

Judge Richard O'Neill had no choice, except to put the trial on hold, until Sapp's competency was resolved one way or the other. Also, so that he could find another attorney outside of Clark County with the proper credentials to represent Sapp—and to give the new attorney time to get up to speed on the case.

The judge appointed another Dayton attorney, Gary Hruska, to replace Sharon Ovington.

Meanwhile, after being postponed twice, Jamie Turner's competency hearing finally took place in April 1998, almost two years after he was arrested the second time. Four psychologists testified during the proceedings. It was the opinion of two of the psychologists who testified in Judge O'Neill's courtroom that Jamie Turner was not competent to stand trial. It was the opinion of the other two that Jamie was competent to stand trial.

During the hearing Jamie periodically turned and scowled at the handful of people seated in the gallery.

Four months later, Judge O'Neill ruled that Jamie Turner was competent to stand trial for his involvement in the murders of Phree Morrow and Martha Leach.

On August 18, 1998, David Marciszewski, "bulked up" at 170 pounds and now wearing glasses, testified in front of the Clark County grand jury for the second time. He was, as usual, a mild-mannered and very nervous man.

Schumaker: There was another individual that we really weren't able to talk to you about last time by the name of Bill Sapp?

David: I knew his mom and his younger brother. I didn't know him very well, but I seen him around and stuff. (Sapp's mother had been David Marciszewski's neighbor years earlier, before he lived on Light Street.)

Schumaker: Now, what about Martha Leach and Phree Morrow? How do you know them, David?

David: I didn't know them.

Schumaker: Okay, did you meet them that night?

David: Oh, yeah.

Schumaker: Where did you first see them?

David: The bakery. I was the only—the one that went in and got the cookies for the two girls. And the girls was waiting outside. One of the guys had a van. We all went in the van and drove over [to Linden Avenue]. Well, the girls were forced in the van.

Schumaker: And who all was in the van?

David: Bill Sapp. And I was in the van too. Jamie Turner, Alex Boone, John Balser.

Schumaker: And how were they forced in the van, David?

David: Well, I didn't force any of them. I helped one in the van, the smallest one. I'm not sure how to put this. . . . They like were picked up and almost thrown in there.

Schumaker: Okay, and who did that?

David: Sapp. He did one. Sapp was driving, but see, he put them in the van first.

Schumaker: How did you happen to go to Linden Avenue?

David: Well, we was supposed to be—John and I were supposed to be doing a job for the landlord over there. That's where everything went down. . . . What I mean is, the two girls was molested up there on Linden Avenue. Sapp, he . . . I don't like the—use the word; that's why I said "molested." And I was trying to help one of the girls, but it didn't work out the way I wanted it.

(David testified that John Balser was "holding one of the girls" and that Jamie Turner "had the legs" of one of them.)

Schumaker: Okay, and what, if anything, was Mr. Boone doing?

David: Same thing. He was holding them by their leg. That's when Sapp, he molested them.

Schumaker: Okay. Having intercourse with one?

David: Right. I don't like . . . I don't like the word, I guess.

Schumaker: I understand. But you have to understand. We have to know exactly what's going on. At this point in time, he was putting . . . Was he putting his penis in her? In one of them?

David: Yeah. Then that's when the girls was . . . They started howling, screaming and stuff. We tried to shut them up, so they took them—put them in the van. Well, we all put them [back] in the van; we carry them.

Schumaker: As much as you can remember, did you carry one?

David: I tried to—I had a bad ankle.

Schumaker: Did you help somebody else carry one?

David: Yeah. John.

Schumaker: So you and John were carrying one. Who was carrying the other?

David: Alex and Jamie. We went over to behind Schuler's.

Schumaker: Now, at this point in time, are the girls awake?

David: Yeah, they were. They was . . . They were beaten—been beaten.

Schumaker: And who all, prior to going down to the pond, who had hit them?

David: Well, as you already know, I hit one of them. Not meaning to. I thought it was one of the guys trying to hurt me, so I come back like this on one. Everybody did.

Schumaker: Okay, now I don't want you to just, you know, lump everybody in. Who do you specifically remember hitting them?

David: Alex Boone hit one. Jamie Turner and Sapp.

Schumaker: Okay. So you get down to the pond behind Schuler's Bakery?

(David nodded yes.)

Schumaker: What do you remember first happening down at the pond? Just take your time.

David: I'm trying to. Well, the girls, I don't think they was—from Linden Avenue—I don't think they was, you know, alive or even awake.

Schumaker: They were unconscious? They'd been knocked out?

(David nodded again.)

David: Took the girls up there by Schuler's—behind Schuler's. Sapp, he was telling everybody that everybody was going to have to have something to do with it, see. I myself, I tried to pick up a rock, which was kind of heavy for me because I had a bad ankle like that, and dropped the rock to the side on one of the girls. I didn't actually drop it on her.

Schumaker: Now, has anybody else arrived there at that point?

David: Oh, we went to get . . . We went to get one of them.

Schumaker: And when did that happen?

David: That was after everything had gone down.

Schumaker: Was that when you first got to the pond or was that later?

David: Later.

Schumaker: So by the time you had gotten them, you had already dropped a rock, or had you dropped a rock yet before Wanda and Robby are there?

David: No, we dropped it afterward.

Schumaker: Okay, so you get to the pond and there's a lapse of time; then you go and get Wanda and Robby. What happened during that time period before you get Wanda and Robby? Anything?

David: I don't remember. I'm trying to remember all this, so . . .

Schumaker: I know, just take your time. All we want is the truth, the whole truth, and nothing but the truth. Why did you guys decide to go get Wanda?

David: I don't know who decided to do that. Anyway, in my point, that was stupid for going to get Wanda. We all went except for one person—Sapp. We went to get Wanda and then we took Wanda and Robby over to Schuler's Bakery—behind Schuler's, I should say. And before the rock was dropped on one of the girls, Wanda took their pulse. And she said that "you're going to have to kill them now."

Schumaker: Okay. That's important. Wanda said that?

David (nodding yes): Everybody was standing around at that time. Trying to figure out how to do stuff. So that's when I grabbed the rock and tried to . . . dropped the rock on the girl's head, and I couldn't do it because my ankle was sore that day. It really didn't hit the side of her face; it just landed on the side. I don't know. I'm saying I don't know if it hit her face or not. Everybody had something to do with the murder of the two girls. Jamie Turner, John Balser, Alex Boone, and all, you know, all the rest. Each one of them picked up a rock and a rock was laid—left on their heads.

Schumaker: Okay. Did everybody hit the girls or what are you telling me, David? I'm not clear on what you're saying here. You say everybody picked up the rock?

David: Yeah. Because Sapp, he turned around and said

everybody had to have something to do with it. So that's what happened.

Schumaker: Okay, and you guys were following his orders?

David: Well, I wasn't really—didn't want to even have nothing to do with it. But I was at the scene, so . . . pretty much.

Schumaker: Now, was anybody doing anything with the girls sexually at that point, at the pond? Anybody do anything as far as touching them or having intercourse with them or anything like that?

David: I don't remember. Huh-uh. I'm trying to help.

Schumaker: I don't want you to try to help. All I want you to do is try to remember—whatever's the truth.

David: That's what I'm saying. I'm trying to remember.

Schumaker: Okay. So do you actually see everybody drop a rock?

(David nodded yes.)

Schumaker: You're watching the whole time?

(David nodded yes again.)

Schumaker: What's Wanda doing at this point?

David: Like I said, she took the pulse and Wanda dropped a rock, tried to drop a rock on one of the girls.

Schumaker: Okay. Now are you and Wanda still married?

David: As far as I know, we are. I don't know for sure.

Schumaker: What happens after everybody drops a rock? What happens next?

David: That's when we started covering the girls up, 'cause the girls . . . It wouldn't have been right for us not to cover the girls up so the animals and the, you know, birds and stuff like that would have got ahold of them, the girls. You never know what will happen. Leaves, branches, and a couple skids. I covered up the one. I had help with the one skid putting it on top—John.

Schumaker: Do you know what Mr. Turner did?

David: He grabbed a skid too, because he fell in the water the same time John and I both fell in the water.

Schumaker: Three of you guys fell in the water?

David: I should say Jamie Turner jumped in the water. That's one thing I do not know—why he jumped in the water, but I know I got soaking wet and John got soaking wet.

Schumaker: What about Mr. Boone?

David: He was trying to help Jamie with the other skid.

Schumaker: What about Mr. Sapp?

David: Well, he was standing there at the time watching all this go down. Make sure everything was going down right.

Schumaker: Okay, he was standing in charge?

David: Yeah.

Schumaker: Now after they were covered up, where did you guys go?

David: Went back over to Lagonda. Oh, no, I take that back. We went to the Lion's Cage.

Schumaker: Wanda and Robby were with you?

David: Yeah, at that time they was with us. 'Cause they was down at the scene, so they had to be with us. We took the shorts—the two pairs of shorts and a bike and threw it down in the lion's pit.

Schumaker: Did everybody walk back there? Did some people stay in the van, or how did it work?

David: I think some stayed in the van.

Schumaker: Where do you go after that?

David: Over there on Lagonda. That's where we was sittin' in the backyard—me, Robby, Wanda, and John—everybody was. [Talkin'] about the murders and stuff—they said that nobody should be talkin'— shouldn't be talkin' about it.

Schumaker: And who was leading the discussion, or who was in charge at that point?

David: William.

Schumaker: Sapp?

David: Yeah.

Schumaker: Okay, did you ever see Sapp after that?

David: No.

Schumaker: Okay. Now, David, I got a real tough question for you, okay. I don't know if the officers talked to you about this or not. You know we have talked before and you never told us about Mr. Sapp. Now, why didn't you tell us about Mr. Sapp before?

David: Well, see, I was afraid of Sapp. 'Cause he threatened me—he threatened to kill me if I told. In fact, he threatened all of us.

Schumaker (to the jurors): Okay. Do any of you have any questions?

Grand juror: Did you go to Schuler's with the intent of meeting the two girls there? Had arrangements been made to meet them there?

David: Yeah, one of the guys made the arrangements to meet the girls there. That was Alex.

Grand juror: Okay. And then you went in and bought cookies?

David: Yeah, see, we wanted doughnuts anyway. At least I wanted doughnuts. I went in and bought the doughnuts and cookies. I bought the two cookies for the girls because I am a kind person. A lot of people could tell you that, that knew me. We was over on Light Street. And one of the guys, Alex, turned around and says, "Well, I got to go meet some girls." I thought he was talking about older . . . you know, that's what I thought he was talking about. But it didn't work that way. It was just little girls.

By this time I had been corresponding—mostly by telephone—with David Marciszewski for several months. He would not talk to me about the crimes at first. He was paranoid that someone at the prison might be listening in on our conversations. I tried to explain to him that he had already pleaded guilty, so it didn't really matter if they were listening. Finally, a couple of weeks after he testified in front of the grand jury, he admitted his role in the murders to me. He stressed to me that he did not rape the girls. That seemed to be his main concern. He did not want me to think that he had raped them.

When I started writing this book, on some level I also thought, perhaps, I could prove that the mentally retarded men were innocent, especially David. Instead, I became totally convinced of their guilt.

28

*The one thing we found out . . . we found that these in-
dividuals, mentally handicapped people . . . they're very
manipulative. . . . They're fiercely loyal to one another.*

—Captain Steve Moody

Later that day, after David Marciszewski testified in front
of the grand jury, indictments were returned against Wanda
Marciszewski and Alexander Boone in connection with the
deaths of Phree Morrow and Martha Leach.

Fifty-two-year-old Wanda, wife of David Marciszewski and
mother of John Balser, was indicted on seven charges, including
four counts of complicity to aggravated murder, one count of
tampering with evidence, and two counts of abuse of a corpse.

Alex Boone was indicted on fifteen charges, including four
counts of involuntary manslaughter, two counts of complicity
to rape, two counts of complicity to kidnapping, one count of
tampering with evidence, two counts of felonious assault, two
counts of abuse of a corpse, and two counts of gross sexual
imposition.

When Sergeant Barry Eggers went to arrest Wanda Marciszewski that afternoon at her home, he couldn't help but
think of Al Graeber: "Al should have been here. Because he
wanted her bad—out of all of them, he wanted her bad."

Wanda, wearing a white T-shirt with an imprint of a horse's
head surrounded by pink flowers on it, was handcuffed and
escorted to the Clark County Jail.

She was held on $500,000 bond.

Alex Boone, clad in a pale yellow sport shirt and jeans, turned himself in voluntarily and was released on his own recognizance, which stipulated that he was to return for trial and that he was not to leave Clark County. At the arraignment one of his attorneys entered a plea of not guilty on his behalf. (Boone was the only defendant in this case who did not have a court-appointed attorney.)

The following month, his lawyers, Richard Mayhall and William West, filed a motion to dismiss all charges, claiming that Boone had been denied his constitutional right to a speedy trial.

According to the document filed in common pleas court: "Rather than have the right to clear his name through a trial by jury, Boone has lived under a cloud of unresolved criminal charges for nearly as long as Bill Clinton has been President."

The attorneys also claimed that the death of Sergeant Al Graeber eliminated any possibility of a fair trial: "The most important evidence against Boone is a statement extracted from him by Graeber on March 2, 1993. No jury can evaluate the reliability of that statement or properly weigh its evidential value absent a thorough cross-examination of Graeber."

On Wednesday morning, November 4, 1998, in Judge Gerald Lorig's courtroom, Wanda Marciszewski—her long hair now almost completely gray—appeared in a dark blue jail uniform and pleaded guilty to involuntary manslaughter as the result of a plea bargain. All the other charges were dismissed.

When the judge asked if she wanted to enter a guilty plea, she replied, "I want to enter it so I can leave." She informed Judge Lorig that she could not read or write. She signed the plea agreement with an "X" in place of her name. She was then sentenced to twelve to twenty-five years in the Ohio State Reformatory for Women.

The fact was that Wanda could sign her name—and had done so many times when she had given statements to the detectives. However, she needed to be looking at her ID, which she didn't have with her in the courtroom, to see how to spell it.

That afternoon, in Judge Richard O'Neill's courtroom, Jamie Turner pleaded guilty to two counts of involuntary manslaughter (instead of aggravated murder) and three counts of rape. The remaining nine counts against him were dismissed.

Jamie had also been accused of raping three other children, a girl and two boys under the age of thirteen. He was granted immunity for those rapes, which occurred between 1991 and 1996, as part of the plea bargain.

The agreement saved Turner from possibly facing the death penalty.

Jamie Turner, twenty-seven, was sentenced to two life terms in prison; he would have to serve twenty years before being considered for parole.

The plea bargains required that Wanda and Jamie cooperate with the authorities and to testify in any future trials, if necessary.

Immediately after the plea agreement was "signed" in Judge Lorig's courtroom, Sergeant Eggers interviewed Wanda again. With very few exceptions, she repeated the same story she had told the investigators in the past:

John called her at Eleanor's and he said he had to talk with her. Wanda left Eleanor's and "ran to the scene." John said he was at a phone booth and she must "come quick." He told her to come to Main Street and he would meet her. Wanda went to the corner of Lagonda Avenue and Main Street and John was there. He told Wanda to quit running because she was out of breath. He said to come with him and they walked to the scene. She saw the girls "laying facedown." David and John said, "The white trash has to die."

John, David, Turner, and Boone were all there. Dave took a brick and hit Martha in the side of the head. Martha had not said anything, or even moved, to cause Dave to do this. Wanda believed David was making sure she was dead.

Phree grabbed Wanda by the pants leg and asked her to "get her daddy." John then picked up a big rock and hit Phree. He told Wanda that if she said anything, she and Willie would die.

A few minutes after John hit her, Wanda took Phree's pulse and "pronounced her dead." Wanda didn't take Martha's because she was sure she was already dead.

The scene was already a "mess" when she arrived. Their clothes were torn off and there was blood everywhere.

Wanda left because Eleanor was home alone. John told her to come straight home after work. About an hour later, Joe Jackson came to Eleanor's and picked her up and took her back to Light Street. It was beginning to get dark. Wanda got home on Light Street and sat down.

Boone drove John and David over in a truck to get Wanda. By then, it was completely dark outside. John and David came in the house and Boone stayed in the truck.

John and David said she had to come with them back "to the scene." John told her the girls had to be buried. She got in the truck and went to the scene a second time. Dave also told Wanda that if she ever spoke to the police, she and Willie would die. Wanda claimed she never saw Robby, Willie, or Sapp at the scene, but she said that John told her that Robby and Willie were hiding there. Wanda said it might be that she just couldn't remember seeing them there.

When they arrived back at the scene, John, David, and Boone began to cover the bodies with pallets and leaves and bushes. They laid flashlights on the ground so they could see what they were doing, covered the girls, and left. They went home and Wanda took a bath and went to bed.

After she did the laundry the next day, David told her that she had washed the blood out of his and John's clothes. Wanda claimed she didn't know there were bloody clothes in the laundry basket.

Wanda said when John was moving the flashlight, she saw a male in the bushes, but she claimed she couldn't see well enough to see who it was.

When she first arrived on the scene the first time she was there, she and Boone just stood next to each other and watched Dave and John hit the girls with the rocks.

She never saw Boone do anything to the girls except help cover them up, the second time she was there. She said that if Boone ever assaulted the girls, it had to have happened before John called her. John and Dave later told Wanda that the truck they used belonged to Boone.

Wanda told the detective that she felt that she had blocked a lot of this out of her mind and that may be why she couldn't remember some of the details. Wanda said she wanted to be put under hypnosis "to see if I can remember all of this."

Sergeant Eggers questioned Jamie Turner that afternoon in his jail cell. It was the very first time that Jamie related what happened with no hesitation, without acting—as he had in the past—like he couldn't think straight.

He told the detective that, other than himself, Alex Boone, John Balser, Wanda and David Marciszewski, and Bill Sapp were present behind the bakery when the girls were killed. It was the first time Jamie had said "Bill Sapp" to any of the investigators.

Jamie claimed that he had just met Sapp earlier that day at John's house. John told Jamie that he had two girls (women) set up. Jamie went home to eat and Bill came by later and picked him up, driving a Dodge van. They picked Alex up at his house and then picked John and David up at their house on Light Street.

Jamie was in the back of the van and couldn't see out to know where they were headed. Bill was driving and he stopped the van and told the girls to get in. They wouldn't, so Bill and John got out and made them get in. They cruised around for a while drinking beer.

Everything was fine until they got to [behind] the bakery. They got out and Bill started arguing with one of the girls. Bill told Jamie to come over to where he was and hold the girl while he "had sex" with her (Martha). John also came to help. Jamie said Dave and Alex stayed with the other girl (Phree). He didn't know what they were doing because he had his hands full holding Martha. Sapp hit her several times with a rock and killed her after "having sex."

David and Alex kept Phree over by the van during the assault on Martha, so Phree didn't know that Bill was raping Martha. When David asked Bill if he killed Martha, Bill said yes. Phree heard them and started screaming, so Bill put his hand over her mouth to keep her quiet.

They all took her over by the pond. Bill started "feeling her privates." Phree was fighting. Bill "had sex" with her while Jamie and Alex held her down. Jamie thought John and David were covering Martha's body up at that time, but he wasn't sure because he wasn't paying attention to them. Bill was on top of her (Phree) while Jamie held one leg and Alex held the other.

After raping her, Bill picked up a rock and hit her. Blood splattered on Jamie's shirt, so he jumped in the pond and tried to wash it off. Then John, Jamie, and David took turns hitting Phree with the same rock. Jamie said he never did see Alex hit any of the girls, but he (Alex) did "feel around" on Phree's breast.

Suddenly Wanda "appeared from nowhere." Wanda took one of the girls' pulse and, talking to Bill, said, "She is still alive, kill her." Bill picked up the same rock and hit her again. Jamie described the rock as being about 2½ to 3 feet across.

Jamie claimed he saw David Marciszewski "having sex" with one of the girls, but he wasn't sure which one. He also said that David hit Phree with a big rock.

Jamie said he held one of the girls—once again, he wasn't sure which one—while Bill killed the other.

He wasn't sure what Boone did, if anything. Jamie was busy holding the girl.

Bill "had sex" with both girls and killed one with a rock and a stick. She fought him a little, but not much.

Jamie, Bill, John, David, and Alex covered the girls with sticks, bushes, branches, and crates. Jamie thought Wanda had left the scene by then. Bill took Jamie home and dropped him off and then left to take Alex home. John and David stayed behind.

Jamie at no time ever saw Willie or Robby at the scene and claimed "to this day" he did not know them.

Wanda knew Bill was at the scene because she spoke to him several times. Jamie said Wanda lied when she said she didn't see Bill there.

While Sergeant Eggers did not believe that Jamie had told him everything, and some of what he told wasn't true, it was the first time he had ever talked to Jamie and Jamie was able to provide any information without having to stop and go "pee." That was Jamie's usual defense mechanism when the questioning got uncomfortable for him.

In a very general way, and remembering that Jamie's concept of "having sex" varied with each instance, this version of what happened on the night of August 22, 1992, is probably close to the truth. He, of course, omitted how Wanda got there and the fact that she was there twice. He also didn't mention going to the Lion's Cage—or Linden Avenue.

As Alexander Boone's trial date drew near, his attorneys filed a motion to suppress the statements that Alex had given to the detectives, claiming the police had coerced Boone into giving a false and involuntary confession.

After Judge Gerald Lorig denied the motion to dismiss and the motion to suppress, a plea bargain was reached. On February 25, 1999, Alexander Boone pleaded guilty to tampering with evidence and abuse of a corpse in Judge Lorig's large second-floor courtroom in Clark County Common Pleas Court. Thirteen other charges were dropped in exchange for his guilty plea: four counts of involuntary manslaughter, two counts of complicity to rape, two counts of complicity to kidnapping, two counts of felonious assault, one count of abuse of a corpse, and two counts of gross sexual imposition.

Steve Schumaker informed the judge that although Phree Morrow's parents agreed with the plea bargain, Martha Leach's family did not.

Boone, clad in a brown-and-gold-striped sweater, his hair shorter and not quite so unruly, was sentenced to two years in prison.

After the court proceeding, Alexander Boone still maintained his innocence, even though he had accepted the plea bargain. If he had gone to trial and had been found guilty of the other charges, he would have faced the possibility of a maximum sentence of life in prison.

There was no physical evidence against Boone. The prosecution would have had to rely almost completely on the statements of the other mentally impaired defendants. The prosecution believed that Boone had played a very small role in the deaths of Phree Morrow and Martha Leach, compared to the other defendants.

Although neither side was truly satisfied with the outcome, it seemed to be the best possible solution.

In April 1999, two years after William Sapp confessed to the three murders and the vicious attack on Helen Preston, he was brought to Springfield again so Judge O'Neill could decide whether or not he was competent to stand trial.

Since Sapp was considered to be a very high security risk, the county purchased a physical restraint belt (stun belt), at the cost of $700, for him to wear in the courtroom. He was the first defendant in Clark County to wear the device, which can send an electronic charge much like a stun gun. The receiver is worn on a thick, wide belt, weighs two pounds, and is placed over the left-side kidney area of the prisoner. One of the deputies would be in charge of the remote control, which can deliver a shock from as far away as three hundred feet.

During the six-hour hearing Sapp was also handcuffed and shackled, and there were four sheriff's deputies present in the courtroom. Courtroom observers were not allowed to sit in the front row of seats.

The defense called Dr. Kathleen Burch, a clinical psychologist, to the stand. Dr. Burch testified that she had interviewed Sapp four times and that she had interviewed Karen, Sapp's wife, once over the telephone.

Dr. Burch explained that she had administered several tests, including a personality test, an IQ test, and a projective psychological test. She claimed that Sapp was "borderline psychotic."

Preoccupied with sex. Poor impulse controls. Internalized emotions. Unable to bond. Grandiose. Watchful and on guard.

Sapp had told her, "I'm gonna bring down the town. I'm gonna wreak havoc on the world."

Sapp also told her that he had another personality named Bob. But Dr. Burch said that it was "not likely" that he had multiple personalities.

She testified that Sapp was unable to have a positive and working relationship with his lawyers: "He is intimidating and threatening because of mental disorders."

Severe disturbances in thought process. Severe borderline. Antisocial with schizophrenic tendencies. Severe mood disorder. Grandiose. Depressed.

When the defense attorney asked her if his condition was treatable, she replied that it would be "very difficult." She went on to say that Sapp had a lifelong belief that the world was punitive and "ungiving." He felt that he must be intimidating to have any personal power.

On cross-examination by Schumaker, Dr. Burch admitted that personality disorders were not mental illnesses. She also admitted that Sapp was "faking" multiple personality disorder. And that he was faking on his intelligence quotient test, which showed he had an IQ of about 74. According to her, the truth was probably closer to 85 or 90—low average.

She testified that Sapp had written letters to her that were threatening and intimidating.

Schumaker elicited the information that Sapp was not only preoccupied with sex, but was also preoccupied with homicidal rage toward women.

On redirect by the defense attorney, Dr. Burch told the court that Sapp signed his letters "Maggot."

He had an inability to cooperate. Wished to die. Get police to kill him.

On recross-examination by Schumaker, she admitted that Sapp had an "intense desire to be in control."

Dr. Burch quoted Sapp: "I'm going to die by a bullet during my trial."

The first witness for the prosecution was Dr. Nancy Schmidtgoessling, another psychologist. She testified that she had interviewed Sapp on January 22, 1999, for two hours and forty-five minutes. During the interview, for security reasons, he was in a "cagelike apparatus" (reminiscent of Hannibal Lecter in *The Silence of the Lambs*), and his hands were handcuffed behind his back.

She told the court that Sapp was "selectively cooperative."

He didn't care about his life and wanted to die. Somewhat irritable. Angry. Did not seem to be scared of the circumstances he was in.

Very quick-thinking. Alert. Bad dreams. Withholding. Evasive. Boasting. Competitive. Thought he could outsmart "them."

He declined to discuss charges. Bright man. Picked up on details. Calculating. Self-protective.

Dr. Schmidtgoessling went on to say that William Sapp was difficult to interview. In her seventeen years as a psychologist, he was one of the most difficult persons she had ever interviewed.

She said that he repeatedly referred to the death penalty and that he was very competitive toward the prosecutor. No symptoms of bipolar. Inconsistent. He said he lied.

Seeing other people scared or uncomfortable was important to him. He was capable of working with lawyers if he chose to. He needed to be in control. He was competent.

She quoted Sapp: "I know stuff they don't know. I'm not going to tell them. Let's see if they can figure it out.

"I'm in control of myself. I'm not mentally ill.

"I've been involved in so many murders—I won't even tell you because it would make you vomit."

Dr. Otto Kausch, a forensic psychiatrist, was the next witness for the prosecution. He also told the court that Sapp had the ability to cooperate with his lawyers if he chose to do so.

He testified that Sapp was not suicidal despite the fact that he had cut his wrists when he was seven years old.

Sapp felt he was not worthwhile. Would force police to shoot him. His lifelong dream: to sit in the electric chair. Destiny to fulfill: going to the electric chair.

Dr. Kausch: "I think he probably would like to kill other people."

The following Monday, April 26, 1999, Judge Richard O'Neill ruled that William K. Sapp was competent to stand trial for his alleged crimes.

29

*Our pastor was with us throughout the trial. I mean, he
actually sat in the courtroom and he could feel it . . .
that this man was full of nothing but evil. . . .*

—Karlene Anderson,
Belinda Anderson's sister-in-law

It took a full week to seat the jury in the case of the *State
of Ohio* v. *William K. Sapp*. On the morning of September 22,
1999, the six women and six men who were chosen to decide
Sapp's degree of guilt (his lawyers would never claim he
was innocent) were taken on a jury view of eleven of the sites
related to the crimes.

That afternoon, before opening statements began, common
pleas court judge Richard O'Neill issued the rules for the spectators in his third-floor courtroom. There was to be total silence,
absolutely no whispering. No visitor was allowed to walk
directly behind the defendant. Once visitors were in the courtroom, they could leave anytime they wanted, but they could
only return during the pause between witnesses or during a
break. And there was to be no loitering on the third floor.

"It is the hope of the attorneys and the court that this matter can proceed to its conclusion without any interrupting
events," Judge O'Neill stated.

In his opening statement Schumaker told the jury that during Sapp's taped statement on April 2, 1997, he told Sergeant
Steve Moody and Detective Al Graeber that "all the bitches
have to die."

Schumaker then picked up individual eight-by-ten pictures of Phree Morrow, Martha Leach, and Belinda Anderson and showed them to the jury: "This is who Sapp was talking about."

He also told the jury that even though Helen Preston had survived the attack by Sapp, he had raped her and left her for dead, with her skull depressed and her throat cut.

He listed the mistakes that Sapp had made: He struck close to home. He did not bury Belinda deep enough. He left his semen in Phree and Martha. He left his "signature" by cutting Phree's shorts and Helen's pants in a very distinctive manner. Helen's cut pants alerted the investigators.

Schumaker informed the jury that they would observe Sapp, on fourteen hours of videotape, attempt to rationalize his actions during his confession to detectives.

When Dennis Lieberman, Sapp's defense attorney, rose to make his opening statement, he acknowledged his client, Bill. This was no doubt an effort to try to humanize the monster that the jury would hear about during the trial.

Lieberman claimed that Bill had been tortured and raped by his mother 2,246 times. This, of course, was the number Detective T. C. Davis from Jacksonville, Florida, had arrived at during the interrogation of Sapp on September 26, 1996.

He said that since Bill's birth on March 22, 1962, he had been raped, tortured, burned, and cut. He also alleged that Bill's biological mother had poured hot candle wax on his genitals and that she forced him to have oral sex with her and she with him.

He told the jury that Sapp's mother had set his younger brother on fire and that she had watched, and done nothing, as another brother drowned.

He claimed that these childhood experiences created a rage in Sapp: "It's a rage so deep that he reacts in the way that he did. Unlike the prosecutor's characterization of his acts."

Lieberman claimed that when Sapp was seventeen, his stepmother bought him a bus ticket and told him, "Get out of town!"

According to the defense attorney, perhaps one of the detectives had said, "All women deserve to die."

He went on to say that his client was not capable of premeditation. He also said that the detectives promised Sapp psychological help and asked leading questions during the interview.

William Sapp sat and listened, scowling, with his arms folded across his bright red-and-black-plaid shirt, sporting a Fu Manchu mustache and a goatee.

After the opening statements Judge O'Neill called a fifteen-minute break because Sapp had become increasingly agitated while his attorney related to the jury the horrible things his mother had allegedly done to him. As they were leaving the courtroom, Sapp told a deputy, "Doesn't matter what I want or what I like."

The first witness for the prosecution was Martha Leach's mother, Jettie Willoughby Whitt (who had since married Tim Whitt), an attractive woman with long blond hair. When she was asked to identify the picture of her daughter, she covered her face with her hands and wept.

After regaining her composure, she also identified the picture of Phree Morrow. She testified that the last time she saw the girls alive was when they left to go to the bakery, between 4:30 and 5:00 on the afternoon of August 22, 1992. She said that it possibly could have been as late as 5:30.

Jettie told the jury about the search that night for Martha and Phree. She said that a police officer stopped them about midnight near the Lion's Cage and asked them why they were there.

She also testified that she did not know David Marciszewski. Or John Balser. Or Jamie Turner. Or Alex Boone. And that she did not know William Sapp.

The prosecution's second witness was Susan Palmer, Phree Morrow's mother, a "streetwise" brunette whose features had hardened over the years. She unsuccessfully fought back tears as she identified the pictures of Phree and Martha, after which she, too, needed a few moments to regain her composure.

She said that she had sent Phree to get her some cigarettes around noon and that the last time she saw Phree and Martha alive was about 3:00 in the afternoon when she and the others left to go swimming.

She testified that she did know David Marciszewski, but only as a casual acquaintance. And that she did know Wanda Marciszewski and John Balser because they had lived next door to her when she lived on Light Street. She did not know Jamie Turner. Or Alex Boone. Or William Sapp.

Not surprisingly, the defense had no questions for these two brokenhearted witnesses.

There was no reason for the prosecutor to ask about J. R. Lilly, Sapp's brother, since he was not involved, but Susan had known him for about eight years. She made the comment to me, outside the courtroom, "J.R. would do anything for you."

Jettie shared with me, also outside the courtroom, that she knew Martha was dead when she didn't come home because "she wouldn't do that."

The next witness was nineteen-year-old Keith Casey, a student at the University of Toledo. He testified that on Sunday, August 23, 1992, his family went to a church picnic at Saint Bernard Catholic Church on Lagonda Avenue. He was twelve years old at the time. He and his younger brother rode their bikes to the pond and there they found the bodies of two young girls. They rode their bikes back to the picnic, but they were unable to find their father.

Keith and another boy, Jay Martina, rode their bikes back to that area and that's when they saw the fire truck and told the firemen. Keith and Jay went with the firemen to the pond and then went back to the church.

On cross-examination, Keith stated that he saw no one else around the bodies.

On the second day of the trial, Clark County deputy coroner Dr. Robert Stewart told the jury that Phree Morrow had suffered at least eight blows and Martha Leach had suffered at least seven blows. Both girls died from blunt trauma, mainly to the head: "We're talking about the type of force where you would free-fall from a second-floor window—from that height onto a concrete surface."

He couldn't determine if the assault on the girls was by more than one person, but he said they could have been injured by more than one weapon. The evidence showed, including the semen, that the girls were sexually molested. No alcohol or drugs were found in their systems.

The next prosecution witness, Marcy Lavelle, testified that at about 4:00 P.M. on the day in question, while driving close to the bakery on East Main Street, she and a friend had seen two little girls lean a bicycle against a newspaper stand and go into Schuler's. The girls were wearing shorts and summer tops.

She also observed a "gentleman" standing on the sidewalk and another man coming out of the bakery. There was a van parked across the street—a 1970s trashy, glass "paddy wagon" type.

She and her friend had planned to stop at Schuler's, but her friend said, "Never mind. That guy really looks creepy."

On further questioning she said the bike she had seen was small and was lavender or purple. She then identified the bicycle in the courtroom as being the one she had seen.

There was also a stipulation that she had previously identified David Marciszewski and John Balser as the two men she had seen outside the bakery.

Two witnesses gave testimony relating to the discovery of Belinda Anderson's body.

Molly Warner lived on South Fountain Avenue. She testified that Belinda Anderson had been her neighbor when she lived on East Liberty Street and she identified the picture of Belinda.

She related to the jury that on July 8, 1995, she had lived in the house on South Fountain Avenue for about a year and that the house had been vacant for about five years before that. While cleaning out the garage, she picked a door up from the floor and saw a tennis shoe.

Since then, they had the garage torn down. She said she couldn't stand to look at it anymore.

She said that she did not know William Sapp—except in the news.

Robert Warner told the jurors that he also saw the tennis shoe—toes down, heel up. He identified the picture of Belinda and said that she used to groom their dog when they lived across the street from her on East Liberty Street.

He also told the jury that a knife had been found on the sanctuary roof of the First Baptist Church (located on the corner of South Fountain Avenue and Miller Street) on the side toward Miller Street. When the roof was torn off, the knife went in with the debris.

On cross-examination Warner said that he had seen the knife.

During one of the breaks in the proceedings, Jettie sympathized with Christine Anderson, Belinda's mother, about not knowing for almost two years. Christine said, "If Molly hadn't decided to clean out the garage, Belinda would still be there."

The prosecution called Robby Detwiler, now twenty-one years old, to the stand on Friday. He said that he did know Wanda Marciszewski; she was his aunt. And David Marciszewski was her husband. And that John Balser was his cousin. And that Willie Jackson, now nineteen years old, was also his cousin. He said he knew Jamie Turner because he used to come over to his aunt's house on Light Street.

Robby timidly admitted that he had told many different stories because he "didn't want to face reality."

He said, "I told a lot of lies. I don't remember the lies."

He testified that he had left [the house on Light Street]

with Wanda, John, David, Willie, and Boone in an old black van with windows, to go to the crime scene.

He identified William Sapp and said that Sapp was with one of the girls in front of the pond when they got there. John, David, Jamie, and Sapp were "feeling the girls and rubbing them." He was about ten feet away and Willie was in the parking lot.

Embarrassed, he told the jury that Sapp grabbed his hand and put them on the girls' "privates."

Wanda told them to kill the girls. The girls were unconscious and he didn't hear them say anything. Balser hit one of the girls with a rock. Marciszewski threw a smaller rock off to the side of one of the girls' heads.

He then saw Sapp with a rock in his hands. When Sapp lifted the large rock over his head, Robby turned away.

Robby admitted that he helped carry the crates.

Sapp told Willie and Robby he would kill them if they told. "He just killed two girls. What would you think?"

They left in the van and went back to Light Street. Robby said that he listened to the radio and he called his dad the next day and went home. He didn't tell anyone about Sapp because of the threats.

"I tried to pretend like it never happened."

On cross-examination Robby testified that he had talked to the police eight or nine times and that he had given testimony to the grand jury twice.

When Officer Chuck Schreiber of the Crime Scene/Evidence Collection Unit took the stand, he testified that he was in his twenty-fourth year on the police force. He had videotaped the crime scne in and around the garage where Belinda Anderson's body had been found. The videotape of Belinda's remains being carefully excavated from the shallow grave was played for the jury.

The next witness was Dr. Lee Lehman, a forensic pathologist with the Montgomery County Coroner's Office. He was deemed by the court to be an expert witness. He testified that

Belinda Anderson's body weighed only sixty pounds when it was found. She had on tennis shoes, a purple top, a bra, and no pants. She had a tattoo of a shooting star on her right ankle and one of a cross on her left ankle.

He told the jury that Belinda's cheekbone and the bone under her eye were fractured. The back of her head had an H-shaped laceration all the way through her scalp. There was a 1½-inch bruise on the right side of her chin.

Her voice box was injured and she had broken cartilage in her neck and her neck was also bruised. He testified that she was still alive when these injuries occurred.

He went on to say that she had suffered a broken rib and that she had a two-inch bruise on her right side by her breast.

The cause of death was multiple traumas to her head and neck, a combination of blows. All of the wounds were inflicted upon her before her death except for the broken rib.

There was no semen sample possible because of decomposition. The toxicology tests showed that there was a Valium-type medicine and cocaine in her system.

Deborah Anderson, Belinda's sister, testified that Belinda was wearing a short-sleeved purple silk top and shorts and sweatpants the last time she saw her.

When the defense attorney cross-examined her, he asked: "Did you tell Belinda not to bring crack into your house?"

Deborah replied: "I thought she was getting back into it."

The last two witnesses of the day testified about the morning they found Helen Preston near death in the Clark State parking lot by the YMCA.

Jim Wilson* told the jury that when he first saw Helen on December 8, 1993, "I thought she got hit by a train." From a distance she "looked like a clown." Then he realized that her throat had been "sliced from ear to ear." He indicated to the jurors, using his thumb and index finger, that the wound to her neck was about 1½-inches wide.

She had rocks embedded in her face, which was swollen black and blue. "One eye stayed wide open."

He said that she had on a shirt, but no pants, and she smelled like urine.

She was sitting on the curb in the parking lot, and when he approached her, she said, "Help me." He asked if she had been raped and she nodded her head yes.

He found out later that he had met Helen on a couple of occasions.

"It was like something you'd seen from a movie. It was hard to recognize her at first. She was beat so bad."

Corey Heaton* testified that he saw Helen sitting on an "island" in Clark State's parking lot and that she had been "beat to a pulp."

When the trial resumed on Monday, September 27, 1999, Helen Preston limped to the witness stand. The jurors were shown photographs depicting the injuries to her head and face and the stab wound to her abdomen.

Helen told the jury: "It doesn't look like me."

Schumaker asked her to step down and stand in front of the jury box and lift her head, so the jury could see the dreadful five-inch scar across her throat.

She testified that she was thirty-eight years old and lived on South Limestone Street at the time of the attack. She remembered leaving John's Bar after having a fight with her boyfriend. The next thing she remembered was crawling to the railroad tracks near the YMCA. She also remembered waking up in the hospital and seeing some of her toes missing.

As Helen testified, she cautiously glanced at William Sapp from time to time, but she said she had no memory of the person who assaulted her.

It was easy to see that Helen had once been a pretty woman. Sadly, even though plastic surgery had done wonders, it was also easy to see that she would always be disfigured. Each and every time she looked in the mirror—and each and every time she caught someone staring at her—she would be reminded. During his confession Sapp had said "There's somebody out there walking around right now, with my heart signature on them. . . ."

Sergeant Barry Eggers testified that although Helen Preston was badly beaten, she kept trying to tell him details about her attacker by holding her hands as if looking through binoculars. He believed she was trying to tell him that the person who assaulted her wore glasses.

Ernest Whitehead, one of the paramedics who responded to the call for help that morning, told the jurors that it was difficult to tell what race Helen was because of her condition: "Her body was too black and blue. Her face was extremely covered with blood. She had numerous cuts. She was completely disfigured. Her body was beaten upon to the point where we couldn't tell, from any observations we made, what color she was."

He also said the wound to her throat was so severe he could see her trachea.

The next witness was Dr. William O. Smith, a neurological surgeon, who was also deemed to be an expert witness. He testified that Helen Preston was brought to the emergency room of Community Hospital in the late morning of December 8, 1993. She had been exposed to freezing temperatures for several hours. The worst injuries were to her head and face. She had an opened and depressed skull fracture behind her right ear, which caused pressure on the brain. He lifted pieces of bone out of the fracture and put them back.

Dr. Smith told the jurors that Helen's cheekbones were so badly fractured that they were "free floating"—no longer connected. Her jawbone had multiple fractures and she had a five-inch cut across her throat. She also had a deep wound at the base of her nose.

He also stated that she had a stab wound in her upper abdomen. She had gangrene from frostbite; her toes were turning black. Her face had to be reconstructed and they had to remove some of her toes.

The doctor testified that Helen had been close to death and

the hypothermia probably saved her life. He called her recovery "almost miraculous."

He went on to say that her memory of the attack was "nonexistent." The worse the trauma and the longer someone is unconscious, the worse the amnesia.

Officer Schreiber took the stand again, this time to testify regarding Helen Preston. He described the scene where Helen was found as a grassy island in the parking lot near a loading dock. Among the items collected at the crime scene: a cigarette butt, a pair of socks, a piece of paper, broken cigarettes, Helen's cut-up jeans, white tennis shoes, broken dentures, broken bricks, and leaves and twigs with blood on them. They also took swabs of blood from underneath the nearby loading dock.

In February 1998 he and Sergeant Michael Haytas watched the videotapes of Sapp's confession. As a result, they were able to locate the weapon used on Helen: a piece of steel cable (rebar), which was found in a catch basin in the Clark State parking lot.

A sheriff's deputy who had been on duty on the fifth floor of the jail on April 17, 1997, testified about a conversation he had overheard between Sapp and another inmate, Tony Hanover*.

Because of Sapp's leg shackles, Hanover was heard to say, "You must be somebody important."

Sapp replied, "Yeah, I guess."

The deputy also testified that Sapp said, "I'm going to make national news."

Hanover asked Sapp: "What'd you do?"

Sapp answered, "Killed several people, but mostly it's about two little girls."

On cross-examination the deputy admitted that he didn't write a memo regarding what he had overheard until July 2, 1998, over a year later.

At the end of the day, there was a stipulation that DNA tests conducted by the FBI revealed Sapp's DNA matched the semen that was recovered from the bodies of Martha Leach and Phree Morrow.

On Tuesday, a former inmate of the Clark County Jail, Clint Sothard*, testified that the previous summer he had been in jail on a probation violation. He told the jurors that during his incarceration he was housed across from Sapp on the fifth floor of the jail.

According to Sothard, Sapp talked to him about the assault on Helen Preston and the murders of Phree Morrow, Martha Leach, and Belinda Anderson, and he also told him that whenever he got the urge to kill someone, he acted on it.

When the prosecutor asked Sothard why he had come forward, he explained: "I've got a daughter who just turned thirteen. If he did to my daughter what he did to those girls, there wouldn't be enough room in this world for both of us."

He also told the jury that he heard Sapp talking to himself late at night.

When Mr. Lieberman cross-examined him, Sothard admitted that he "didn't like it" when he was written up because Sapp reported to the jailers that he had medication in his cell.

Detective Robert Hinson of Jacksonville, Florida, told the jury that Sapp had mentioned an attack on a Springfield woman to him. Sapp blamed it on an alter ego named Bob. However, they were unsuccessful when they tried to get Bob to come out and talk to them.

He went on to say that he believed Sapp needed psychological help.

When the questioning turned briefly to Sapp's abuse as a child, William Sapp became angry and patted the stun belt—hidden from view under his shirt—and asked the deputy if it was activated. He was assured that it was.

On his way out of the courtroom, Sapp was heard to say, "Why don't they leave sleeping dogs lie?"

30

*I was a good mother to Martha. I've never done drugs.
. . . I don't drink. . . . If Susie wanted to drink, that was
her business. . . . Didn't give him the right to kill Phree.*

—Jettie Willoughby Whitt

On Wednesday, day six of the trial, Schumaker called Lieutenant Steve Moody to the witness stand. Through his testimony, the videotapes of Sapp's confession were introduced into evidence and played for the jurors.

Sapp's only response to seeing himself on the large screen was to become agitated when his childhood was being discussed and to turn away when he saw himself crying. Although, most of the time, he looked bored or half asleep, he watched with great interest when the questioning turned to how he had cut the pants and left his "signature."

It took almost five days to view all of the videotapes.

At the conclusion, the following Tuesday afternoon, Lieutenant Moody testified that Sapp told him, "I had to make sure you had your act together."

Sapp also told Moody: "Tell Jimmy Boy (John Balser) it's okay to tell."

When Schumaker questioned Lieutenant Moody about the techniques used in the interview of Sapp, he explained to the jurors that the cabinet was "to keep Sapp off balance." He and Sergeant Graeber talked about Sapp's past with his mother "to get him talking again."

The detectives referred to Phree and Martha as "young women" so Sapp wouldn't think of them as children.

Sapp, wearing a pale blue-and-white-plaid shirt, listened intently at the defense table, now sporting a Hitler-style mustache.

The next day, on cross-examination, Lieberman, referring to the other defendants, their sentences, and plea bargains, asked Lieutenant Moody: "You wouldn't be a party to these pleas if you didn't believe these people were guilty, would you?"

Lieutenant Moody replied that he would not.

The defense attorney seized the opportunity to introduce a chart that he had prepared showing what each of the other defendants had previously admitted to:

David Marciszewski:
1.   Hit w/hand and board (Martha).
2.   Had sex w/her (Martha).
3.   Covered girls (Martha).
4.   Threatened to kill (Martha).
5.   Hit Martha's head w/rock.
6.   Hid evidence.
7.   Dropped rocks on heads.
8.   Left big rock on Phree's head.

Wanda Marciszewski:
1.   Took pulse—had none.
2.   "Kill them."
3.   Phree pulse and none on Martha.
4.   Hid evidence.

John Balser:
1.   Hit girls in head w/rocks.
2.   Sex w/both girls.
3.   Hid evidence.
4.   Covered girls.
5.   Hit girls w/hand and a limb.

Jamie Turner:
1.   Jamie raped.
2.   Hit girl.
3.   Hid evidence.
4.   Hit girl w/hand and boards.
5.   Hid evidence.
6.   Covered girls up.
7.   Dropped rock on one.
8.   Hit w/pipe.

Alex Boone:
1.   Hid evidence.

Lieberman included Robby Detwiler on his chart, even though Robby had never been charged:

1.   Touched girls.
2.   Covered girls.

Lieberman asked whether or not they had advised Sapp that he was being videotaped. Lieutenant Moody replied that it wasn't necessary.

On redirect Lieutenant Moody told the jury that the plea bargains were made in an attempt to find the semen donor. William Sapp was the seventy-fifth person on whom DNA tests were conducted in relationship to this investigation.

He testified that the concept of "intercourse" was different with each one of the other perpetrators.

Steve Moody told the jury that on April 4, 1997, the day after they concluded their interview with Sapp, he went to see John Balser and told him, "Jimmy Boy, he said it was okay to tell the truth."

The prosecution rested its case.

At all times, I avoided making eye contact with William Sapp, but during a break in the proceedings, I came face-to-face with him when the old courthouse's single, excruciatingly slow, elevator stopped and the doors opened as I waited to enter. There he stood, facing me, flanked by a deputy on each side. As I quickly looked away, I caught a glimpse of the emptiness—of the nothingness—in his eyes.

William K. Sapp did not take the stand. The only "testimony" the jury heard from him was his videotaped confession. In fact, the defense did not call any witnesses. They did, however, introduce into evidence an exhibit of records from Children's Services pertaining to Sapp.

There was no rebuttal.

Dennis Lieberman asked the court for a directed acquittal on all counts. Judge O'Neill denied his request. The defense attorney then asked the court for a directed verdict on three counts of abuse of a corpse and one count of rape. He claimed there was no evidence that Belinda Anderson had been raped.

Assistant prosecutor Steve Collins reminded the court of the testimony from the former jail inmate who said that Sapp had admitted to him that he raped Belinda before he killed her. Collins also reminded the court that Belinda was naked from the waist down when her body was found.

Judge O'Neill ruled that there was sufficient evidence to allow the jury to determine if Sapp was guilty or not of the rape charge and the three counts of abuse of a corpse.

Closing arguments were then scheduled for the next day.

William Sapp appeared some days in the courtroom wearing a striped shirt and other days he appeared wearing a plaid shirt, but he continued to change his appearance. Now clean shaven, he listened vigilantly during the closing arguments.

Schumaker began what would become a very passionate statement by reminding the jury of the specifications: purposeful killing of multiple victims, rape—principal offender, and kidnapping—principal offender. Rape with force—victims under age thirteen.

Phree's shorts were Sapp's "signature." He cut the shorts

before she died—prior to the deathblows. Another child found the bodies, a child the same age as Phree and Martha.

He showed the pictures of the girls' bodies to the jury. "This is staging—posing—not rage. This is a perverse individual getting his kicks. He was meticulous. Their heads were in holes.

"He was playing a game—a murderous game."

They took the bike and the shorts to the Lion's Cage. The shorts were wrapped in a brick. Meticulous planning—meticulous getting rid of evidence. It showed planning. It showed control.

After the murders they met at the Lagonda Avenue house. A pair of panties was found in the cistern.

"Now what does Dr. Stewart—the forensic pathologist—tell us? Phree Morrow—at least four blows to her head—one to the lip—one to the neck—one to one hand—one to the other hand—two to the shoulder—contusions of the thigh—lacerations. Hemorrhages to the wounds—she was alive. These are not postmortem. She is alive when all of these wounds are struck and all of these blows contributed and are a cause of her death.

"Martha Leach—two blows to the back of the head—one blow to the right front—two to the shoulders—one to the ribs—abrasions—multiple trauma. Eggshell fracture of the skull.

"The force required on both: at least an unrestricted second-story window fall straight down on concrete.

"The question that haunted law enforcement for years: Who put the semen in those girls? They didn't have that answer. When they were prosecuting those other individuals, they did not have that answer. Well, we got that answer and we've presented it to you. The DNA stipulation—no contest."

Schumaker pointed to Sapp: "It's his semen in those girls! This man chooses victims of opportunity and who, for some reason, are vulnerable."

He reminded the jurors of Robby's testimony: "The individual who did not leave? That man! You want to talk about sudden rage? He's still there. He's still there when the others come back. And what is he doing? He is molesting the girls. He is still—after all that he has done—having his fun. Rage? Or somebody who is enjoying—perversely—what he is doing?

"The scene talks to you, ladies and gentlemen.

"That's not sudden rage! That's a perverse individual enjoying the act of rape—enjoying the act of murder. Because we know that after that point in time other blows were struck to those girls. When that man participates in those last blows—and Robby sees him with the rock over his head and turns away—he has a significant period of additional time to think about what he was going to do—and do it. That is called prior calculation and design.

"Robby didn't tell us the truth for a long time. He was a scared kid. It was tough for Robby to admit what he did. I think you could see that."

Schumaker referred to Belinda Anderson: "There wasn't anyone else at this scene to blame anything on. The Valium and cocaine in her system shows she had a weakness, a vulnerability."

Close proximity. Relive crimes. Secluded area where he's comfortable. Areas where he's in control. Not sudden rage. Not coincidence. He got trash bags and went back and dug the shallow grave.

They thought Helen Preston had been hit by a train. When asked if she had been raped, she nodded yes.

"That is called an 'excited utterance.'"

Helen lost her watch and Sapp said he threw a watch away. It was a game at first: "Bob did it."

Schumaker held up Helen's stiff, blood-soaked pants for the jury to see and then laid them aside: "He took her back to that dock—he thought she was dead—and shoved her under that dock. And by all accounts, she should have been dead. But she crawled out of there. She was discovered. And the officers discovered some chilling evidence—those pants."

Helen was sitting on her cut-up pants. It took Sapp seven to twelve minutes to cut them.

"He knows what he's going to do. He's done it before."

Helen indicated glasses. The pants were not disposed of because he was interrupted. "Something happened to interrupt him—that caused him to run from the scene before he had done everything he would normally do. In fact, this time—unlike the others—he ran so quickly, he disposed of one of his prize knives on the church roof. He was interrupted. Someone was in the area."

He told Lieutenant Moody and Sergeant Graeber where the weapon was hidden that he used on Helen. The prosecutor gripped the rebar firmly in his right hand: "This is what he clubbed the face of Helen Preston with. This is what he shattered virtually every bone in her face with. He completely shattered the orbital floor, which caused the entire side of her face to droop down."

Sapp said he did not come inside Helen, but he left his "signature."

"Uh-oh. What'll I do?"

"He was haunted so bad, he went out and killed again!"

Phree said, "Are you going to kill us or just fuck us?" This showed prior calculation.

"Let's tie in Mom! Let's blame Mom!" And he tried to throw the rock to the other side of the world.

Phree told him, "You'll be sorry!" His response was, "Like hell I will!" Sapp told the others, "Don't return to the crime scene." Sapp was in control.

Schumaker quoted Sapp talking about Belinda: "Blond. Pretty face. Pretty body." And then later, "How many times do you have to hit someone before they don't get back up?"

And "Like opening up a Christmas present!"

He was like a child at Christmas. Prior calculation. Not a coincidence. Isolated areas. Weakened people: "It's about a man looking at victims of opportunity as Christmas presents—to rape and kill for his pleasure.

"That's why—when you look at all these counts, whether they charge prior calculation, whether they charge in the course of a rape, whether they charge in the course of kidnapping—the man's guilty.

"Thank you very much, ladies and gentlemen."

Dennis Lieberman gave the closing argument for the defense.

"I'm convinced you'll not find him guilty of charges that carry the death specifications. I'm convinced you'll find him guilty, but not of those.

"This is not about innocence. Find him guilty of the ones he did and not guilty on the ones he didn't."

He told the jury they could find him guilty of murder, or manslaughter, or involuntary manslaughter. The principal offender was the person who personally performed each act. There can be more than one. Bill Sapp was not the principal offender, but he was certainly guilty of rape of two girls under thirteen.

He referred to the "defense board": "If this is true, David Marciszewski is the principal offender."

There was no evidence Belinda was raped—consensual sex.

Prior calculation? Rocks were there. Out of control.

Lieberman asked the jurors, "Who are you? We are what our parents made us."

Child abuse. Foster families: "What if that excuse is true? What if that excuse is real?"

According to Children's Services records in 1972: "He has hostility toward all women he comes in contact with."

He was born innocent. He didn't have a chance. His stepmother beat him with fists all day. "This man never had a chance."

Profound hatred for women. Voluntary manslaughter. Guilty, but not as charged.

Lieberman quoted Sapp: "They should never have done that to y'all. I'm sorry."

As Lieberman finished his closing statement, Sapp demanded from the defense table: "You're gonna have to let me out of here or shoot me! That's all you got left!"

After Judge O'Neill quickly had the jury removed from the courtroom, he called a break. When court reconvened, he scolded the spectators about whispering.

Before the jurors were brought back in, Sapp made the unusual request that the handcuffs and shackles—utilized during transportation of the prisoner—be left on him. It was rare for a jury to see a defendant bound in any way, the concern being that it could prejudice the jurors.

Judge O'Neill: "Have you talked to your attorneys about this?"

Sapp shrugged and answered: "It needs to be."

"So ordered."

Judge O'Neill also ordered that no family members of the victims were allowed to sit in the first row.

Assistant prosecutor Steve Collins presented the rebuttal argument. He addressed the issue of Sapp's dysfunctional family: hot-tempered father and lazy mother—highly exaggerated. He had very little contact with his mother since early age. He claimed that Sapp was the one who set Paul on fire.

With clenched teeth Sapp spoke out loud in the courtroom, "That's not it."

Collins continued to say that the abuse by Sapp's (biological) mother was not supported by the facts. He then quoted Sapp: "If you're a liar, gotta do it right."

He killed because he enjoyed it. He was a cold-blooded killer who had a fascination with death.

The assistant prosecutor pointed out to the jurors that what they had seen on the confession tapes, regarding Phree's shorts, was Sapp's reliving of the experience. And when Sapp demonstrated cutting Helen from ear to ear, again he was reliving it.

Collins told the jury that Sapp was full of self-pity, not uncontrollable rage: "This defendant's a coward."

At the defense table Sapp was visibly angry. His jaw was

clenched and his legs were continuously shaking up and down as they had done many times during the trial when he was upset.

Collins continued, saying that Sapp chose vulnerable victims: "Those are the actions of a coward."

As Collins ended his rebuttal, Sapp, even though he was still handcuffed and shackled, seemed to try to leap out of his chair. He shouted in the direction of the deputy who was holding the controls to the stun belt, "What the fuck you doing, man? It didn't fucking work, did it?"

The deputy shrugged. "I didn't touch it!"

Again the jury was removed from the courtroom immediately and there was a break in the proceedings. It was determined that the stun belt had malfunctioned and accidentally shocked Sapp, although not with full force.

Lieberman asked Judge O'Neill to instruct the jury about the belt incident. When Sapp was brought back into the courtroom, he was shackled but no longer wore the belt. Sapp, his mood obviously lighter and speaking to no one in particular, stated, "Just call me 'Jingles.'"

Some of the other investigators who had worked on the case would later say that they were "sure" Al Graeber was sitting in the courtroom with them listening. Sharon Graeber told them, "That's probably why the zapper went off—just to let Sapp know he was there!"

Judge O'Neill read the jury their instructions for deliberation, including the death penalty specifications and the charges against William K. Sapp.

The specifications: the murders of two or more persons, murder during the commission of rape or kidnapping, principal offender, and prior calculation.

The charges:

1. Aggravated murder—Phree Morrow.
2. Aggravated murder—Phree Morrow—during commission of rape.

3. Aggravated murder—Phree Morrow—during commission of kidnapping.
4. Aggravated murder—Martha Leach.
5. Aggravated murder—Martha Leach—during commission of rape.
6. Aggravated murder—Martha Leach—during commission of kidnapping.
7. Rape—Phree Morrow.
8. Rape—Martha Leach.
9. Kidnapping—Phree Morrow.
10. Kidnapping—Martha Leach.
11. Tampering w/evidence—Phree Morrow and Martha Leach.
12. Abuse of a corpse—Phree Morrow.
13. Abuse of a corpse—Martha Leach.
14. Aggravated murder—Belinda Anderson.
15. Aggravated murder—Belinda Anderson—during commission of rape.
16. Aggravated murder—Belinda Anderson—during commission of kidnapping.
17. Rape—Belinda Anderson.
18. Kidnapping—Belinda Anderson.
19. Tampering w/evidence—Belinda Anderson.
20. Abuse of a corpse—Belinda Anderson.
21. Attempted aggravated murder—Helen Preston.
22. Attempted aggravated murder—Helen Preston—during commission of rape.
23. Rape—Helen Preston.
24. Kidnapping—Helen Preston.
25. Tampering w/evidence—Helen Preston.

On counts one through six and fourteen through sixteen, the jury had the option of finding Sapp guilty of murder, voluntary manslaughter, or involuntary manslaughter (felonious assault). On counts twenty-one and twenty-two they had the option of finding him guilty of attempted murder.

And, of course, on all the counts, they had the option to find him not guilty.

The jury deliberated for about an hour that day and about 3½ hours the next morning.

On Friday, October 8, 1999, William K. Sapp was found guilty as charged on all counts.

Sapp smiled slightly as Judge Richard O'Neill read the verdicts. And before he was escorted from the courtroom, he stopped and posed with a big grin on his face as Marshall Gorby, the *Springfield News-Sun* photographer, snapped his picture. His lawyers, Dennis Lieberman and Gary Hruska, shook their heads in dismay.

The penalty phase of the trial was scheduled to start on Tuesday, October 12, 1999. During this segment the defense may call witnesses to testify in front of the jury in an effort to convince the jurors to recommend to the judge a life sentence in prison instead of the death penalty.

But this stage of the trial had to be postponed after one of the female jurors became ill. Judge O'Neill stated, "It would be the best circumstance to have all of the original twelve. We'll do all we can to keep the jury intact."

The court was also informed that Sapp had broken open an ink pen in his cell and ingested nontoxic ink. Even though the ink was harmless, he was no longer allowed to have pens in his cell.

The next night, even though Sapp was on high-security watch requiring deputies to check on him every fifteen minutes, he managed to remove the metal band that held the eraser on a pencil and cut his wrist. The injury required three stitches.

As a result, Sapp was moved to a special isolation cell and was watched constantly. He had to wear a paper gown and was not allowed to have anything in his cell.

One of the paramedics, Tom Freeman, would later tell me, "I had to wrap his arm up and I was that close to him—he made the hair on the back of my neck stand up. He has no color in his eyes. They're black. They're black like a shark's eyes."

31

Sapp has no idea how much pain he has caused our family. He's killed every one of us inside.

—Richard Anderson, Belinda Anderson's brother

Finally, on Monday, October 18, 1999, everyone was back in Judge Richard O'Neill's courtroom for the penalty phase of the trial. William Sapp was present and, once again, was wearing the stun belt. It seemed that he was making an attempt to grow his mustache and beard back. Or perhaps it was just five o'clock shadow.

Courtroom observers were not allowed to sit in the first row of seats.

After listening to the testimony, the jury would have to decide whether to recommend the death penalty or life in prison for William K. Sapp. The three possible sentences were death, life with eligibility for parole in thirty years, or life with eligibility for parole in twenty years. The judge would then make the final decision.

Not only would the jurors need to consider the aggravating circumstances—the murders of two or more persons, whether or not Sapp was the principal offender, rape and kidnapping—they would also have to consider the mitigating circumstances: the character of the defendant, duress, provocation, and mental disease.

The testimony during this phase of the trial revealed the extremely dysfunctional relationships within Sapp's family.

In his opening statement Dennis Lieberman told the jury

that "so far you have been looking through a door with a peephole," only seeing a small part of what Sapp had been through, but "we're going to open this door wide open."

He stressed that "it's not going to be pretty. It's not going to be fun. It's so you can decide what to do with this man."

Sapp was the oldest of five children. J.R. (Kessler Lilly Jr.) was the only sibling who testified. His brother Paul had been in a mental institution since he was a toddler. His half sister, Katrina, lived in Oklahoma. Charles, his half brother, died when he was seven years old.

J.R., whose physical resemblance to his older brother was uncanny, testified that he was thirty-four years old, unemployed, was being treated for mental illness, and still lived at home with his father on East Main Street.

He stated that when he and Bill were children, they were unsupervised most of the day because their mother stayed in bed until 2:00 or 3:00 in the afternoon. He also stated that his mother had hit both of them with her hand and with a belt. She had forced Bill to have sex with her. And she had burned Paul.

At some point his father put them in the Children's Home "until he could do better for them." He testified that his dad had never abused him or Bill, physically or sexually. "Dad would work two or three jobs at a time to keep food on the table.

"All I ask is . . . please don't kill my brother."

Kessler Lilly Sr. (Sapp's father) testified that he was sixty-four years old, unemployed, disabled because of diabetes, heart trouble, and Parkinson's disease. When asked if he knew Bill Sapp, he answered, "Yes. He's my son."

He stated that he himself was born in Blue Jay, West Virginia, and was one of twelve children, seven boys and five girls. His father was a minister, "strict, very religious." When Kessler senior's father died at the age of fifty-four, Kessler was only nine years old. "Mom went wacky. Completely changed." He said that she suffered from untreated mental illness.

When asked by Lieberman if anyone else in the family was mentally ill, Lilly stated, "Me." He added that his mother's two sisters had killed themselves and that his brother, Benny, had threatened their mother with a gun. Benny "hated" their mother.

One morning "during squirrel season," Benny came to the house and kicked the door in. Kessler shot him seven times with a .22 rifle. Kessler was seven years old at the time.

Several years later, Kessler was outside and heard a "muffled sound" from within the house. All the doors and windows were locked. When he finally got inside, he found his mother "against a wall." She had "blown her brains out" with a twenty-gauge shotgun. Their dog started "licking the blood." Kessler choked the dog to death.

Sometime later, Kessler "built a fire—set the house on fire." (It's not clear whether it was hours, days, or years.) He then moved to Springfield, Ohio. In 1961 he met Margaret (Sapp's mother). Margaret was from San Francisco, California: "Her mother deserted her; she was adopted."

Kessler and Margaret had three sons: Bill, J.R., and Paul. Kessler said that Bill was "my shadow." Referring to Paul: "He's a vegetable."

Charles (Margaret's son, fathered by Kessler's older brother) died while they were living in Chillicothe, Ohio. The seven-year-old boy drowned in a pond while his mother was sleeping. The only reference to Margaret's daughter, Katrina, was that she was "by a truck driver" and that she lived in Oklahoma.

According to Kessler, someone in the family "set Paul on fire" when he was three months old. He remembered him having a bandage on his head. Someone called Children's Services. He then took the boys to West Virginia and "gave Paul" to one of his brothers "until he was one and a half years old."

Kessler claimed that Margaret didn't feed the kids or bathe them. She "slept all day." On one occasion Bill tried to ride his tricycle to where his dad worked. When the police found him, he had been gone for four hours and his mother hadn't even noticed.

Lieberman: What did she do to your kids?

Kessler: Just let your mind run wild. As I understand it—as little as they was—she even tried to have sex with them.

(The prosecution strenuously objected and the objection was sustained.)

Lieberman: Did you personally witness sex?

Kessler: No.

Lieberman: Did you see evidence of beating or burning children?

Kessler: Yes.

Lieberman: Did you see any of them hit with a frying pan?

Kessler: Yes.

Lieberman: Cutting?

Kessler: Never seen.

Lieberman: Burning?

Kessler: She burned Bill's hands on the stove because he played with fire.

Kessler Lilly then told the jury that when Paul was about 1½ years old, he took him to Mercy Hospital because he was screaming. Somehow he had taken an overdose of medicine. He was committed to an institution and was still there. He had to wear a helmet because he "breaks glass." Kessler took Bill and J.R. to the Children's Home "until I could get on my feet."

It's not clear when Bill and J.R. returned to live with their parents. Kessler and Margaret filed for a divorce and Kessler's girlfriend, Patricia, lived in the same house with them until the divorce was final. He testified that Patricia beat both Bill and J.R. and even broke J.R.'s arm with a plastic bat.

When asked if he had a temper, Kessler Lilly responded:

"Yes, I have an explosive temper, but I've learned how to control it." Then, "I'll fight in a minute."

In further testimony about Margaret, Kessler said that she had given alcohol to Bill when he was only nine years old because she said it would "calm him down." He also said that she had been committed to a mental hospital because she had thrown "a screwdriver, a knife, and a chair." He claimed that the police told him to "beat her up." She spent six weeks in Mercy Mental Health and then went to counseling for a while. Kessler Sr. felt that they were "wasting their time" because "Margaret was not going to change."

Also, he caught her "stripping for some guy in front of the window." At some point after that, the guy she had been stripping for (her boyfriend) stabbed Kessler. This was while they were still married.

Back to his girlfriend, Patricia: "She was a sexpot. She'd have sex with anybody." He claimed that he saw Patricia having sex with Bill and threw her out. (But later he married her, making her Sapp's stepmother.)

On his way out of the courtroom, Kessler Lilly patted his son on the back.

Karen Sapp, a petite woman with long sandy brown hair who wore glasses, testified that she met William Sapp in Jacksonville, Florida, and they were married in 1988. She said that on their first date he was "clean-cut, polite, friendly, and showed me respect." According to her, he was like a "scared little boy."

Karen went on to say that she was from a violent, alcoholic family. Her father sold her for $58.45 when she was only four years old. It took her mother six weeks to find her.

She claimed that hers and Bill's marriage was "pretty good" for a while. They had three children—two boys and one girl—ages: ten, five, and four. They had been placed in foster care.

She told the jury that she had seen the scars on Sapp's body and that he had nightmares about his childhood and would wake up screaming and in cold sweats. After these episodes he would go for up to two days without sleeping: "Most of the time he kept his distance from me. Other times he would grab me by the throat, slam me against a wall, or jump on top of me on the bed. I just told him to 'calm down and get off of me.' " She said they were together for eight years and it didn't happen very often. "He put his hands on me about six times."

> Lieberman: Did you tell the prosecutors that Sapp never beat on you?
> Karen: Yes.
> Lieberman: What do you call the choking?
> Karen: Choking.
> (She also informed the court that a homosexual named Al Sapp had adopted Bill in Florida. William Sapp was nineteen at the time.)
> Karen: Just spare his life.

Steve Collins, the assistant prosecutor, had a few questions for Karen.

> Collins: On July 7, 1998, you told Sergeant Barry Eggers that Sapp only slapped you once. You didn't tell him about the choking incident.
> Karen: He didn't ask.
> Collins: You don't believe choking is abusive?
> Karen: Not where I came from.
> Collins: But you weren't afraid of him, were you?
> Karen: No, sir.

Periodically during Karen's testimony—when the lawyers were at the sidebar—Sapp made faces at Karen and she giggled.

The next defense witness was Dr. Kathleen Burch, the same clinical psychologist who had testified for the defense at Sapp's competency hearing. She was an expert witness—despite the fact that Steve Schumaker questioned her "expertise."

She testified that she was appointed to the case in September or October of 1997 and had six direct contacts with the defendant. She also reviewed the confession tapes, Sapp's medical records, Children's Services records, etc. The results of her testing showed that Sapp had "very severe mental-health problems, mood disorder, severe personality disorder, neurological dysfunction, and an inability to control his impulses."

She claimed that Sapp had bipolar mood disorder (manic-depressive), which caused his thoughts to "race one hundred miles per hour," and caused him to have "lack of judgment and driven, inappropriate behavior."

She went on to say that he also suffered from a chemical imbalance causing him to have suicidal thoughts: "This is a very serious personality disorder."

It was her opinion that Sapp also had an antisocial personality disorder: "He has a disregard for the rules of society and a disregard for his own safety and the safety of others. He came from an antisocial family, where he learned to be hostile and abusive."

In addition, she testified that he had borderline personality disorder, the new name for "psychotic." This disorder caused him to be "very dependent, can be clingy," and "very angry," and to have difficulty having relationships.

"Hurt, wounded, angry; unstable mood; impulsive; unstable sense of self. He thinks he is the 'the scum of the earth' and refers to himself as 'the maggot.'" She noted he can also be grandiose and "swings from idealizing to hating the person he's attached to.

"These people think they have a special way of seeing things. He said he could communicate with dead people and spirits."

There had been many arguments, fights, and suicide attempts in his life.

She explained that "bipolar" was a mental illness; the others were personality disorders, which cause an "inability to conform" and cause "emotion to overrun thought."

She explained how "these are symptoms of an abused child and characteristics of an aggressor."

She also related to the jury that all three components of the homicidal "triad" of symptoms were present in Sapp's behavior: enuresis (bed-wetting beyond the appropriate age), fire starting, and cruelty to animals. She said that Bill was "filled with anger" and had a "high problem of acting out violently." She quoted one of his teachers as saying that "this little boy hates women."

Dr. Burch also claimed that at some point Sapp's mother had "taken a knife and cut the seam of his pants." This was a scene that he had reenacted later during the attacks on his victims.

During cross-examination Dr. Burch admitted that she was not a medical doctor and that neurological tests showed no abnormalities in William Sapp and that he was faking multiple personalities. Inkblot tests showed that he was preoccupied with sex and with killing women.

She went on to say that Sapp practiced self-mutilation and that his cuts and burns were possibly self-inflicted. He had been abused by his mother and his stepmother and "various other women that were in and out of the house"—and men. He was raped in prison in 1982, in Florida.

Even though Sapp claimed he never got any help, Dr. Burch told the court in detail about the counseling and declined opportunities for counseling that he had had over a period of almost twenty years. One of his teachers described him as "extremely intelligent," but his IQ tests showed a range between 73 and 79. Dr. Burch estimated an actual score of 90, which is at the bottom of the average range.

When questioned further, Dr. Burch admitted: "Yes, I believe he was faking on the IQ test."

Sapp told her during their interviews, "Something big is going to come down in Springfield when I go to trial."

The next day, Tuesday, October 19, the defense called Richard Emmons to the witness stand. He had been a police officer for nineteen years and then went on to become a private investigator. He testified that he had inspected Sapp's body and found many scars. He found twenty-six cigarette burns and one knife wound. On Sapp's testicles there were three larger scars, two on one side and one on the other. He claimed that these scars were consistent with "hot candle wax being dripped on them."

The prosecution objected and the jury was told to disregard the remark about the hot candle wax.

According to Emmons, there were also scars on Sapp's testicles that were irregular, slightly raised and discolored, and were consistent with burns.

During cross-examination Emmons admitted that he had no personal knowledge of when or how the scars got there. When the prosecution elicited the information that Sapp was a smoker, the defense emphatically objected, "No foundation!"

The prosecutor responded, "It's on tape!"

Next, the exhibits were admitted into evidence: these included Sapp's school records, Children's Services records concerning Sapp, J.R., and Paul, and the convictions of David Marciszewski, John Balser, Alexander Boone, Jamie Turner, and Wanda Marciszewski.

Lieberman announced that William Sapp did not wish to make a statement and the defense rested.

The aggravating circumstances had already been established during the guilt phase of the trial and the prosecution's evidence was complete at that point. Under Ohio law, during the penalty phase, the prosecution was restricted to rebuttal of the mitigating circumstances that the defense put forth.

So, in a rather bizarre turn of events, the prosecution called its first witness, Reverend Margaret Lilly, to the stand: "I'm his mother." The plump, matronly woman with reddish long hair identified Sapp and stated she did not wish to see her son receive the death penalty.

Sapp watched her with a look of disgust on his face.

She told the court that she suffered from mental illness and that before her divorce from Kessler, she had a nervous breakdown. She spent five weeks in Mercy Mental Health. She didn't see much of Bill after the divorce: "Not as much as I'd like."

Margaret: I could have done better [as a mother].

Schumaker: Was the house dirty?

Margaret: Dirty enough. I didn't cook when I started breaking down.

Schumaker: Did you hit the kids?

Margaret: Both of us used wet washrags.

Schumaker: Why?

Margaret: Nerves.

Schumaker: Did you have sex with Bill?

Margaret: I did not.

Schumaker: Was he sexually abused?

Margaret: No, sir.

Schumaker: Did you drip candle wax on him?

Margaret: No, sir.

Schumaker: When did you become a minister?

Margaret: February, this year. I've always been interested in becoming a minister.

Schumaker: Do you have a congregation?

Margaret: No. I prayed and asked if there was any way a woman could become a minister. A certificate came in the mail about a month later.

Schumaker: Is it your testimony that you did not sexually abuse your son?

Margaret: That's true.

When the defense had its turn to question this very strange woman, Lieberman asked her about the certificate she had received in the mail.

Reverend Lilly claimed that it was unsolicited: "I didn't ask for it and didn't send any money for it."

Lieberman: Do you believe you're a minister?

Margaret: Yes.

Lieberman: You also didn't molest your children?

Margaret: No. (She named all of her children.) I don't remember Katrina's father's name. Charles's father is Kessler's half brother.

Lieberman: Is Charles the one that drowned?

Margaret: Yes.

Lieberman: Were you asleep?

Margaret: No, wide-awake.

(And then, regarding Paul, she said she had never visited him. She claimed she had made an effort, but "they wouldn't let me in.")

Lieberman: Did you try?

Margaret: No. Kessler visited Paul.

Lieberman: You never saw him again, did you?

Margaret: In the Children's Home, a couple of times.

(Paul had been taken out of their home when he was 1½ years old. He was institutionalized when he was three.)

Lieberman: What was his diagnosis?

Margaret: Don't know.

Lieberman: He wears a helmet. Did you abuse Paul?

Margaret: No.

Lieberman: Did you hit him?

Margaret: No. He fell out of his crib.

Lieberman: How do you explain J.R.? Was that because of you?

Margaret: Agent Orange. All the kids are that way.

Lieberman: Did you ever have sex with Bill?

Margaret: No!

Lieberman: Did you ever hit him with a frying pan?

Margaret: I held his hands over the flames to take the soreness out.

Lieberman: Were you ever sexually molested?

Margaret: No.

Lieberman: Did you hit Bill with a razor strap?

Margaret: Not true.

Lieberman: Did you burn him with cigarettes?

Margaret: I never done that to him.

Lieberman: Kessler, J.R., and Karen are lying?

(The prosecution vehemently objected and the objection was sustained.)

Lieberman: Did you report any child abuse to Children's Services?

Margaret: I have no idea how stuff got in the records.

Lieberman: Was your house dirty?

Margaret: It wasn't exactly clean. My house today's not ever clean.

Lieberman: Who got them up for school?

Margaret: No one, I guess.

The next prosecution witness, Sergeant Barry Eggers, testified about the interview with Karen Sapp on July 7, 1998. He said that Karen indicated to him that Sapp had slapped her on one occasion when they lived on Miller Street, and specifically denied any other mistreatment.

On cross-examination Sergeant Eggers said that the interview was not recorded. He had taken handwritten notes.

Lieberman: You didn't ask her if she was choked?

Eggers: No reason to.

Lieberman: If stuff was thrown at her?

Eggers: No reason to.

Lieberman: Did you explain "abuse"?

Eggers: No.

Lieberman: She was not under oath, was she?

Eggers: No.

On redirect Sergeant Eggers told the jurors there was no reason to be specific. Karen had no fear of Bill and she controlled the situation.

Lieutenant Steve Moody also gave testimony pertaining to the same interview with Karen Sapp. He stated that when asked about physical abuse, she firmly maintained that there had been one slap.

Lieberman, on cross-examination, asked Lieutenant Moody if he had explained "abuse" to Karen.

Lieutenant Moody answered no.

In his closing statement Stephen Schumaker reminded the jury about the aggravating circumstances: two or more victims, principal offender, committing or attempting to commit rape.

He also reminded them that when Phree Morrow told Sapp that "you'll be sorry," Sapp's reply was "Like hell I will!"

There were four victims: Phree Morrow, Martha Leach, Belinda Anderson, and Helen Preston. "How many do you have to have? Can mitigation even come close?" Schumaker implored. He told them to give the mitigating circumstances weight only if they were credible.

Referring to the other defendants: "Reject this. Give it little or no weight. Especially with Belinda Anderson. Plea agreements were made with David Marciszewski and John Balser in an attempt to find that man!

"The weight of the aggravating circumstances cannot be overcome."

Dennis Lieberman presented a fervent closing statement, with the hope of saving his client's life: "My mom was there for me. I bet you had good mothers. What kind of mom do you think Bill has? Do you think she fixed him a cup of hot chocolate? Do you think she was there for him? She said the boys were that way because of 'Agent Orange.' She says she's a minister. This is 'Margaret Lilly.' Do you believe Margaret Lilly in anything she says? Her presence on the stand should tell you who William Sapp is.

"His father found the stepmother in bed with Sapp.

"Why should we care whether we give him the death penalty or five life sentences? If we take the life of mentally ill people, what does that make us?

"Sapp's family is not dysfunctional. It's nonexistent! This is not a family. The home was filthy. Mrs. Lilly doesn't even see Paul. The child abuse was real. Mrs. Lilly's mentally ill. It's sad. What do we do? Do we burn a burn?

"Karen is a tough woman. She was sold. She was sexually and physically abused.

"Is it a coincidence that Bill turned out the way he did? He didn't have a chance to be different. Bill acted out the way he was taught. What if you do spare his life? It will be one hundred thirty to two hundred thirty years before he's eligible for parole. He will be in a jail cell for the rest of his life. He will be one hundred sixty-six years old before he's eligible for parole. That's what he deserves.

"Marciszewski and Balser raped Phree and Martha. Marciszewski and Balser killed Phree and Martha. Is there equality in our justice system? That's for you to decide. Why should he be treated any differently? This isn't a numbers game (referring to Belinda Anderson). What Marciszewski and Balser did is absolutely terrible! What he did is absolutely terrible!

"He is the victim of child abuse. He has the scars. It's in the documents. The only psychologist that testified in this case said that he has mental illness, bipolar, and personality disorder. He did not have the ability to conform his actions to the law.

"His kindergarten teacher was quoted, 'He hates women.'

"Only you can decide whether he should die or be in jail for the rest of his life. Thank you for your dedication and commitment. Should you take another's life? I wish I could find the magic words to tell you not to kill him. I wish I could think of an argument that might convince you to give him a life sentence. I hope I have."

In his rebuttal Schumaker told the jurors: "You must follow the law. We wanted you to see Margaret Lilly because you deserved to see her. J.R. didn't grow up to be a killer. Sapp turned away from help. You must follow the law!"

It was close to midnight, after five hours of deliberation,

when the jury returned with their recommendation. None of the victims' family members were present in the courtroom to hear their decision because at about 10:30 that night the jurors had told the judge that they thought they should get a motel room for the night. Therefore, the family members and other interested parties who had been waiting in the prosecutor's office left for the night.

While waiting for arrangements to be made to accommodate them overnight, the jurors continued to deliberate and came to a unanimous decision. After some discussion the members of the jury agreed they should announce their recommendation that night.

I had spent the evening waiting with Belinda Anderson's family. I left the courthouse when they did. After I got home and changed into my nightclothes, my phone rang. It was Wes Wilson, the reporter who was covering the trial for the *Springfield News-Sun.* He was excited and out of breath, calling me on his cell phone as he hurried back to the courthouse. He had gotten word that "the jury was in."

Not knowing whether or not I would be able to get back into the locked courthouse, I grabbed my clothes, threw them back on, and rushed downtown. I parked across the street in the post office parking lot and jaywalked across the now-quiet street. As I quickly approached the building, I could see through the glass door one of the deputies in the hallway. He recognized me and let me in.

It was perfect timing as they were just then putting Sapp on the elevator. No one else is allowed on the elevator while the deputies are transporting a prisoner and, quite frankly, I had no desire to be in arm's reach of him, anyway, so I waited while they escorted Sapp to the third-floor courtroom. Then I followed, anxious to hear what the jury had decided.

When they came into the courtroom and sat down in the jury box, it appeared that one of the female jurors had been crying.

The jurors had decided that William K. Sapp should get the death penalty for each of the three murders: one for the murder of Belinda Anderson, one for the murder of Martha Leach, and one for the murder of Phree Morrow.

As the deputies escorted Sapp from the courtroom, he exclaimed, "I won, baby, I won. That's what I wanted!"

32

While this court is not an advocate of capital punishment, it is sworn to uphold the law.

—Judge Richard O'Neill

Prior to Judge Richard O'Neill announcing his decision on Thursday, October 21, 1999, Richard Anderson was informed that Sapp "hoped that Richard would try to be a hero," and that Sapp "hoped he would try something with him."

Richard Anderson shared this with me outside the courthouse just before we entered. When I asked him, "You're not going to do that, are you, Richard?" He answered, "No—not that I wouldn't like to."

Many people were waiting to get into the courtroom while sheriff's deputies once again checked to make sure there were no weapons hidden under the seats or anywhere else in the room. When the public was finally allowed in, the family members of the victims were not allowed to sit in the section behind where Sapp would be sitting.

No one was allowed in the row directly behind the defense table except law enforcement officers who wanted to be present to hear the sentencing, even though many of them were not directly involved with the case. The presence of the uniformed officers, detectives, and additional deputies reinforced the already very secure courtroom.

The only juror who came back to hear the judge's official ruling was the young woman who had been crying the night the jury had recommended death for William K. Sapp. Just by chance, we were seated next to each other. She was curious about who I was and why I was there. I was curious about her tears. It is a heavy burden—even when the guilt of the defendant is so obvious—to have a say in the destiny of that person.

Before the deputies brought Sapp into the packed courtroom, the judge admonished the audience very strongly that there were to be no outbursts and that if anyone felt that they couldn't restrain themselves from showing emotion or having outbursts, they needed to leave. He had instructed the deputies, and had verified that there were enough of them to carry out his order, that people be removed if there were any problems.

Richard Anderson felt that Judge O'Neill was looking directly at him and he nodded at the judge to indicate that he understood. Most of Belinda's immediate family were present: her parents, Christine and Richard senior; both of her sisters, Patricia and Deborah; Richard's wife, Karlene, and his son, Jake; her two daughters, Kim and Stephney; and the grandchild she never got to see.

Phree Morrow's grandfather, one of her aunts, and her half sister Dawn Wilson represented Phree's family. No one from Martha Leach's family was present for the sentencing.

William Sapp chose not to make a statement prior to being sentenced.

Judge O'Neill upheld the jury's recommendation and sentenced William K. Sapp to death for each of the aggravated murders—three death sentences.

Sapp, wearing a blue shirt, smiled and looked very pleased with himself. ("Blue was a happy color.") He raised his middle finger in the direction of the television news camera.

His execution date was set for September 1, 2000.

Judge O'Neill filed a written decision that he did not read in the courtroom. The document was six pages long and read, in part:

"The murders of Phree Morrow, Martha Leach and Belinda Anderson were cold-blooded, senseless acts of cruelty committed with prior calculation and design and while perpetrating upon these victims the offense of rape. Further, the Defendant engaged in a course of conduct which not only took the lives of these three individuals, but nearly took the life of a fourth victim, Helen Preston.

"While the Defendant suffered tragic child abuse in his early years, and the extent of the abuse shown does merit some weight as a mitigating factor, the Court finds that this factor does not carry sufficient weight to balance the scales when compared to the aggravating circumstances. Even when the factor of his mental illness and defect, which likely resulted from this abuse, is added, these factors are insufficient to overcome or equal the weight of the aggravating circumstances.

"While this court is not an advocate of capital punishment, it is sworn to uphold the law. The aggravating circumstances of these offenses are grave and carry great weight. The mitigating factors, while tragic in their effect not only on the Defendant, but now on so many others, do not rise to the weight of the aggravating circumstances.

"Thus, this Court hereby shall impose upon the Defendant a sentence of death for the commission of each of the three aggravated murders, with the specifications of aggravating circumstances, as set forth in the indictment."

After the court proceedings Sapp was returned to the Southern Ohio Correctional Facility in Lucasville, Ohio, where he had been serving his sentence for the attack on Ursula Thompson. Sometime later, he was transferred to Mansfield Correctional Institution in Mansfield, Ohio, and placed on death row.

Prior to 1995, death row was located at the Southern Ohio Correctional Facility, but it has since been relocated to the Mansfield Correctional Institution. The "death house" and execution chamber remain at the Southern Ohio Correctional Facility.

* * *

It is unlikely that anyone will ever know for sure whether William Sapp and the others were in a van or Karen's Mercury Marquis on the night of Phree Morrow and Martha Leach's murders. Or whether there was a black pickup truck involved. Perhaps all three vehicles were involved in some way or another.

If all of them—Sapp, Balser, Marciszewski, Turner, and Boone—met on Linden Avenue to "go partying," they could have arrived there in different vehicles. They may have left together in the van, gone to the bakery, then returned to the Linden Avenue house with Phree and Martha, and the initial attack took place there. They probably took more than one vehicle to the pond area.

But were Phree and Martha forced into the van at the bakery, then taken to the house, where they were knocked unconscious? And then later raped and murdered at the pond? Or were the girls already at the pond and the whole attack took place there?

Although there are still unanswered questions and conflicting statements, a picture does emerge of what happened that hot summer night.

The picture is much clearer—if Sapp's version is to be believed—of what transpired the fateful night that Belinda Anderson crossed the path of a serial killer. And the night that Helen Preston turned to a stranger for comfort.

According to Sapp, all of his victims "offended" him in some way. Were they chance encounters? Or did he troll whichever neighborhood he lived in at the time, always on the lookout for the common denominator—a vulnerable female?

Did Sapp plan the murders of Phree and Martha? Or did things just "get out of hand"?

According to Joe Jackson, John Balser's uncle and guardian, in one of his statements to the detectives: "John has told me they knew on Friday it was going to happen."

Did one of the mentally impaired men set up the meeting with Phree and Martha? Or was it Sapp? At any rate, Jamie knew about it ahead of time because he told his friends that he had a "date with two whores." Alex also knew about it beforehand because he told the others on Light Street that he had to "go meet some girls."

Phree and Martha told their friends, Deon and Matthew, that they were "going to a party" that night. The girls may have agreed to meet the guys because Phree knew John Balser. Or maybe because they wanted to have some "fun" with them. Or maybe they had no idea they were supposed to "meet" these guys anytime, anywhere. The guys had arranged earlier to meet Sapp on Linden Avenue to "go partying." Perhaps he had told the others they were going to "meet some girls."

Many nights I've fallen asleep trying to picture exactly how everything played out that night—how it all came together.

One of the most unusual facts in this case is the involvement of the mentally retarded men. Sapp's younger brother, J.R., John Balser, and Jamie Turner had all gone to Town and Country Day School. Most likely, they all "looked up to Sapp" because he befriended them despite their handicap and he was "normal," at least in their eyes. And, perhaps, he befriended them because it made him feel superior.

The strange letters, which were received by Phree and Martha's families, the police, and the newspaper, were most likely written by John Balser. They "sound" like John. Did Sapp tell John to write the letters?

Was it because Sapp coached him that John went to the police every few months with a different name? A different vehicle? Was Sapp in the background orchestrating the investigation? He was certainly the one in control on the night of August 22, 1992.

Even though there was much talk in various statements (and even "confessions") about which ones raped the girls— besides Sapp—they would have had to wear a condom. It is very doubtful that it happened that way. It is believed that Sapp controlled the mentally retarded men to the point that he did not allow them to "have sex" with Phree and Martha.

374 Carol J. Rothgeb

Sapp made sure they covered their tracks so well that very little of any evidentiary value was found outside the pond area and the Lion's Cage. In fact, very little was found at the crime scenes. Fingerprints were wiped off the skids and the bicycle—and anything else that they might have touched.

And the fact that no evidence was found at the house on Linden Avenue doesn't mean that nothing happened there. If the girls were only knocked unconscious at that location, there could easily have been no blood to find.

No doubt Sapp was aware that David Marciszewski put a pair of underpants in his pocket, or maybe he found out later. John and David were so sure the panties were in the "hole" next to their house on Light Street, but the investigators found no evidence at that location. Did John or David tell Sapp that was where they hid them? Did Sapp take them out of the "hole," in another effort to taunt the police?

And did Sapp then "hide" other clothing, including a pair of underpants that had nothing to do with the case, in the cistern at the house on Lagonda Avenue?

That house is where Wanda was working, taking care of Eleanor, the night Phree and Martha were murdered. The backyard of the house is where Sapp and the others went after they went to the Lion's Cage. It is where Sapp threatened them and they planned what to say if they were ever questioned. Sometime after the murders, Wanda and John moved from Light Street to the upstairs apartment in this same house.

In Sapp's confession he talked about being at John's house on Lagonda Avenue. Since John didn't live there until after the murders, it's obvious that they were still in contact with each other.

Sapp also said he saw Wanda remove Martha's necklace. Perhaps he was so certain of his control over Wanda that he just "let it go." Even after Wanda's plea bargain, she wouldn't mention Sapp's name.

But, of course, Sapp's downfall was that he left a minute

part of himself inside Phree and Martha. Perhaps he thought it was another way to mock the police, to see if "they had their shit together."

There were several opportunities for the others to call the police that night and they chose not to: John could have called the police instead of calling Wanda. Wanda could have called on her way back to Eleanor's or after she got there. It is believed that Sapp was left alone with Phree and Martha while all of the others later went to Light Street to pick up Wanda and Robby (and Willie?). Any of them could have dialed 911.

If indeed they were in more than one vehicle from Linden Avenue to the pond area, the person driving the second vehicle could have driven to a pay phone or the police station or the hospital. Even if Sapp was right behind them, he was outnumbered, and the girls were still alive at that point.

The truth of what happened that night, no doubt, lies in the combination of their stories. The deeds that John attributed to Damien Tyler, Lloyd Tyler, Frank Fisher, Jason Holmes, Jake Campbell, etc.—replace those names with William Sapp.

Profilers generally group serial killers into one of three categories: organized, disorganized, and mixed.

Although there are differing opinions among the professionals, a close look at Sapp's methods reveals that he could be considered "mixed":

Even though the bodies were left at the scene of the murders, he did try to conceal them, with much success in the case of Belinda Anderson.

The weapons he used were whatever was convenient, but he then took the weapons away from the scene and hid them—with much success—especially with the third lava rock, which still has not been found. It's unlikely that the piece of rebar used in the attack on Helen Preston would ever have been found if he had not told the detectives exactly where it was hidden.

Sapp must have thought he was very clever, revisiting the crime scenes, and even returning two of the lava rocks to the pond area.

He did not take all of each victim's clothing; he took the pieces with his "signature" on them. Belinda's pants were never found. In the case of Helen Preston, because the area was not as secluded as the other crime scenes, he may have thought he heard someone coming and panicked.

He managed to manipulate or force his victims into secluded areas, rendering them even more vulnerable, before the onslaught of his attacks.

If the initial assault on Phree and Martha did indeed occur on Linden Avenue and was then finished in the pond area, this proved just how much William K. Sapp was in control of his "rage."

For the most part, Sapp was able to depersonalize his victims, raping them after they were dead or at least unconscious. He seemed to have a more difficult time depersonalizing Belinda Anderson: "I'd never seen her before . . . but [she] sure was pretty. . . ."

It is a rare serial killer that has a wife and children during the period in which he is committing his horrendous crimes. Sapp's son, Aaron, was only three years old when Phree and Martha were murdered. Karen probably was just realizing she was pregnant with Vanessa when Helen Preston was viciously attacked and left for dead. And Brad was born the month before Belinda Anderson's decomposed body was found buried in the garage on South Fountain Avenue.

Karen is believed to have been the dominant personality in hers and Bill's relationship. And, in fact, on the day that he attacked Ursula Thompson, when Karen had told him to go to the Laundromat and he returned home with the unwashed clothes, she was livid.

There was much speculation among the authorities: "At what point in time would he have killed her?"

It is also very unusual for a serial killer's victims to be in different age groups. Sapp's known victims range in age from eleven to fifty-eight. The characteristics they all shared were their vulnerability and availability: He was able to manipulate, dominate, intimidate, and overpower them.

There was a time when the authorities very much believed that Sapp was responsible for the attack on Caitlin Levalley on Penn Street Hill and the murder of four-year-old Avery Bailum as a result of the arson on Miller Street. But now, for reasons that cannot be revealed here because of ongoing investigations, he is no longer considered to be a suspect in these cases.

There are differing opinions about the murder of Gloria Jean White: Some still believe Sapp is responsible for her death; others do not. Although he has since "confessed" to her murder, he was not able to describe the crime scene.

He was never considered to be a suspect in the case of Peggy Casey, but he has also "confessed" to her murder. There is no reason to take his confession seriously. Peggy Casey was killed by someone who was extremely organized. All of Sapp's known victims were found "in his own backyard." And even though his crimes were violent to the point of "overkill," none of his victims had been dismembered.

In 1993 a bill granting condemned prisoners in Ohio the option to choose either death by electrocution or death by lethal injection was passed and signed into law by the then governor, George V. Voinovich. Seven days before the scheduled execution, the death row inmate would be asked to choose between the two methods. The law stipulated that if the prisoner did not choose, the default method of execution would be death by electrocution.

On March 23, 2000, a motion was filed on behalf of William K. Sapp for a stay of execution to appeal the convictions and the death sentence. His first execution date of September 1, 2000, came and went.

A little over a year later, on November 15, 2001, Governor

Robert Taft signed House Bill 362, eliminating the electric chair as a form of execution. Therefore, a condemned prisoner can no longer choose his (or her) method of execution.

In February 2002, Ohio's electric chair, nicknamed "Old Sparky," was disconnected from service.

This, of course, destroyed Sapp's chance to "fulfill his destiny." It seemed that his "lifelong dream to sit in the electric chair" would never come true.

Epilogue

When Captain Steve Moody went to visit William Sapp on death row in the spring of 2002, Sapp claimed that he had converted to Catholicism and had taken the name Francis, after Saint Francis of Assisi.

Captain Moody said, "Well, Bill, you know who else's name was Francis, don't you?"

Sapp replied, "Yeah . . . Al Graeber." (His full name was Francis Albert Graeber.)

Sincere? Or another game?

Rumor had it that he had "mellowed somewhat."

Periodically, he confessed to a murder that the authorities knew he couldn't have committed. But he succeeded—for a moment, anyway—in getting their attention. And it probably helped break the monotony of being on death row.

Karen Sapp was nowhere to be found. Most likely, she moved back to her home state of Mississippi, where she lived before she moved to Florida—before she met and married Bill Sapp. She no longer had custody of her children. They were placed in foster care and—rumor had it—adopted by a "good family."

The families of Belinda, Phree, and Martha continued to try to heal.

No one seemed to know for sure where Helen Preston was now living.

Sadly, Ursula Thompson could still be found in the downtown area of Springfield—still accepting rides with men she'd never seen before.

Sergeant Michael Haytas retired in December 2002, after more than twenty-seven years on the force, most of them spent doing crime scene investigations. He had a woodworking shop named C.S.I.—Country Styled Images. His wife, Carol, was a retired nurse. Over the years, because they both witnessed sad and disturbing events in their professions, they were able to talk to each other and support each other.

Both of their sons, Matthew and Joshua, were now police officers with the Springfield Police Department. Their daughter, Heather, was a full-time mother.

I still correspond with him and his wife by e-mail on a regular basis.

Sergeant Barry Eggers, his hair and mustache prematurely silver, continued to head the Crimes Against Persons Unit. Several years ago they combined the adult and the juvenile sections of this unit, so he was a very busy man. (But he always answered my e-mails!) He took advantage of the on-site (Public Safety Building) weight room, which helped him to cope.

On January 1, 2003, Steve Moody became the chief of police of the Springfield Police Department.

As a captain he continued, even though it was not required, to go to crime scenes, even if it was 2:00 in the morning. He didn't do this to take anything away from his men, but rather to be there in case they needed anything and to make sure they had the resources they needed to do their jobs.

He still loved coming to work.

I interviewed him on August 23, 2002, the day after the ten-year "anniversary" of the homicides of Phree Morrow and Martha Leach. These were his words:

"I drove down to the pond last night. It was about midnight—and just stood there and looked. It hasn't changed that much. You look at things like this and you take it personally that someone would do this in your community. And not so much just 'How dare they?' I think you have to take it personally to be able to successfully go about your job objectively—do the right thing. Because you're also talking about taking somebody's freedom away for the rest of their life—or the death penalty. So, I mean, you don't want to half-ass it."

Afterthoughts

All the books I've read and all the movies and documentaries I've seen did not prepare me for the experience of watching a true sociopathic personality at work in the courtroom.

The only things the lawyers talked about that mattered to William Sapp were the ones that involved his feelings and his childhood and anything about him.

He listened to the testimony of the two little girls' mothers and saw their tears and their heartache. He saw the chilling crime scene tape of how Phree and Martha were found, their skulls crushed with a huge rock.

And he watched as Belinda's sister, Deborah, told of the last time she saw her alive. He surely heard Christine Anderson's sobs after the viewing of yet another crime scene tape, in which Belinda's badly beaten body was exhumed from her shallow and improper grave in the dirt floor of a garage.

He saw the woman whom he had savagely beaten and had left for dead limp into the courtroom—a woman whose physical scars would forever remind her of that horrible encounter.

He watched with interest, but absolutely no emotion or reaction—and certainly no remorse. It was as if all the pain and tragedy visited upon these victims and their families had nothing to do with him. It was as if he were the only one who had any feelings.

It is difficult not to take this case personally. I was born and raised in Springfield, Ohio. I have two granddaughters almost exactly the same age as Phree and Martha, and I have a daughter the same age as Belinda—the ages they were when they were so viciously and senselessly murdered.

Although I have concerns—for the most part I believe in capital punishment—but in the case of the *State of Ohio* v. *William Sapp,* there is no doubt about his guilt. He confessed to killing a "bag lady" in Florida. He confessed to killing Phree, and Martha, and Belinda. He confessed to leaving Helen for dead. Instead, he maimed her for life.

I wonder how many others suffered that we'll never know about. As of this writing, Sapp was still awaiting his fate in a cell on death row.

Also, I can't help but wonder how many of us have nodded at a stranger as we passed him on the street, or brushed against a shadow in a theater, or had a friendly conversation about the weather with the nice man standing in line with us at the grocery store—or the bakery—and didn't have a clue that we were in the presence of evil.